INSIDE THE SPACE RACE
A SPACE SURGEON'S DIARY

LAWRENCE E. LAMB, M.D.

INSIDE THE SPACE RACE: A SPACE SURGEON'S DIARY
PUBLISHED BY SYNERGY BOOKS
2100 Kramer Lane, Suite 300
Austin, Texas 78758

For more information about our books, please write to us, call 512.478.2028, or visit our website at www.bookpros.com.

Publisher's Cataloging-in-Publication
(Provided by Quality Books, Inc.)

    Lamb, Lawrence E.
      Inside the space race : a space surgeon's diary /
    Lawrence E. Lamb.
      p. cm.
      LCCN 2006920200
      ISBN-13: 978-1-933538-39-6
      ISBN-10: 1-933538-39-2

      1. Lamb, Lawrence E. 2. United States. National
Aeronautics and Space Administration--History.
3. Astronautics--Biography. 4. Physicians--Biography.
5. Space race--History. 6. Astronautics--United States--
History. 7. Astronautics--Soviet Union--History.
8. Astronautics and state. 9. Aviation medicine.
I. Title.

    TL789.85.A27 2006   629.45'0232'092
                      QBI06-600019

10 9 8 7 6 5 4 2 3 1

"To Mrs. Glenn and members of the Glenn family go my deepest sympathy. It was my pleasure to have known John Glenn. This nation and the entire world share his loss with the Glenn family. Space scientists will revere his pioneering spirit forever." John F. Kennedy, President

Fortunately, this message was never required. But it was prepared in the event his flight took his life. The government must always prepare contingency plans for events that hopefully will never occur. This statement reveals it was understood at the highest level of the government that John Glenn might not survive. All the astronauts knew the risk they were taking. They took this risk during a national crisis, when the freedom of the United States was in jeopardy. All the astronauts were heroes. HEROES. May God bless and keep them forever.

ACKNOWLEDGEMENTS

 First, I want to acknowledge that the United States Air Force made it possible for me to spend 11 exciting years working with pilots and astronauts, a group of very intelligent and dedicated individuals. I was literally a 28-year-old whippersnapper when the USAF Surgeon General entrusted me with developing medical support for Air Force flying personnel, which ultimately led to my role with NASA. Both Air Force and NASA leadership were, "top drawer." The fact that we did not always agree with each other does not diminish my respect and appreciation for them and their dedication.

I would like to express my appreciation for the friendship Lyndon Johnson extended to me in those years and the memories that will be part of my life as long as I shall live. The entire Johnson family and the staff that I knew will always be part of my fondest memories.

Dr. Janet Travell, President Kennedy's personal physician and, most importantly, a wonderful friend, provided many of the items from newspapers at the time these events occurred. They enabled me to keep events in the perspective of national and world events that occurred at the time.

The Lyndon B. Johnson Library staff was of great help, particularly Claudia Anderson and Philip Scott, in locating important documents and graphics that have added significantly to the book.

Then there were people who had a direct influence in my writing the book. Duane Unkefer, a fellow writer, made it through the first very rough draft and pointed out my many faults as a writer. A long time friend, Nancy Dean, a former English teacher, used her red pen on the manuscript and reminded me there was such a thing as punctuation, correct and incorrect. Chuck Maurer of Alternative Inc., prepared all the graphics other than those from the Lyndon B. Johnson Library. Bob Craycraft, a friend of many years, strongly encouraged me to have the book published. Tim Metzinger, a very bright attorney friend in Santa Barbara, California, insisted that I use photos and actual letters in the book. The end result is a unique history of events at the beginning of man's escape from Earth's gravosphere to explore the universe—a history I have felt an obligation to record.

"...Let us create vessels and sails adjusted to the heavenly ether, and there will be plenty of people unafraid of the empty wastes. In the meantime, we shall prepare, for the brave sky travelers, maps of the celestial bodies. I shall do it for the Moon, you Galileo, for Jupiter." *John Kepler, 1610*

CONTENTS

To Harry Lamb
with high regard and appreciation
from his friend - Lyndon B. Johnson

U.S. Air Force photo

President John F. Kennedy giving the dedication address for the new facilities at the nation's Aerospace Medical Center in San Antonio, Texas, November 21, 1963, the day before he was assassinated in Dallas. This was his last official address as President, and the official reason for the trip to Texas. He addressed the future of space and the plans for the nation's moon project.

PROLOGUE

～ We live on a giant space station, planet Earth. It spins on its axis, creating night and day as it orbits around the sun. Earth is shielded from the hostile environment in space by its atmosphere. The sheer mass of Earth produces a gravity field enveloping the planet that gives weight to the particles comprising the atmosphere. The atmosphere is sufficiently porous to allow life-giving solar energy to bathe Earth, but dense enough to prevent harmful radiation from destroying life. We are prisoners of our planet and have been locked to its surface since the beginning of mankind. That changed with the advent of aviation and finally, the ability to launch space vehicles to explore the vistas beyond the near-earth environment. Now we are at the threshold of exploring the solar system in person, beginning with building a permanent crew-occupied base on the moon. NASA's Crew Exploration Vehicle (CEV) will be used for the mission.

The dream of exploring the planets of our solar system is centuries-old, exemplified by the writings of the great scientists of the Middle Ages, such as Galileo and Kepler. Step by step, those dreams are being realized. The journey has not always been a peaceful one. There was a real danger that the Soviet Union, under a repressive dictatorship, would gain control of space, and only the United States had a chance of preserving freedom. The race was on between the Soviet Union and the United States. *Inside the Space Race* is a behind-the-scenes history of the early competition between the United States and the Soviet

Union to dominate space and consequently the world. It was a war: a war the United States almost lost.

I was part of that exciting adventure at the beginning of the conquest of space, in the days before *Sputnik I* startled the free world. The space and technology age made it possible for the United States to astonish the world with its quick victories in Afghanistan and later, "shock and awe" in Iraq. Today, the world is united by orbiting satellites that provide global positioning, essential to modern warfare, the Internet (without satellites there would be no Internet), our communications system with cellular telephones and other essential space hardware of this new age.

During these years, I frequently enjoyed spending time at the Lyndon B. Johnson ranch and had the opportunity to be with the Johnson family during their more relaxed times, when they escaped from public view to the Texas Hill country. Lyndon Johnson was my friend and a patient.

Lyndon Johnson was the leading national figure who made the space program possible. His actions at the national level and vision in the early days enabled the United States to prevail in the space race. This story relates his major role in these achievements, beginning in 1952 as Senate Majority Leader through the end of his administration as President in 1968: 16 years later.

President Kennedy made the Space program a major instrument of national policy, and in his short three years as President, he was its champion. His last official address on November 21, 1963, dedicated the new facilities at the Aerospace Medical Center in San Antonio, Texas, the day before he was assassinated in Dallas. That was the official reason for his trip to Texas. Both Lyndon Johnson's and President Kennedy's speeches emphasized that the survival of the free world depended on the United States overcoming the Soviet's shocking lead in space. Comments by Khrushchev, and Soviet achievements serve as milestones as the history of the space race unfolds.

Inside The Space Race is really about the people behind the scenes involved in this effort, which President Kennedy called the greatest adventure of the 20th century. I recount the story based on my own personal experience as physician to Lyndon Johnson, consultant to NASA, Chief of the Clinical Sciences Division of the Aerospace

Medical Center for the Air Force, and my personal interaction with the top decision makers in the Air Force, NASA, the Kennedy and Johnson administrations. I developed a team of scientists and physicians who carried out the medical evaluations for the selection of the astronauts, participated in training the medical monitors for the first manned space flights and was a key scientist for the Air Force and NASA's man-in-space program.

Those eleven years required all my ability and time to cope with the events. There were strong, determined and ambitious individuals participating in the power games I became involved in. Much of this remained hidden from public view. Only occasionally would a particularly onerous problem become public knowledge. All of this was going on while the world remained in conflict and different political parties grappled for control, even of the White House. It was a tumultuous time.

The conflicts between NASA and the Department of Defense (DOD) are supported with news items of the time. Dr. Janet Travell, President Kennedy's personal physician and a close personal friend of mine, provided many of the newspaper stories that I have used in this account. The Air Force, in particular, wanted a military role in space. They had established the first Department of Space Medicine under Dr. Hubertus Strughold, the "Father of Space Medicine," and they were far along in developing a space plane, the Dyna-Soar or X-20, that would fly into space and orbit. There were conflicts between groups within the Air Force and between individuals. Some of these seriously threatened national security and the success of the effort to send a man to the moon. One of the most serious of these concerned the seventh Mercury astronaut, Deke Slayton, who was not allowed to pilot a Mercury flight for medical reasons. There was an attempt to cover-up the medical problem, which led to President Kennedy's personal involvement. Slayton held me responsible for disqualifying him. A reporter told me, "Slayton hates your guts." I tell the real story for the first time and provide important documentation of my role in advising President Kennedy about this difficult situation. It had become a national and international news story.

A series of crises bedeviled the man-in-space project. One involved a chimpanzee's (Enos) heart irregularity during a space flight that nearly scrubbed John Glenn's orbital mission. I was able to establish that Enos' heart irregularity was not caused by weightlessness, allowing Glenn's flight to proceed. The lack of information about the influence of weightlessness was a major concern before the first manned orbital flights were achieved.

The conflicts I experienced included a confrontation with USAF Surgeon General Oliver K. Niess—in part because of the Slayton problem—and over a missing $500,000 that I was determined to find. General Niess was so angry he wrote, and disseminated, a letter complaining about my activities. He was also concerned about my relationship to Vice President Johnson and the Kennedy administration.

President Kennedy's role in promoting the man-in-space project is highlighted. It includes a chapter relating his visit to the Aerospace Medical Center in San Antonio, Texas, the day before he was assassinated. I had corresponded with Lyndon Johnson a year earlier, regarding President Kennedy's trip to Texas.

Despite all the contentious confrontations and turf wars related in *Inside The Space Race*, project Apollo was a tremendous success. As the story unfolds, the conflicts subside. Even information on weightlessness and space flight was exchanged between the Soviet and American scientists. Early reports from the Soviets suggested man could not survive the weightless environment long enough to go to the moon. *Was it a real threat or a Soviet effort to derail the American moon project?* This cloud was dispelled largely by data from my team's research on the effects of bed rest to simulate the effects of weightlessness.

The story details the United States' apathy before the shock of *Sputnik*, and a dog orbiting around the world alarmed the nation. It ends with the final climactic achievement of Neil Armstrong landing on the moon—the end of the real danger the Soviets would dominate the world by dominating space. The United States came from behind and accomplished the greatest single achievement of the 20th century. No other nation has ever landed anyone on the moon. That achievement stimulated many technological advances that have changed the way we will live forever.

The lunar landing was the first major step to what will ultimately be mankind's colonization of the moon, leading to the exploration and conquest of the universe. The moon could well become the base used to defend planet Earth from such dangers as an impact from a large, killer meteorite from outer space.

President Kennedy was right when he said it wasn't just astronauts going to the moon, but the entire American people. The Soviets' contribution to space exploration was equally important in many respects. In that sense, it was an achievement of all mankind: astronauts, cosmonauts, the scientists, political leaders of vision and the multitudes who made it possible. The world is a much better place today because of the achievements associated with the space race. The people involved, and their struggle to make this incredible conquest of space possible, is what this book is about.

1

WAR IN SPACE

1

⟿ The world got a glimpse of the importance of space in warfare when the United States projected its military might cross the globe to defeat the Taliban regime and al Qaeda forces in Afghanistan. That impressive achievement was heavily dependent on the United States' capability in space. The global-positioning satellite system was used to help protect forces on the ground. Satellites were essential to communications and even to view the battlefield from remote locations. Satellites were essential for the success of precision weapons. General Tommy Franks said that 10,000 of the 18,000 bombs, missiles and other ordnance used in the Afghan war were precision-guided munitions, and that 5,000 of these were laser-guided bombs, steered to targets by orbiting satellites.

The Afghan campaign was followed by "shock and awe," as the United States military machine humbled Saddam Hussein's defenses. Satellites made possible an air war that demolished Iraq's ground defenses before the advancing coalition forces arrived. Space technology demonstrated that previous war methodology was obsolete. Old wars involved destruction without regard for civilians or infrastructure. Germany blitzed London, and later, when the Allies gained air superiority, they returned the favor to Germany. The United States fire-bombed Tokyo, and the atomic bomb devastated Hiroshima and Nagasaki. But space technology has changed all of that. Early wars were totally dependent upon a sledgehammer approach, while modern warfare can be more like using a scalpel with surgical precision, destroying a nation's military capability while avoiding much of the death of the civilian population and destruction of infrastructure that occurred in previous wars. Unfortunately, guerilla warfare, used by terrorists, remains a scourge to entire populations.

Today, satellites orbit planet Earth to provide global communications of all types. Satellites map weather patterns, survey evidence of military activity and are an essential part of modern warfare. They enable our troops to communicate with one another instantly and are essential to planes flying combat missions. The Afghan campaign wasn't *Star Wars,* with orbiting satellites dropping nuclear bombs on targets or zapping cities with death rays as once envisioned, but it is hard to imagine the world today without utilizing space—for the Internet, for global positioning, and yes, for defending the free world. Dominating space and denying it to enemies is essential to the free world's survival.

None of these things would have been possible, had it not been for the pioneering efforts in space by the Soviet Union and the United States. The world was fascinated when the Soviets launched *Sputnik I* in 1957, and many were frightened when *Sputnik II* was launched a month later. The competition between the United States and the Soviets in the new frontier of space was heating up. The conquest of the cosmos requires rockets that provide enough power to thrust a space vehicle beyond Earth's gravity field. An American rocket scientist, Robert Hutchings Goddard, pioneered the early stage in developing such rockets. The key to his success was using liquid fuel, and he developed the first rocket engines to use a liquid mixture of oxygen and gasoline. His first successful test using the engine was on his Aunt Effie's farm in Auburn, Massachusetts, on March 16, 1926. The rocket achieved only a brief liftoff, but it was a start. In many ways, this first achievement for rocket flight was comparable to what the Wright brothers' first airplane flight in 1903 was to aviation. In 1935, Goddard launched the first liquid-fueled rocket that traveled faster than the speed of sound.

The Germans used Goddard's research to develop rockets that achieved an altitude of one mile in 1931 and 1932. Wernher von Braun, the German rocket enthusiast, was head of a small group that developed Germany's rocket capability during World War II. Later, he headed the project to build rockets for the United States, including the rockets that propelled American astronauts into space to land on the moon.

Goddard was not the only man to dream of, and develop, rockets that were the prelude to manned space travel. Actually, the Chinese were using rockets powered by gunpowder for fireworks by 1232. It is also believed the Arabs used rockets on the Iberian Peninsula in 1249. Serious scientists began considering actual manned space flight about the time Galileo recognized that planet Earth orbited around the sun, and Earth was not, in fact, the center of the universe. John Kepler wrote Galileo in 1610,

"...Let us create vessels and sails adjusted to the heavenly ether, and there will be plenty of people unafraid of the empty wastes. In the meantime, we shall prepare, for the brave sky travelers, maps of the celestial bodies. I shall do it for the Moon, you Galileo, for Jupiter."

Galileo was the first person to use a telescope to view the skies. He observed that planets moved across the face of the Sun. This was contrary to accepted dogma that Earth was the center of the universe. That concept was the brain-child of Ptolemy, an Egyptian astronomer and geographer of the second century A. D. The idea that planet Earth was not the center of the universe was anathema to the self-anointed intelligentsia of the time. Galileo proved that the theory of Nicolaus Copernicus, an astronomer of East Prussia, was correct. Earth did rotate on its axis daily and rotated yearly around the Sun. For flying in the face of learned professors and the Catholic Church's teachings of the Scriptures, Galileo was reported to the Inquisition for "blasphemous utterances." He was forced to recant his published observations, and spent the last of his years under house arrest.

John Kepler, a contemporary of Galileo, was a German astronomer who formulated laws of planetary motion. Two were included in his published *Commentaries on Mars*. Copernicus, Galileo and Kepler were the awesome trinity of early scientists who changed the views of the universe, providing the fundamentals for planetary exploration by manned and unmanned space vehicles.

The problem with the early rockets was their dependence on gunpowder—solid fuel. The forms of solid fuel available then could not produce enough energy to propel rockets far enough or fast enough for space travel. The early, air-breathing engines that were subsequently developed could not propel a rocket much beyond 90,000 feet.

None of the early scientists could match Jules Verne for his fantastic vision of the future. In his science fiction novel, *De la Terra a` la Lune*, 1865, and in English, *From the Earth to the Moon*, 1873, he envisioned, correctly, that a rocket would be launched from Florida for a trip to the moon. He accurately forecast the effects of weightlessness that astronauts would experience.

The Russians, too, had their claim of being first to envision space travel in Konstantin E. Tsiolkovsky, who recognized that a liquid fuel of hydrogen and oxygen would provide much more power than black powder, but Goddard was the first to develop and use a liquid-powered engine to boost rockets. Tsiolkovsky's publication, *Investigations of Space by Means of Rockets,* 1903, also proposed a closed biological systems using plant life to provide oxygen during prolonged space flights. This concept was seriously considered in the early days of the American man-in-space program.

Another early space travel enthusiast was Hermann Oberth, actually a mathematics teacher in Germany. He set fourth the potential for manned space travel in his 1923 publication, *The Rocket into Interplanetary Space*. He recognized that rockets had the potential to travel at great speeds, essential for manned space travel. In his 1929 publication, *Way to Space Travel*, he provided designs for huge interplanetary space vehicles powered by a cluster of liquid-propelled motors.

Goddard's liquid-fueled rocket that traveled faster than the speed of sound in 1935 took advantage of the markedly increased thrust that could be obtained with liquid fuel. His early work, in 1916, was financed by the Smithsonian Institution. Later, his champion to obtain funding for his work was Charles Lindbergh, who helped raise funds for him from 1930 until the mid-1940s. Oddly, the United States government provided little support for Goddard's rocket developments and even the news media, in all its wisdom, referred to his concepts of travel beyond the Earth as a fantasy of "Moony" Goddard.

During World War II, Hitler demanded progress in developing new weapons, including an atomic bomb. Walter R. Dornberger and Wernher von Braun were charged with developing rockets to deliver explosives. They used much of Goddard's work to develop engines for the large V-2 rockets. The rockets were approximately 47 feet long and weighted over 13 tons, including the one-ton warhead each would carry. They were first fired against Paris on September 6, 1944. The V-2 rockets were very fast and traveled at a speed of one mile per second. Because of their speed, there was no warning that the rockets were coming. They rained down on London and other targets. In all, over 4,000 V-2 rockets were launched against Allied targets during the course of the war.

In 1944, I joined the Navy's program to train new doctors for the Navy's anticipated needs, should the war drag on. I finished the premedical requirements to enter medical school in the early summer of 1945, and was scheduled to enter the University of Kansas Medical School that fall. My classmates, who were also in the Navy program, and I were assigned to a naval hospital near Memphis, Tennessee, to serve as hospital corpsmen for the summer. By then, the war in Europe was nearing its climactic end. The plan to win the war in Europe first before concentrating on the Pacific war had been a success, and at midnight on May 8, 1945, the war in Europe was officially over. The nightmare of Hitler's attempt to establish his Third Reich was finished. That was none too soon, as Germany was making significant progress in developing nuclear weapons that could be delivered by rockets. Hitler was close to having weapons of mass destruction and the means to deliver them.

In the final days of the war in the European theater, the United States and the Soviets competed to obtain the personnel and resources for the Germans' rocket project. The Soviets captured a large number of technicians involved in rocket development. To avoid being captured by the Soviets, Dornberger and von Braun, with at least 100 specialists, headed south to surrender to the United States Army. The United States also captured V-2 rocket components. There were enough to enable them to assemble 100 V-2 rockets. About 70 of these were fired at the White Sands missile range in New Mexico in 1946, providing experience for the American military. The United States had done very little in rocket development during the war.

Those Germans who could escape from being captured by the Soviets did so, including war criminals who made it to South America. The aeromedical scientists also escaped, including Dr. Hubertus Strughold, who had been in charge of aeromedical research for the German Air Force. He was often referred to as the "Father of Space Medicine." Later, as events unfolded, he would be my patient when I became a key scientist for the American man-in-space program. Many members of the German medical group were sent to the School of Aviation Medicine, then at Randolph Air Base near San Antonio, Texas. That would be where I would start developing the medical program to support the Air Force flying personnel and later the man-in-space program. I knew most of them. Kurt Reissmann was among the group. I worked with him when he was assigned to the University of Kansas Medical School and I was starting my career in cardiology in 1951.

It was super secret at the time, but on July 16, 1945, the United States exploded an atomic device near Alamogordo, New Mexico. We had won the race to be the first to develop the atomic bomb. The entire world knew it shortly afterward, on August 6, 1945, when the United States dropped its first atomic bomb on Hiroshima. Immediately, Stalin declared war on Japan—August 8, 1945—just days before the second atomic bomb was dropped on Nagasaki. Japan accepted the surrender terms and a formal surrender was signed on September 2, 1945. Japan surrendered separately to China on September 9, 1945, in Nanking. The nightmare of World War II appeared to be over, but there remained the problem of the Soviet Union, ruled by Joseph Stalin, a communist dictator bent on world domination. That led to the Cold War. The struggle to preserve the independence of the free world was not over.

All of us at the Navy hospital were thrilled when the atomic bomb promised an early end to the war. There was no longer any need to plan for a long war that would require a lot more doctors. We returned to the University of Kansas for one semester and were discharged from the Navy in February of 1946.

***

I was a cardiologist at the U. S. Air Force's School of Aviation Medicine in 1957, when *Sputnik I* was launched. I had gone there as a civilian scientist to develop a program to support flying personnel. Suddenly, I found myself in the trenches of the national effort to send men into space, something I had never considered before. Those early days in the conquest of the cosmos have changed the world. In a way, it is ironic that the National Aeronautics and Space Administration (NASA) was formed because the Eisenhower administration wanted space to be used for peaceful purposes and not as a new arena for military activity. The war against the terrorists has demonstrated how impossible that idealistic view was.

The United States was caught napping when *Sputnik I* was launched by the Soviets and was far behind their efforts to utilize space. It was several years before America could catch up to the Soviets. Finally, the United States succeeded—through difficulty—in landing men on the moon. That achievement, led by Presidents Kennedy and Johnson, produced the necessary advances for both the commercialization of space and its use in maintaining and projecting military power. The first astronauts and cosmonauts were the pioneers in man's attempt to escape from the gravity field of planet Earth.

There are stories to tell about those early days that made today possible. There were political struggles at the highest levels of the government. There were turf wars between the teams that developed the capability to send men into space and land on the moon. Before there were astronauts, there were men of vision who made it possible for the United States to win the race to the moon. One of those men was then Senator Lyndon B. Johnson. He obtained funding for the future Aerospace Medical Center at San Antonio, Texas, in 1952, before the Eisenhower administration was in place. Because of his efforts and knowledge, President Kennedy had the Space Act changed by Congress in April 25, 1961, to name the Vice President, then Lyndon Johnson, to head the National Aeronautics and Space Council, overseeing the nation's entire space program. The Aerospace Medical Center provided extensive support to the man-in-space effort. It was where President Kennedy gave his last official address as President—the day before the assassination—once again emphasizing the importance of the nation's space program.

My role in this great adventure—landing on the moon—was one of the high points in my life. It was a most unlikely story. I was a Kansas farm boy who grew up during the Depression, without plumbing, electricity and usually without a phone. By age 28, I was responsible for an important Air Force program that led to my attending Lyndon Johnson as a physician, helping to set Air Force and NASA medical standards for flight crews, heading the medical evaluations for the selection of the astronauts—including everyone who has ever gone to the moon—participating in training the physicians stationed around the world to monitor the first manned space flights and helping to resolve the medical crises that frequently arose during those years. It was quite a sweep, involving politics, power struggles, medicine and space science.

The conquest of space was the greatest adventure of the 20th century, and I was along for the ride. No, I wasn't in a spacecraft. I was in the trenches, along with many others who made the man-in-space project possible. I was, so to speak, on top of a rocket when somebody lit the damned fuse. And it was a bumpy ride. Don't get me wrong—I'd do it all over again, and hopefully do a better job. I dealt with the top people who guided this great mission, including Presidents, the men who ran NASA, a host of wonderful scientists and astronauts.

I became chief of the clinical sciences division for the School of Aerospace Medicine at the Aerospace Medical Center, responsible for evaluating medical problems that occurred in flight crews. The recommendations in these cases often involved multimillion-dollar decisions, determining whether or not it was safe for a pilot to fly very expensive aircraft. Grounding the pilot was an expensive loss, but letting him crash a multimillion-dollar aircraft was even more expensive, not to mention the risk to human life. But I hadn't seen anything yet.

The world got a wake-up call on October 4, 1957, when a small satellite, *Sputnik I*, startled the world. The Soviets had succeeded in launching a man-made object into orbit around planet Earth. Its *beep-beep* signal reminded the world that the Soviets were first in space and would soon be in control of the skies above, well beyond the altitude fighter-bombers could prowl. Dr. Strughold came to my office and we talked about it and what it meant.

Some scoffed at the Soviet achievement as a stunt and seemed unperturbed about it. But their cavalier attitude changed to concern when the Soviets launched *Sputnik II*, a much larger space vehicle with Laika, a live dog, on board. Suddenly, the future of mankind hung in the balance. Fighter-bombers were not going to be a match for intercontinental ballistic missiles (ICBMs) and orbiting satellites armed with nuclear weapons. There was a real danger the Soviets would threaten the entire free world. This was no science fiction thriller—it was the real thing.

It would be several years before the United States could answer the Soviet threat from space. The road for the Americans would be long and hard. Risks would be taken in an effort to jump-start the American space effort. Although I had never even thought of such a possibility, suddenly I would be directly involved in the national effort to make it possible for men to function in space and land on the moon. It was an exciting challenge: one that would require all my energies and abilities to fill the role these events demanded. The national effort to cope with the Soviet's conquest of the cosmos would change my life forever.

2

DURING THE MISSILE GAP

had raised questions concerning the School, that Air Force Secretary Talbot had then gone to San Antonio to make a personal inspection, that he had ordered a restudy, and that this restudy had brought about the cancellation..

We are going to get to the bottom of this high-handed action. We will see what can be done about it.

Secretary Talbot's efforts to cancel the School of Aviation Medicine were not successful, and congressional action—under Lyndon Johnson's guidance—prevailed. The outcome of this important struggle was reported in a joint statement, released by Senator Johnson, Senator Daniels, and Congressman Kilday on July 21, 1954:

Secretary of the Air Force, Harold E. Talbot, in a conference Wednesday, informed us that he had reviewed the circumstances leading to the recent announcement that the Aero Medical School at Brooks Air Force Base, San Antonio, was to be canceled.

In the light of this restudy, Secretary Talbot has assured us that the project will be continued.

This is, of course, most gratifying to us, in view of our conviction that cancellation of the project, authorized by Congress, was ordered without prior notice to Texas Senators or to the Representative from the San Antonio district and also in view of our conviction that it is a most worthy project.

It is hoped that this important project will now move forward without further delay.

Much later, as I came to know Lyndon Johnson, I recognized what that meeting with Secretary Talbot must have been like. When Lyndon Johnson became certain that something had to be done, he was a force to be reckoned with. Thank God for Lyndon!

At the end of World War II, the Air Force was "pushing the envelope," developing new planes that flew faster and higher than ever before. It was essential to know what a man's limits were and how to protect him. There were a lot of unknowns. Just how fast was it safe for man to fly? There was great concern that it would not be possible to fly faster than the speed of sound: break the sound barrier. Air Force Captain Chuck Yeager settled that question once and for all on October 14, 1947. He was probably the Air Force's hottest test pilot and a survivor in any situation. He flew a new breed of aircraft, the X-1, the first in a series of rocket planes that would eventually fly to the edge of space. The rocket planes were carried under the wing of a mother ship, then dropped to begin their flight. By 1953, Yeager flew the X-1A at Mach 2.5—or 1,612 mph—and that was just the beginning.

Suddenly, the military needed to make a big push in technology. During the Truman administration, in the lull that followed World War II, the government was particularly stingy about spending money on the armed forces. While the Soviets were busy advancing rocket development, much of the activity in the United States was shut down. There was no research at all on Intercontinental Ballistic Missiles (ICBMs) from 1947 until 1951. That caused the "missile gap" between the United States and the Soviets, and the United States was on the short end of the stick. The "missile gap" led to the "space gap."

Both nations were still in the World War II bomber mentality mode. Both were armed with nuclear weapons. The question was, who would strike first? Some advocated that the United States should make a preemptive strike and end the Soviet threat. Much later, after the fall of the Soviet Union, papers revealed that the Soviets considered a preemptive strike against the United States. The world was teetering on the brink of a nuclear holocaust.

Just before the end of my year in Geneva with Dr. Duchosal, I got a letter from Archie. He wanted me to come to Washington as soon as I got back to discuss going to work for the Air Force. He said they needed me and I was the only person he knew who could do the job. I wasn't certain what "the job" was, but I looked forward to seeing him again. I wanted to do research in cardiology and I didn't see how I was going to do that working for the Air Force.

When I returned to the States, I went directly to Archie's home in Washington. His wife, Gert, was a great cook and I enjoyed staying with them. The next morning, Archie and I drove to the Surgeon General's Office in his little Volkswagen. Archie was still smoking, still overweight, and just as enthusiastic as I had remembered him. The surgeon general's staff included Archie, who was in charge of internal medicine, and physicians in charge of surgery, ophthalmology, psychiatry and other specialties. I met all of them.

Archie briefed me about what they wanted. The Air Force was particularly concerned about the pilots in the Strategic Air Command (SAC)—these were the guys who really defended the nation. They could fly over the Soviet Union and drop nuclear bombs, and they could repel any such attack on the United States by the Soviets.

Archie told me that the average age of the SAC pilots was 37. There was practically an epidemic of heart attacks in the United States. It was the leading cause of death in American males, and many SAC pilots would soon be in the age group likely to have one. SAC was the first line of defense of the nation. ICBMs for defense and offense were not yet a reality, but SAC bombers were. The country needed to depend on SAC pilots for the foreseeable future. My job: go to the School of Aviation Medicine and develop a program to ensure the pilots who flew the Air Force's bombers and hottest aircraft were healthy enough to do so, and develop what needed to be done to keep them that way.

I felt like I had stepped into a strange new world. I was just a 28-year-old physician, a budding heart specialist, somewhat intimidated by sitting in the Office of the Surgeon General, discussing matters of the greatest importance to national security, and about to take on a major responsibility for the country.

The Air Force recruited me because of my record during the Korean War, taking care of patients with heart problems, and because of my research background. The Air Force had previously been part of the Army—as the Army Air Corps. When it became a separate service, there was a shortage of physicians in the Air Force who had experience in the cardiovascular field. That was how I became the answer to the need of the moment.

3

BEFORE MERCURY

Left: Dr. Lamb, 1957; Dr. Hubertus Strughold, "Father of Space Medicine," formerly chief of aviation medical research for the German Air Force during World War II and General Otis O. Benson, Commander of the School of Aerospace Medicine.

Janet Travell, personal physician to President Kennedy and White House physician.

3

⤙ It was the 15th of August, 1955, when I arrived at the School of Aviation Medicine. What a shock! It was nothing like I had envisioned. It was an obsolete relic left over from World War II. The School was a small tenant on Randolph Air Force Base, a relatively large military installation to train pilots, located just north of San Antonio, Texas. The School consisted of two rather old, small, two-story office-type buildings and a few old, wooden, temporary barracks-type buildings—temporary on a permanent basis. I had expected a modern research facility with up-to-date classrooms where bright young physicians would learn about the medical aspects of aviation.

The medicine department was a bad joke. There were two rooms for two doctors and enlisted personal, and one room that could be used to examine patients. About the only equipment was a machine to take electrocardiograms. In fact, before I came on board, the plan had been to close the department entirely. The School was rapidly becoming a basic science school, with little or no activity involving patients or pilots. There was a 50-bed hospital for the base military personnel and their families, which was not part of the School. It was next to the building where the medical department was located. I was able to use it for laboratory work or for X-rays, and even to admit patients when necessary.

The sad state of the School's medical facilities was a grim reminder of how things could deteriorate in peacetime, when there was no apparent national urgency. In those days, there wasn't even a hint of interest in sending men into space—except in comic strips. The Air Force was intent on developing missiles and new, hot aircraft to fly faster and higher than ever before. There was no way the School could provide top level medical support for the flying personnel, or for a national requirement such as the man-in-space project. I would have to start from scratch to put together the capability needed to evaluate flying personnel. What had Archie gotten me into?

At the time I took the job, many of my academic friends thought I had lost my mind. After looking over the situation, I tended to agree with them. But there are lots of advantages in starting from scratch: You don't have to overcome a lot of obstacles that are already in place. I was excited about being able to do my research and to learn more about what happened to relatively healthy people exposed to environmental stresses. I had already become intrigued with preventing heart attacks.

Suddenly, the leading cause of death in the United States was heart attacks. That was quite a change. In 1900, the three leading causes of death were all infectious diseases. Tuberculosis was the main cause. Heart attacks were thought to occur only in "old people," not in relatively young, vibrant men who would be flying airplanes. With the epidemic of heart attacks, a young, apparently healthy man could drop dead suddenly, without any previous warning. The nightmare for the Air Force was the possibility that a man would die at the controls of an airplane.

After World War II, Dr. Paul Dudley White of Harvard and Dr. Ancel Keys of the University of Minnesota did a worldwide study of heart attacks. Many of the countries where people ate less, exercised more, and ate less meat simply didn't have many heart attacks. But in more-developed countries, like the United States, where the living was easy, heart attacks had become a major epidemic. No small number of them occurred in relatively young men. The idea that blood cholesterol levels were important was a new thought. The study by White and Keys established the importance of diet in heart disease, a concept that evolved in the years that followed.

I liked the idea of studying what happened to people before they got sick. At the time, traditional medicine dealt with healing sick people, rather than looking for ways to prevent diseases. The exception was the progress in preventing infectious illnesses. Cardiology usually dealt with patients with obvious heart diseases. The question facing most doctors was whether their heart patients were well enough to be passengers on commercial aircraft, not whether they could fly jets. Doctors examined patients in an examining room, on a table or in a hospital bed. The idea of studying human capacity during activity, such as flying, was a very exciting and challenging frontier.

Shortly after I arrived, I looked up from my desk and there was Dr. Hubertus Strughold. He was a legend in his own time, the "Father of Space Medicine." He had been in charge of aviation medicine research for the Luftwaffe during WW II. At the end of the war, both the United States and the Soviets recruited key German scientists.

The Air Force was already anticipating a future in space and Dr. Strughold was chairman of the nation's first Department of Space Medicine, established at the School in 1949. He was really the senior member of the group of German physician-scientists who had been with him in Germany during the war. Strughold was a dreamer. His small department was mainly a one-man think tank. Strughold defined the changes in the atmosphere at increasing altitudes and coined such concepts as the "biosphere," the near-Earth environment that could support life, and the effects of the "biological clock."

Much later, after his death, Dr. Strughold was accused of having been a war criminal, primarily because of the human experimentation done by the Germans during World War II. It is hard to imagine that this gentle, kindly old professor, who was more philosopher than physician, really had any significant involvement in such events. No doubt he was powerless to do anything about whatever happened in Nazi Germany.

Dr. Strughold became my patient. When I arrived at the School, he was 57 years old. His white, thinning hair had a windblown appearance, and his slightly wrinkled face and slow movements suggested a man of much older years. But he had a twinkle in his blue eyes. I often found him sitting quietly in his office, apparently in deep thought, but always ready to stop and talk to me about his recent theories regarding space. He usually began such conversations with, "Now, Lomb," never having lost his German accent, or learned to say 'Lamb.'

Things began to change soon after I was on board. The Surgeon General's Office had to make the final decision regarding pilots who had problems that could affect flight safety. Archie began sending such problems for me to examine. These were pilots who might or might not have had heart attacks, and those with irregular heartbeats, high blood pressure, fainting, or other problems that could compromise flying safety. A pilot usually won't survive if he faints while flying high-performance jet aircraft. A lot of money was invested in training pilots to the level of being able to fly such advanced aircraft. If they crashed, there was a high risk the pilot would be killed and the expensive aircraft would be lost. My job: to make recommendations on the disposition of such cases to the Surgeon General's Office.

One of the first things that needed to be done was to get an electrocardiogram on all air-crew members. It was unbelievable, but there were jet pilots in SAC—our first line of national defense—and other commands who had never had an electrocardiogram. All officers were required to have one at age 40, but there was nothing special for flight personnel. I began the long effort to require at least one electrocardiogram on all flight crews and have them sent to the School. This was the beginning of the Air Force's library of electrocardiograms. It proved invaluable in finding men with problems at an early age, and also to learn what changes occurred in normal men who really didn't have any significant heart disease.

The man-in-space mission had its roots deep in the earliest days of aviation. A great deal of information, which was essential for ordinary and high-performance flight, regarding how flying affects the body had already been discovered, before and during World War II. You didn't just blast off a Chuck Yeager in a rocket plane faster than the speed of sound without having developed the life support equipment to protect him! The effects of the changes in altitude, speed, motion, and gravity (g forces) were among the most important stresses.

You couldn't even fly in a commercial jet if the cabin wasn't pressurized to protect you from the decreased atmospheric pressure at altitude. The higher you go, the lower the atmospheric pressure is. When you get far enough away from the Earth's surface, there is no atmosphere and life cannot be sustained. The first thing a pilot notices as he is exposed to increased altitude is decreased vision. He has to breathe deeper and more rapidly (hyperventilation) to inhale the same amount of oxygen as he would at sea level. As atmospheric pressure decreases further, gases that are dissolved in the tissues are released, forming gas bubbles. These can cause simple aches and pain in the joints, but if they form in the brain or nervous tissue, they may cause a stroke or even death. At sufficiently high altitude, the blood will actually boil, and if you decrease atmospheric pressure fast enough—called explosive decompression—the body will explode.

The astronaut's familiar pressure suit and helmet prevents all of these dangers. It was originally developed for pilots engaged in high performance, high-altitude flights. The astronauts' flight suits maintain a pressure equivalent to 27,000 feet altitude and provide 100 percent oxygen. That combination supplies more oxygen to the lungs than the 20 percent oxygen in the air we breathe at sea level.

The pressure suit also helps protect astronauts and pilots from increased g forces. As a pilot pulls out of a dive, it's like pulling out at the bottom of a dip on a roller coaster—only much stronger. The pull of gravity in that case is from head to foot and will pull the muscles of the face down. That is *vertical g*, and the downward force is parallel to the spine. Blood and body fluids are pulled to the lower part of the body. The pressure suit squeezes the legs and abdomen enough to prevent this. Otherwise, at high g levels, there would not be enough blood flow to the brain and the pilot would black out: something you don't want to happen when flying high-performance aircraft. A momentary loss of consciousness during air maneuvers—even for just a few seconds—can be fatal.

Blasting astronauts into orbit would involve a different g force stress. The pressure would be from front to back—*transverse g*, perpendicular to the spine—rather than from head to foot as occurs when a pilot pulls out of a dive. A mild form of transverse g occurs when an airplane gathers speed going down the runway for takeoff.

You feel yourself being pushed back into the seat. The faster the plane speeds down the runway, the greater the force. I felt really pushed back into my seat during takeoff in the F 104 Starfighter jet when I flew at Mach 2 with one of the Thunderbird pilots. When astronauts are lying on a couch for launch, the mighty upward thrust of the rockets, blasting the spacecraft into orbit, causes a crushing pressure against the chest and abdomen. We needed to know how much transverse g force the astronauts could safely tolerate, and for how long.

Unexpected events often affected my career. In the spring of 1956, during my first year at the School, Dr. Grey Dimond invited me to return to the University of Kansas to lecture in a postgraduate course for practicing physicians. He was my professor when I began my training in cardiology. Near the end of the week, a guest lecturer from Cornell arrived. She was sitting in the audience while I was presenting a lecture. That day we had lunch together, and that was the beginning of our friendship. Later, she wrote of our first meeting in her book, *Office Hours: Day and Night*, about her years in the White House, "Likewise on the panel was a young physician-scientist, Lawrence E. Lamb, who was helping to build the first School of Aerospace Medicine in San Antonio, Texas. Larry and I became friends on the spot."

She was Dr. Janet Travell, then-associate professor of pharmacology at Cornell. She spoke about chest-wall pain and how it often simulated a heart attack. She was one of the most magnetic and charming personalities I had met in many years. Her eyes twinkled and her face was full of expression. She was obviously enjoying life. We joked about my life in San Antonio and I invited her to come see me. Afterward, she was kind enough to send me some reprints of her articles on the areas of work we had discussed. Of course, I couldn't have known then that one day she would be the first woman to serve as White House Physician—an appointment made by President Kennedy—or that we would share so much during the early days of the man-in-space program. I would soon begin seeing Vice President Johnson, and she would be President Kennedy's personal physician. Naturally, we became close friends and confidants. I often stayed with her and her husband, Jack Powell, when in Washington, D.C., during those years.

While the United States wallowed in complacency after WW II, the Soviet Union had quietly developed its rocket expertise, and was taking the first steps to use and explore space. The stumbling block to space was power: rockets with enough thrust to lift objects against the pull of gravity and hurl them into orbit around Earth. The object would be much like a ball attached to a string. As the ball is whirled in a circle at sufficient speed, centrifugal force causes the ball to pull outward, away from the center. The pull of gravity holds objects to Earth's surface. Without it, we would float off, into space. If you can launch an object at sufficient speed around Earth, the outward centrifugal force balances the inward pull of gravity and a weightless state exists. When the speed is too slow, the outward force diminishes and the object is pulled back to Earth by gravity. That is what happens when a spacecraft slows down for reentry to return to planet Earth. If its speed is too great, the outward force is greater than the pull of gravity and it flies out of orbit into deeper space. The huge rockets the Soviets had developed could thrust large weights at sufficient speeds to orbit the Earth. When the Soviets launched *Sputnik I* and *II*, the "space gap" was evident. A major cause was the long period from 1947 to 1951, when no work at all was done in the United States on ICBMs, and that neglect was making a huge difference.

Lyndon Johnson grasped immediately the significance of the Soviets' launch of Sputnik. He observed on October 18, 1957:

The real meaning of the satellite is that we can no longer consider the Soviet Union to be a nation years behind us in scientific research and industrial ability.

The mere fact that the Soviets can put a satellite into the sky—even one that goes beep—does not alter the world balance of power. But it does mean that they are in a position to alter the balance of power.

And they will do it if we remain where we are.

On October 19, 1957, he continued to alert the nation with his remarks:

But it does not take an investigation or a long series of facts to realize the central implication of the satellite. At this point, the question of whether the satellite does or does not possess military value is secondary to the basic meaning of its existence.

Again, on November 4, 1957, at the beginning of Senate hearings, he observed that the United States had to take action:

The time has come for bold, new thinking in defense and foreign policy. The objective of this inquiry is not to fix blame or to put anybody on trial. The objective is to determine what steps can be taken to strengthen our position and restore the leadership we should have in technology.

We need to direct the attention of the public into a frame of mind where, without panic, we can explore the real need for changes in our military policies.

The Soviets' second satellite—*Sputnik II*, launched on the 5th of November, 1957—weighed more than 1,100 pounds, at least six times the weight of *Sputnik I*. Inside *Sputnik II* was a dog that could be heard barking through receiving sets around the world. The barking of a dog in outer space struck fear in the hearts of many Americans—so much so that President Eisenhower gave a television address on November 7 to reassure the public about the adequacy of the nation's defenses.

I watched President Eisenhower's televised speech. He was a calm and reassuring father figure. He held a small cone-shaped object in his hand and announced that the United States had perfected a nose-cone, made of specialized material that could survive reentry into Earth's atmosphere without burning up. Most objects in space are destroyed by fire from the heat produced by friction during reentry. This development ensured that a nuclear warhead could reenter Earth's atmosphere and deliver its payload on target. The space race was on, with nuclear overtones. *Who would deliver nuclear bombs first, and on which cities?*

Eisenhower did not point out that the United States had no rockets capable of orbiting *anything* into space, much less a 1,100 pound space vehicle with a dog on board. The best we could hope to do was to fire a much-less-powerful rocket, perhaps with a small nuclear bomb on board, that could land in enemy territory if the distance was not too great. This was the beginning of mating nuclear weapons to ballistic missiles.

Senate Majority Leader, Lyndon B. Johnson sprang into action in the aftermath of *Sputnik II*, and on November 25, 1957 began hearings on the state of the nation's space program. Still later, on February 6, 1958, he was named chairman of a special committee on space and astronautics, as a result of his long-standing interest and activities in developing the nation's capabilities in aviation and space flight.

Senator Johnson commented at the beginning of the hearings:

It is not necessary to hold these hearings to determine that we have lost an important battle in technology. That has been demonstrated by the satellites that are whizzing over our heads.

But to me—and I think to every American—a lost battle is not a defeat. It is, instead, a challenge—a call for Americans to respond with the best that is in them.

There were no Republicans or Democrats in this country the day after Pearl Harbor. There were no isolationists or internationalists. And, above all, there were no defeatists of any stripe.

There were just Americans anxious to roll up their sleeves and wade into the enemy.

Hearings were certainly needed. *Why was the United States so far behind in missile development?* The Air Force did not award a long-term contract to develop ICBMs until the winter of 1954-1955. Intelligence sources had learned that the Soviets were working on ICBMs that could carry nuclear weapons, and that the Soviets also had a hydrogen bomb. At the end of World War II, the United States held the edge over the Soviets with the atomic bomb. Now, things were reversed, and there was a real danger the Soviets could threaten the United States with nuclear bombs launched by ICBMs. Those large ICBMs could also launch a satellite into space to orbit over Washington, D.C., or other cities. Similar satellites could carry nuclear weapons.

Sputnik II caused great excitement at the School. Suddenly, the possibility of sending men into space was not science fiction. We had to start thinking beyond jet aircraft and consider the problems of men in space vehicles. I was thankful we had a team that could adequately study men under all forms of stress. We were just in time for *Sputnik*.

Even before *Sputnik* startled the world, I was being asked about how certain stresses affected man. I was invited to speak on heart disease and altitude at the Western Cardiac Conference, held in Denver, Colorado, in October 1956. I soon learned that the residents of the Mile High City were particularly interested in the subject, and why. There were a number of calls from reporters. I was somewhat dismayed, since I was young and unaccustomed to interviews with the press. I was cornered by Robert Byers, then a staff writer for the *Denver Post*. He asked a number of questions about altitude in preparation for his news story. Finally, he asked the one question which was uppermost on his mind. He wanted a comment from me regarding the advisability of President Eisenhower visiting Denver, in view of the President's heart attack the preceding year. Even I was not naïve enough to consider this an innocuous question on the eve of the presidential election. The nation had been shocked when President Eisenhower had a heart attack while fishing in Colorado. Would he be able to complete his term or run for reelection? Adlai Stevenson, his opponent, even stated on national TV that Eisenhower would not be able to live out a second term. It was clear that if I gave a controversial answer, I could make national headlines the following day. I told Mr. Byers that it was not my habit to discuss patients I had not seen, and I had not seen President Eisenhower. In fact, I had reviewed his electrocardiograms.

The next day, the newspaper account in the *Denver Post* stated that I had declined to comment on the advice of President Eisenhower's doctor, Major General Howard Snyder, that the President should not return to Denver that year because of the possible adverse effects of altitude upon his heart condition. This was the first time I had heard that the President had been advised against returning to Denver, and I was glad I had made no attempt to answer the reporter's question. Dr. Paul White's long-term studies were published about that time, showing that many men survived for years after recovering from a heart attack. Previous medical opinion held that most men survived only two years after a heart attack. Dr. White's timely study changed that view. In fact, Eisenhower was reelected, completed his second term as President, lived to see Richard Nixon elected and his grandson, David, marry Nixon's daughter.

The question of altitude and heart disease was of immediate concern to me. I had just hospitalized our commanding general at the School of Aviation Medicine, Major General Otis O. Benson, for a severe heart attack. In his assignment, he would need, and want, to fly. Although he would only be a passenger in military aircraft, low oxygen levels would have to be a consideration. General Benson had been stationed at the Surgeon General's Office. I had met him in Washington when I was there to discuss developing a cardiac program for flight personnel. He was a very dapper and proper gentleman. His rather sharp face exuded interest and enthusiasm. He had a narrow, well-trimmed salt-and-pepper mustache, and gave the impression of being a very active individual. He had charisma, and his keen interest in everything around him made him very popular with the School's staff.

I had recently seen the general for his annual flight physical examination and was looking at his records when there was an insistent *tap, tap, tap* on the door to my office. The General didn't wait, but opened the door and burst in. He said to me, "Larry, I think I am having a little angina. Could you give me some nitroglycerin?"

I saw he was mildly agitated and he was sweating rather profusely. I told him we had better take a look at him first and put him on the examining table and started recording his electrocardiogram. At first, it looked like it had on his previous examination, but while the recording was being made, the changes of an acute heart attack were evident. His heart rate slowed to less than 30 beats a minute and I knew he was in a critical state. I moved him immediately to the hospital next door and began treatment for an acute myocardial infarction. As he was being carried out on a stretcher, he said to my secretary, "This is a helluva way to leave his office."

I stayed in the hospital with him to keep a close watch on his condition. This was in the days before there were coronary care units to care for patients who had an acute heart attack. He made an excellent recovery and returned to full duty.

General Benson was eager to develop medical programs to serve the needs of the flight personnel—the very reason I was at the School. I began developing a program which my team used later to evaluate candidates for the man-in-space program. I added several doctors to my staff. One was my friend, Dr. Robert L. Johnson, from my Sheppard AFB days during the Korean War. He had left the Air Force, but returned to the service to work with me. I was delighted to have him back, as he was an exceptionally capable individual.

One of the major concerns was whether a pilot was or was not prone to fainting. This proved to be a concern for the future astronauts. *Would they faint after a period of weightlessness, like people who have been at bed rest for a prolonged period of time?* In the early days of manned space flight, the astronauts, including John Glenn, walked across the deck of the recovery ship with someone on each side of them. That was because of their tendency to faint after flights.

We used a tilt-table to evaluate fainting cases in flight crews. The tilt-table was also used to test the astronauts after their space flights. The astronaut would be strapped in a parachute harness while lying on a table that was then tilted feet-down. He would be hanging motionless in the parachute harness. In a way, it was a humane, mild form of crucifixion—without the nails.

The blood pressure and an electrocardiogram were recorded during the test. If the subject was likely to faint, his blood pressure would fall, and often his heart rate would slow markedly. It was not unusual during this part of the test for the heart to stop completely for a few seconds while the subject was holding his breath, causing him to faint. When he was tilted back and breathing normally, the heartbeat would resume slowly, finally returning to normal rates. We used this test to evaluate astronaut candidates.

The tilt-table studies and other tests related to fainting helped improve flight safety. High altitude causes a person to breathe faster and deeper—called hyperventilation—to deliver enough oxygen from the oxygen-deficient air. This is a normal response to altitude. Pilots had been trained to hold their breath if they noted they were over-breathing. No doubt, many unexplained aircraft accidents occurred because of these old instructions. When a pilot fainted and died in a crash, there was no way to tell at autopsy that cardiac arrest was the cause of the crash. There would be no anatomical change to see. As a result of our studies, the instructions were changed. Pilots were instructed to take slow, shallow breaths, but not to hold their breath.

We needed to know how well the heart functioned at maximum physical effort. Dr. Bruno Balke, one of the German physiologists who came to the United States after the War, had been using treadmill exercise to study lung function. The subject would breathe into a bag so the amount of oxygen the body used at maximum exercise could be measured. I liked this approach, but you couldn't take electrocardiograms while the subjects were exercising. I wanted to take electrocardiograms while people were active and while flying. Unfortunately, the electrodes for the chest and arms commonly used for patients in those days were not stable, so you couldn't get a decent record during exercise.

We had to lick the electrode problem. The engineers at the School helped us. They designed very small electrodes that could be securely attached to the chest. Soon, we had our first subject hooked up. The treadmill started and he began walking. The record was perfect. We watched as the angle and speed of the treadmill increased. The subject's heartbeat increased as he walked faster and faster, as if he were walking uphill: 140...160...and finally 180 beats a minute. We were at about the top level of exercise for a young, healthy individual, and the electrocardiogram was technically perfect. The engineers had also included an electrical filter that eliminated electrical artifacts that would have distorted the record. The subject's blood pressure was taken while he exercised. We had just done the exercise electrocardiograms that would become commonplace in the practice of medicine in the years to come. The same techniques were used to record pilots' electrocardiograms during flight, and later to monitor astronauts during space flights.

We also used a complete battery of tests to evaluate lung function. After such examinations, we had a pretty good picture of how a man would perform during maximum physical effort or stress. The program we were developing to test flying personnel was, in fact, ideally suited to evaluate the first astronauts.

conducted research and partnered in the technical side of developing new planes, including the X-series, for the Air Force. The NACA had brilliant scientists, but they were not ready to take on the operational aspects of the nation's man-in-space program alone. That was the root of a lot of the conflict that existed.

President Eisenhower's desire to avoid letting space become involved in the arms race, and to preserve it for peaceful exploration, was also a major factor. It was commonly stated that as an old Army man, he considered rockets as an extension of artillery and thought of space wars being waged—should they occur—with ICBMs. NACA had growing pains and was reaching out to expand its empire. The end result was the NACA became NASA. While NASA won the right to explore space, they still had a long way to go to achieve the operational capability needed to send men into space.

Neither I nor anyone else at the School of Aviation Medicine had any input into the medical evaluation for the selection of the Mercury astronauts. The psychologists involved in determining what would be included in the selection process had a field day with paper-and-pencil tests. Sadly, most of the tests had never been validated. Only a handful had been investigated with proper research methods. In reality, much of the testing was a giant fishing expedition and a means for the psychologists involved to survey areas for their own interests. They were not a meaningful contribution to the selection of the astronauts. Chuck Berry, an Air Force flight surgeon at the School, did go to Wright-Patterson as an observer, and said afterward that there were so many psychologists there; they "were like ants around a sugar bowl."

The purpose of the selection process was to identify the best men available for the man-in-space program, not to do ongoing research with methods that were of unproved validity. The medical and psychological phase of the selection process was supervised by Lt. Colonel Stanley White, a career Air Force flight surgeon on loan to NASA—along with two psychologists, two psychiatrists, an army medical officer doing his two years of obligatory service, and one test pilot.

The Lovelace Clinic was a fine facility, and examined pilots for some of the major commercial airlines. For this reason, they were better qualified to do the examinations than many university hospitals and even many military hospitals. But the duties of civilian pilots were a long way from the type of activities the first astronauts would be required to perform. A number of individuals in the Air Force medical service, including General Benson, were clearly miffed about NASA's contract with the Lovelace Clinic.

The candidates to become Mercury astronauts were not too happy with the nature of the examinations at the Lovelace Clinic, either. This had nothing to do with the Clinic's medical capabilities, but rather, once again, tests that covered everything—including sperm counts. It is hard to imagine that how much sperm a man produced could have any influence on his ability to be an astronaut. It might be of interest after exposure to excess radiation. If women had been considered for space flight at that time, the sperm count test would have been somewhat of a problem.

The astronaut candidates felt their interest in their examinations was being ignored. They complained that when they asked questions, they were often told it was too complicated to explain, or they were put off in other ways. Part of this may have been because the Lovelace Clinic personnel were not used to dealing with military flying personnel. The test pilots were accustomed to military physicians or, as in my case, a civilian physician working with the military; that meant they were treated like equals. The pilots were intelligent, well educated individuals.

The group of applicants to be the first men in space was narrowed down to 32 test pilots. After the psychological and medical evaluations to identify their characteristics and health status, the final selection was made by three non-medical engineers and managerial types from NASA's Manned Spacecraft Center (MSC), which would be home base for the astronauts. The men making the decisions were Robert Gilruth, the Director of the MSC, Charles Donlan and Warren North, along with input from Lt. Colonel Stan White.

It was entirely appropriate for Gilruth, Donlan, and North to make the final decision, as all of the men considered at that stage of the selection process were deemed to be medically and physically qualified. The remaining question was how well they could perform the mission and fill their roles as the nation's first astronauts. This was how the seven astronauts were picked. How well they succeeded, and how they conducted themselves—in success or failure—would have a major impact on our national image in the eyes of the world.

The primary purpose of the Mercury project was constantly ignored. Yes, the United States was anxious to have astronauts in space and to close the "space gap" with the Soviets. But to be successful in this new unknown arena, it was necessary to learn how the space environment—particularly weightlessness—affected man. It was essential to find out what the risks were before man could engage in something more than making a few orbits around the earth—before going to the moon.

There were many stories about how the final Mercury astronaut selections were made, including the question of political influence by patrons of those selected. By some strange coincidence, three Air Force pilots, three Navy pilots, and one lone Marine pilot were chosen. The Marine was John Glenn. He was 37 and the oldest of the seven astronauts. The Army had no test pilots in the program.

The decision that the first astronauts would be military test pilots was reasonable. They were experienced in flying high-performance aircraft and tested the hottest new planes. Also, it would be a bigger problem to obtain adequate security clearance for any civilians applying to become astronauts. The Air Force had trained most of its test pilots at Edwards Air Force Base in California, home of the Test Pilot School. This was where men such as Chuck Yeager, the first man to break the sound barrier, made their mark. This was home to the pioneers of flight—the men who flew the first planes fast enough and high enough to be at the edge of space. This was where the brave men, who were daring and skilled enough to explore the new frontier, came from. The streets of Edwards AFB are named after the brave men who gave their lives in the pursuit of their passion for flying.

Lyndon Johnson's support for the Aerospace Medical Center continued. On June 6, 1958, he went again to Congress to request additional funding for the Center. In his review before the Senate, he said:

These hearings have developed valuable information to help us meet the challenge of the Space Age. They have made us aware that we must open up new frontiers of knowledge in many different, although related, fields.

Among these fields is that of medicine in the space age.

Against this background, Mr. Chairman, it becomes of vital importance—it becomes an urgent necessity—that construction and equipping of the Air Force Aeromedical Center at Brooks Air Force Base, San Antonio, Texas, be pushed to completion as rapidly as possible.

In 1951, seven years ago, the Air Force submitted a complete design for the Aeromedical Center....

After detailing the needs for the center, he concluded his remarks:

In comparison to the total budget, the amount requested for the Aeromedical Center is small. But the policy established will be of transcendent importance, and its effects will be felt for as long as time endures.

While the nation's attention was focused on the Mercury project, the Air Force quietly continued with its plans to operate in the space arena. There was a strong belief that there was a military role in space, that future wars would be fought in space. The Air Force already had the X-15 experimental plane that could fly to the edge of the space environment. The next step was Dyna-Soar. The plan had been on the drawing board for several years, and funding had been provided for feasibility studies.

One of the first steps to give this program momentum was to select the space crews for the Dyna-Soar mission. Since this was an Air Force project, the widespread dissatisfaction in military circles with the Mercury selection was not likely to permit a repetition of that pattern.

To lay the groundwork for the selection of the Dyna-Soar crews, Brigadier General Don Flickinger, the Command Surgeon for the Air Force Research and Development Command, held a meeting in his offices at Andrews AFB, Maryland, in the suburbs of Washington,

D.C., on the June 23, 1959. General Benson was requested to send a representative who could speak for the School in terms of commitment to participate in the medical evaluation of the Dyna-Soar crews. He requested that I go as his representative. It was a high-level meeting, including Dr. Lovelace and representatives from the Office of the Surgeon General and Edwards AFB. I first met Major Bob White, one of the pilots who had flown the X-15 aircraft to the edge of space, at this meeting.

This was the beginning of my personal involvement in the astronaut selection process. By then, the School's consultation service for the Air Force flying personnel was very active, with a team of people trained to evaluate pilots of high-performance aircraft. We had the major experience available in the United States.

It was agreed at this meeting that the medical evaluation for the astronaut selection program was to be phased over to the School, and the responsibility for medical evaluation was to rest solely with the School. That was it: Events had thrust me directly into the first efforts to send men into space.

We agreed that all pilots flying aircraft beyond the level of the X-15 would be classified as astronauts, and all would be evaluated by the medical evaluation for astronaut selection program. The first four candidates for the Dyna-Soar project were to go through the Lovelace Clinic and the rest would be evaluated at the School. I agreed to go to the Lovelace Clinic to review the procedures they had been following. All the pilots who entered the Edwards AFB Test Pilot School thereafter would also have the same examination. When they graduated, they would provide a pool of young test pilots with the engineering and educational background to fulfill future NASA and Air Force requirements for astronauts. I was very excited about the outcome of the meeting and that this important mission would come to the School. It would be great to bring the news back to my colleagues.

The next morning, after my return to Randolph AFB, I met with General Benson and gave him a complete review of what had transpired. He shared my enthusiasm over the importance of the event and its impact on the future of the School. He immediately made arrangements for a meeting to be attended by all of the professional personnel. By the time of the meeting, the news had spread across the campus like a prairie fire. Every seat in the auditorium was taken, and each member of the staff was listening intently to hear about his role in the nation's man-in-space program.

In the next few weeks, I had to integrate all the different activities of the staff that would support the examination procedures. Everybody wanted to include everything possible in the examinations. I knew about the reaction to the excessive psychological testing during the Mercury astronaut selections and discouraged—upon the advise of the School's psychiatrists and psychologists—the inclusion of tests which could not be validated as contributing to a meaningful evaluation. There would be no fishing expeditions.

The first examinations for the "space pilots" were scheduled for August 3, 1959. This was complicated by the planned move in July of the School to our new facilities at Brooks AFB on the south side of San Antonio. Brooks was an old base with many traditions. As President Kennedy noted, it was the place where Charles Lindbergh had taken flying lessons. It was also where the School of Aviation Medicine was first started.

With the new emphasis on space, the School's name was changed to the School of Aerospace Medicine, and the Brooks location was designated as the Aerospace Medical Center. The first buildings for the nation's Aerospace Medical Center, envisioned by Lyndon B. Johnson, were ready. We moved, and on August 3, 1959, the first two crew members of the Dyna-Soar project reported to begin their evaluations. They were Charles Bock and Russell Rogers, both from the Edwards AFB Test Flight Facility.

Everyone was pleased with the quality and scope of the School's examinations. General Flickinger wrote me a nice letter of congratulations. At this point in time, I was chief of internal medicine and also in charge of—after having developed—the consultation service that evaluated air crews. Shortly thereafter, I was named chief of the Clinical Sciences Division. This included all the clinical medical specialties: the departments of surgery, pathology, psychiatry and psychology, ophthalmology, otorhinolaryngology and others. The Clinical Sciences Division had the final responsibility for all the clinical aspects of problem cases referred from the entire Air Force flying population. I learned a great deal from each of the highly-trained physicians in charge of each department. In many ways, it was like a postgraduate course in all the major specialties of medicine.

I couldn't have been happier. My projects were going well. I was affiliated with a fine group of colleagues, and the future appeared to promise nothing but a continuing series of new accomplishments. Everything was coming up roses—yellow roses, since I was in Texas. Things were too good to last. This was when I received a call from Lt. Colonel Bill Douglas, to arrange for Mercury astronaut Donald K. "Deke" Slayton to see me for a consultation about his heart problem.

5

⏎ Finally, all of the School personnel had moved to the new Aerospace Medical Center. Lyndon Johnson's efforts to provide such a facility were realized. General Benson and I planned an International Symposium on Cardiology in Space. There would be a two-day scientific session on November 12 and 13, 1959, that would include a major portion of the work we had done in cardiology at the School. The following day the new facility would be dedicated, and Senator Lyndon B. Johnson would give the dedication address.

The week before the symposium, San Antonio enjoyed brilliant sunshine. The warm weather added to the festive air. Giant mockups of current rockets were erected in the large circle in front of the headquarters building. Physicians, scientists, and dignitaries descended upon the city.

The symposium was a gala occasion for me, and a high-water mark after four years of hard work. The School's large new auditorium was packed. The customary flags hung from their standards at the corner of the stage. The room was full of good fellowship as old friends greeted each other. The noise subsided as Major General Otis O. Benson stepped to the podium. His remarks, as always, were timely and well received. In one succinct paragraph, he underscored the role of cardiology in aerospace medicine:

Medical Center created for the nation. The preceding October, Mr. Sam Rayburn, Speaker of the House, had announced at a press conference in Dallas the formation of an unofficial Johnson for President Committee. The first Johnson headquarters was established in the Littlefield Building in Austin, Texas, and from there the slogan, "All the way with LBJ" emanated across the land. A young senator from Massachusetts was the other contender for the nomination. He was John Kennedy.

The Brooks facility was packed with guests and dignitaries. The largest auditorium was full. Overflow classrooms and other auditoriums were filled to hear Senator Johnson speak. The Chief of Staff of the Air force, General Thomas White, was there. There were good wishes from nationally prominent people, including a telegram from President Eisenhower. Although the Senator had not made any official announcement, almost everyone was certain that he was a candidate for the Democratic nomination for the presidency of the United States. The Senator assured everyone that he was not about to talk politics, then promptly gave one of the best political speeches of his career. He emphasized that two years and two months after *Sputnik* we were still behind the Soviets. He spoke eloquently and with sincerity. He spared no effort to show his feeling about the importance of the space age and his disappointment that the nation had not progressed further. He called the Aerospace Medical Center "one rung of the ladder to the stars" and he said,

Ladders are not built of rungs alone. There must be firm supports. Today, two years after the age of space was thrust upon us, those supports are still not firm. Our national step is uncertain. Our climb is unsure. Our goal is unsettled. Our effort is divided. This is not the way to space. This is not the way of America. Two years and two months have passed.

Here he held up two fingers of each hand to emphasize his point.

There is a space program in the United States. There are space activities. There will continue to be space projects. But the clear and simple truth is that the will of the people has been allowed to dissipate. We are not out

in front—if anything, we have fallen further behind, and you need to be told the truth. We have very nearly defaulted two precious years and, if that course continues, we may default the century.

The reason for this lies not with the American people. It lies with an attitude of some of their leadership.

There are those who would have us maintain our national poise, whatever the peril, by pretending that the greatest advance of the century has not happened. To this, I say: Space is not a side street of the security of the West. Space is the main street of Freedom's survival. We must be able to walk that street, proud and unafraid, if we are to lead all free men to a community of peace.

Our official policy has not been a policy of commitment. It has been a policy of concession—a policy of conceding leadership to the totalitarians and hoping someday later to catch up.

If we are to 'catch up' we must at least 'stay up'—and on our present course we are neither staying up nor catching up.

Never have free men gambled so much for so little cause as our leadership is now gambling in the deliberate lag behind the Soviets.

We have the resources of mind, materials and money to stand first in space. That we do not stand first rests solely on those in our leadership who lack the will to marshal those resources.

In the course of his remarks, the Senator departed from his prepared text to personally recognize many of his friends. One of those recognized was Dr. Howard Burchell, a well-known cardiologist from the Mayo Clinic. Senator Johnson commented that, following the dedication speech, he was going to take the opportunity to have a medical checkup at this new facility. He had survived a serious heart attack at age 49, an attack he sometimes characterized, "As bad a heart attack as a man can have and live."

It wasn't long after the dedication ceremony until Senator Johnson arrived at my office. Dr. Burchell and I met him there. Crowds of well-wishers greeted him along the way and he had a handshake and a "Howdy" for each. It was obvious that the crowd was delighted to see him, and that he was delighted to see the crowd. In part, because of his tall stature, I had the sensation that he was towering over me. I was impressed by his friendliness and good humor. After a blood sample was taken, he turned, looked at me and said, "Well, I see you have some of those dull Republican needles."

Afterward, I took portions of Senator Johnson's electrocardiogram and constructed a miniature record the size of an identification card that he could keep in his wallet. It included one complete electrical cycle for one heartbeat of each 12 circuits (leads) customarily used for electrocardiograms. I wanted him to have this because he traveled extensively. Any other physician who might be called upon to examine him would have immediate access to a previous record. Later, there were references about the Senator's plastic-covered electrocardiogram, which he carried in his wallet, in *Time, Newsweek*, and *The Wall Street Journal,* among other papers.

I had originally designed such a record when I had been attending General Harry Armstrong, the second Surgeon General of the Air Force. On that occasion, it would have been helpful for me to have access to a previous record. He was having some chest discomfort and none of his medical records were available. This caused me to consider the problem of seeing patients with a possible emergency without their medical records. That summer, during the Democratic National Convention, while I was watching the evening news, I was startled to hear David Brinkley say that Senator Johnson had an electrocardiogram in his wallet and was showing it to everyone at the convention, like others were showing pictures of their family. His electrocardiogram at that time was within normal limits and that pleased the Senator. I was thankful that I had not put my name on the back of the card, as I was concerned that the news media would be contacting me about the Senator. I didn't relish that idea and considered the advisability of a trip to Mexico until the convention was over.

In May, the annual Aerospace Medical Association meeting was held in Miami, Florida. A number of papers were presented by the staff from the School. All of us enjoyed a few days in the sun, with an opportunity to exchange scientific information with our colleagues in pleasant surroundings. It must have been the season for a world honeymoon. Premier Khrushchev and President Eisenhower were making friendly overtures toward each other. My own life was relatively tranquil and I did not foresee any major controversies looming on the horizon. The world was a warm and friendly place—or so it seemed.

While we were at the meeting, everything changed. Large headlines screamed the truth. A U-2 pilot, Gary Powers, had been shot down over the Soviet Union. Now it was public knowledge that U. S. "spy" planes, capable of flying at very high altitudes, had been making secret surveillance flights over the Soviet Union. Only a small number of people were cognizant that such a plane existed, or that the Air Force had gained considerable knowledge about man's ability to survive and fly such high-altitude missions.

It was equally revealing that the Soviet Union had developed accurate missiles, capable of knocking down aircraft at high altitudes. The whole event had much the same effect as that of a blue northern blowing in to Texas at the end of summer.

At the height of the Cold War, U-2 flights over the Soviet Union were done to detect any military build up and to assess the military preparedness of the Soviets. This necessity would end once satellites could orbit high above Earth and take detailed photographs of ground operations. The world was still on alert for a possible nuclear strike. SAC bombers remained on alert, ready to deliver such a strike if the Soviets chose to start a nuclear war. Eisenhower was concerned about the U-2 flights and was reported to have seriously considered canceling the Gary Powers U-2 flight. But in the end, the military felt they needed as much intelligence as possible with one last flight.

To all outward appearances the Soviets and the Americans were entering a new era of friendship. Nikita Khruschev visited the United States and the good chemistry between him and Dwight Eisenhower was dubbed as the "Spirit of Camp David." The two leaders planned for an Eisenhower visit to the Soviet Union and a summit conference in Paris. But a U-2 aircraft piloted by Gary Powers was shot down over the Soviet Union on May 1, 1960. Unknown to the United States, Powers was captured alive and a nasty international situation developed. The U-2 incident resulted in Khruschev angrily confronting Eisenhower in Paris and withdrawing from the summit—any semblance of cooperation between the two nations went into a deep freeze. International tensions were decidedly worse.

The Gary Powers incident would add one more project to my

growing list in the not-too-distant future. Soon, selected candidates for the U-2 pilot program and individuals evidently involved in CIA operations came to the School to have the same examination as the astronaut candidates. Only a few essential staff members knew these were not astronaut candidates, since the matter was highly classified. Some of the staff complained about how poorly their medical records had been screened before they were selected for evaluation in the "astronaut project," particularly when one group arrived just after we had completed examining a group of very healthy space pilots.

An interesting footnote to the examinations for the U-2 pilots was the story about the poison pill. Yes, there was such a medication. It had nothing to do with the selection of astronauts. Such a medication was part of the U-2 pilots' emergency gear, in case they were in danger of being captured after a crash-landing in enemy territory. Powers didn't use it. Don Flinn, the chairman of the psychiatry department, and myself were required to state that the U-2 or CIA candidates being evaluated would use the medication under such circumstances to avoid capture. I never knew if this was for only the CIA U-2 pilots or also for U-2 pilots who were not part of the CIA. Such flights were also made over other hostile nations. U-2 flights over Cuba in 1962 alerted the United States to the presence of Soviet missiles. Otherwise, the Cuban missile crisis might have had a much different ending. Satellites have made high-stakes missions, such as the U-2 flights, no longer necessary for national security. Spies in the skies are capable of detecting any significant threat to national security, other than some of those posed by terrorist activities.

6

ASTRONAUT'S HEART PROBLEM

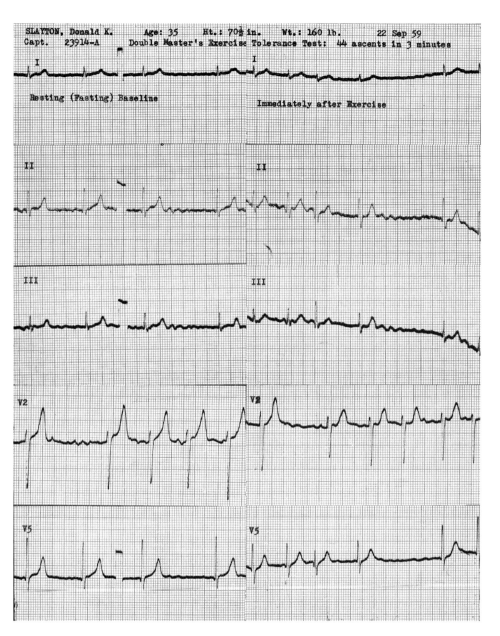

Astronaut Deke Slayton's electrocardiogram after mild exercise. Each sharp, tall complex (QRS) is caused by the irregular electrical stimulation of the heart to contract, causing a grossly irregular heart beat, characteristic of atrial fibrillation. The low amplitude undulations of the base line are from electrical stimulation of the atria, the upper chambers of the heart, fibrillating at a very rapid rate.

6

⤷ Undoubtedly, the one most difficult decision I had to make in evaluating an astronaut's fitness to fly was the case of Deke Slayton, the astronaut who was not allowed to pilot a Mercury flight—and for very good reasons. This was the case that made national headlines and news around the world.

It was September 1959, and I was still basking in the satisfaction of heading the team that had accomplished the first medical evaluations for the planned Dyna-Soar project when I received an ominous telephone call from Lt. Colonel Bill Douglas. He was an Air Force flight surgeon on loan to NASA, assigned to be the personal physician to the astronauts. He called to tell me that one of the Mercury astronauts, Donald K. "Deke" Slayton, had an attack of atrial fibrillation. Douglas thought it might have been caused by a recent viral infection, and he needed to obtain a cardiac evaluation. He asked if he could bring Slayton to see me. We discussed the matter briefly and I assured him I would be glad to do whatever I could. I scheduled an appointment for Douglas and Slayton to come to the school—which they did on the 21st of September.

I would never have anticipated that this would become a national issue at the highest levels of the government—including President Kennedy—or that it would create such divisiveness within the man-in-space community. But it did. It had the potential of undermining the nations' man-in-space program, and that had international implications. That just couldn't happen.

I met Deke Slayton and Bill Douglas in my office at the Aerospace Medical Center. It was the first time I had met any of the Mercury astronauts, or Bill Douglas—one of the early career Air Force flight surgeons.

I had every reason to be sympathetic to Major Slayton's cause. After all, he was one of only three Air Force pilots who had been selected for the nation's space program. I was highly partisan and did not want the Air Force's role to be jeopardized in any way. Deke Slayton was a likable guy, and made a very good personal impression on me. All the astronauts had the capability to present themselves well—when the occasion demanded it, and if they wanted to. *"Would they make good heroes?"* had been one of the considerations of the selection program. The first men the United States sent into space *must* present "a good national image."

Bill Douglas had been with the seven astronauts since their initial selection. He was a tall, rather good looking individual with slightly curly blond hair and blue eyes. He had a friendly demeanor and was easier to communicate with than Deke. Douglas had become closely identified with the group, which he was expected to do in fulfilling his duties, and he enjoyed being referred to as "the eighth astronaut."

Deke appeared to be a healthy, robust individual. His dark brown hair was cut in a short "crew cut" and the sides were clipped rather close. That was the popular style then. His hairline was receding, which made his facial features more prominent, and he had a rugged, muscular look. He was rather stoic, so Bill Douglas did much of the talking. At the age of 35, Slayton had acquired a wealth of experience, and was regarded as one of the nation's top test pilots. Deke was expected to be a standout in the nation's space program, and likely to be the first American astronaut in space. There was no indication that he had any medical disorders when he was initially examined for entrance into the space program at the Lovelace Clinic in Albuquerque, New Mexico.

Deke's problem surfaced on August 27, 1959, when he was tested on a human centrifuge. As the arm of the centrifuge whirls around and around, the gravitational force (g force, centrifugal force) increases the body weight. In manned space flights, the astronaut is lying on a couch during launch. The increased g force is perpendicular to the chest, compressing it and affecting the astronaut's ability to breathe. It required a large g force to accelerate a space vehicle to orbital velocity: at which point weightlessness occurred. It was essential to be sure all the astronauts were able to tolerate the high g loads required for space flights in those days.

Bill Douglas noted that Slayton had an irregular heartbeat during a centrifuge test. Slayton had "not felt up to par" that morning. The irregular heartbeat was obvious to Dr. Douglas when he reviewed Deke's electrocardiogram. The big surprise was that it had not been caused by the increase in g force during the test at all. It was actually present before the centrifuge run started, which was probably why he had not "felt up to par" earlier in the day. The irregularity had occurred spontaneously. Deke had atrial fibrillation. This was the same problem that President George H. W. Bush developed years later, secondary to an overactive thyroid. But the President had a medical condition that could be cured—an overactive thyroid—and he was not a candidate to be one of the first men to blast off into space.

Douglas hospitalized Slayton in a nearby medical facility where he was carefully examined. Nothing of note was found during the studies except for a minor variation in his blood count. That was the main reason the possibility of a virus infection had been considered. When I reviewed the medical records from the Lovelace Clinic, I noted the same variation in the white blood cell count was present when he was examined before entering the astronaut program. It had been there all along and was of no real significance—so much for the recent virus infection theory.

There was nothing definite in Slayton's history to suggest a heart problem. He had fainted in 1946 when he entered the gate of a military installation, and he experienced an earlier episode of fainting during childhood. I had already done surveys of the flying population and learned that such a remote history of a single fainting episode in childhood was not unusual. There remained the possibility that an episode of atrial fibrillation had caused him to faint in 1946. There was also a history of an episode of "heart palpitations" during some air races held in Oklahoma three years earlier. No medical examination had been done, so the significance of this rather vague history was difficult to assess.

Atrial fibrillation is an irregularity of the heart that causes the top part of the heart, the *atria*, to contract or twitch at a rate of about 500 twitches a minute. These are ineffective mini-contractions, which decrease the heart's ability to pump blood. This can cause the lower chambers of the heart, the *ventricles*, to beat so fast they cannot fill adequately. That can cause a person to be breathless or faint. In other cases, only a few of the 500 atrial impulses stimulate the lower heart, allowing the heart to pump adequately for normal activities, but unable to perform at peak levels required during vigorous exercise or any activities that required the heart to perform at its maximum capability.

Atrial fibrillation is most commonly seen in people who have significant heart disease, although it also can occur in individuals who do not. This raised serious and valid questions regarding Slayton's medical fitness to be an astronaut. The problem was not a simple heart murmur, as falsely reported in numerous news accounts based on information from NASA's Manned Spacecraft Center (MSC)— perhaps in an attempt to conceal his real problem.

Slayton was a very active man and had never shown any evidence of physical limitation. After a careful examination, I was unable to find any significant evidence of an important underlying problem. I had hoped we might uncover some temporary cause for his atrial fibrillation that could be treated and prevented from recurring.

The next morning, when Slayton arrived at my office, he greeted me with the information that his atrial fibrillation had started again. The evening before, after eating, he began to have the sensation associated with the onset of irregular beats. He had learned to recognize the attacks, *a fact that suggested he had experienced more than a few episodes in the past*. My examination confirmed his observation. This represented the third documented example of atrial fibrillation in approximately one month, and no one knew how many others had occurred that were not documented.

Despite an extensive medical examination, including removal of a lymph node to look for any evidence of an infection, no underlying medical problems were found. This was very disappointing to me because I knew what the impact of such an intermittent finding would be on the advisability of his remaining in the nation's space program or even stay on unrestricted flight status in the Air Force to fly high performance aircraft.

For years, it was an Air Force regulation that anyone with atrial fibrillation could not be a solo pilot to fly high-performance jet aircraft. The only exceptions—*which had to be granted by the Surgeon General*—were for individuals who had one transient episode, caused by a correctable medical abnormality: such as a complication of acute pneumonia or other temporary illness. There were occasional senior officers of general rank who were permitted to stay on limited flight status, since their overall responsibilities required it. But even in those circumstances, such officers were not responsible for flying high-performance aircraft, and they were essentially passengers.

The plain truth was that if Deke Slayton had been on duty in the regular Air Force—not on assignment to NASA—he would have been disqualified from flying and grounded without a second thought. Period. Bill Douglas knew that very well. Since Slayton wasn't qualified for high-performance flying in the Air Force, how could he possibly be qualified for the first man-in-space flights that were so vital to the nation?

The Air Force's policy on atrial fibrillation had been set for good reasons by some of the foremost cardiologists in the country. While it could occur in individuals with no demonstrable heart disease, that is quite rare. In other instances, the irregularity is evidence of a recent underlying heart attack, rheumatic heart disease, inflammation of the heart, an overactive thyroid gland or a number of other medical disorders.

Even if there was no apparent underlying heart disease, it was not considered safe for such individuals to fly high-performance jet aircraft. Should such an unpredictable attack occur while flying, it could be catastrophic. Atrial fibrillation can cause fainting. That could have been the reason Deke fainted in 1946. You can't faint for even a few seconds if you are flying at twice the speed of sound and survive. All of these aspects of atrial fibrillation had been carefully considered well before the space program began, long before my time.

The United States' man-in-space effort could ill afford the unnecessary risk of letting Slayton pilot a Mercury flight. To do so would jeopardize the future of the entire mission. It was essential to stick to the purpose of the Mercury flights: *to obtain information about how man responded to the space flight environment: particularly weightlessness.* The big unknown in manned space flight was how weightlessness would affect the human body. The man-in-space program was not a contest to see who was the best jet jockey, maneuvering high-performance jets. Astronauts really wouldn't do what test pilots do: loops, rolls, stalls, and other aerobatic maneuvers.

We were severely limited in ways we could collect data during space flights in those early days, and had to depend on an electrocardiogram, blood pressure, respiration, and body temperature. If an astronaut had atrial fibrillation, that alone would affect the heart rate, the blood pressure, and make it impossible to assess the effects of space flight on normal astronauts. There would be no way to tell what was caused by atrial fibrillation and what was caused by space flight. Nothing would have been learned about the effects of weightlessness on normal healthy pilots. The results of a multi-million dollar space ride would not provide any accurate useful information.

Orbiting an astronaut with atrial fibrillation could have made the United States the laughingstock of the world. If a catastrophe occurred, no one would know if it was really because of space flight conditions or from the heart irregularity. It would have been a very bad, ill-conceived experiment, costing millions of dollars. Congress was not all that enthusiastic about providing funds for the man-in-space program, either. Such a fiasco could have made NASA's effort to obtain funds that much more problematic. It didn't matter how much I might have wished it to be otherwise; it was my painful duty to discuss the facts with Deke Slayton and Bill Douglas. I always hated having to tell patients unwelcome news.

At the completion of the examination, I explained to Deke that I doubted very much that he would be able to continue in the Mercury project. Clearly, he understood me. Bill Douglas was with him and most certainly, as a flight surgeon, he understood me. My opinion was a severe disappointment to Deke. Tears welled up in his eyes and ran down his cheeks, visible evidence that he did understand my remarks.

I knew how much it meant to him and was deeply touched by his reaction to such bad news. It was not my responsibility to make the final decision concerning Slayton's role in the nation's space program. It was my responsibility to express an honest medical opinion—which I did.

Not all of the test pilots who were potential Mercury astronauts were exactly thrilled with the opportunity. The initial plans were for a sealed capsule, and the astronaut had little to do except be a "man in a can." That was not what test pilots did or liked to do. They liked to take a plane up and do aerobatics and aerial maneuvers. In addition, pilots tended to dread medical examinations that might uncover some medical problem, which would disqualify them from flying. The potential candidates were afraid that the planned extensive astronaut examination would do just that.

Ordinarily, written copies of consultations on Air Force flying personnel were forwarded to the Office of the Surgeon General for a ruling. In Slayton's case, he was an Air Force officer on duty with NASA. Supposedly, the Mercury astronaut candidates were promised their medical examinations at Wright-Patterson and the Lovelace Clinic would not to be relayed to their parent services—in Slayton's case, to the Air Force Surgeon General. Some apparently believed that the nation's first astronauts were a special category, beyond usual management practices. It is not at all clear that the Air Force Surgeon General's Office ever agreed to such an arrangement.

At the end of my examination of Slayton, Bill Douglas took this opportunity to remind me that the astronauts' medical records were the responsibility of NASA, and I was not to forward copies of the consultation elsewhere. All I needed to do was to prepare a report and give it to him—he would manage all matters thereafter. This was agreeable to me, since I was acting as a consultant to him in his capacity as the physician for the Mercury astronauts. It was his responsibility to forward my consultation to the proper authority. It was exactly this policy that led to the fact that Slayton was not qualified for unrestricted flight status being covered up for quite some time, and resulted in the crisis that followed.

Slayton's medical status was known to General Don Flickinger. He was probably responsible for the policy of not providing the results of the astronaut examinations to the Surgeon General, indeed, if anyone was authorized to make such a commitment. He had been in charge of an earlier meeting to phase over the medical examinations of astronaut candidates to the School under my supervision. Shortly after I had seen Slayton, I received a long distance call from General Flickinger. He reminded me that there could be differences in professional opinions on medical matters, and that it was in the best interests of the nation not to let medical findings reflect adversely upon the selection program of the original seven Mercury astronauts—done at Wright-Patterson and at the Lovelace Clinic. He said it would not be wise to withdraw any of the seven Mercury astronauts from the program, and that Slayton would be retained to utilize his engineering skills.

I had no reason to think that Slayton would be assigned as the pilot astronaut for the planed one-man Mercury flights. General Flickinger told me Slayton's medical problems had been brought to his attention by Dr. Douglas, and I was not to make a specific recommendation concerning the retention of Slayton in the Mercury program for the reasons he had stated.

General Flickinger's conversation with me suggests that he did not inform Air Force Surgeon General Oliver K. Niess. But I do not know if Bill Douglas ever gave General Flickinger a copy of my consultation, either. Flickinger made his comments to me based on Douglas's verbal report BEFORE I had written my consultation. That established that Bill Douglas certainly knew and understood that I did not think Slayton was medically qualified for the Mercury project and had discussed my opinion with General Flickinger. As an Air Force flight surgeon he also knew Slayton was not qualified for unrestricted flight status to fly high performance jet aircraft. That was why Flickinger called me to request that I not make a recommendation regarding Slayton's status in the Mercury project. The subsequent claims that I had cleared Slayton were self-serving fabrications.

After these instructions, from what I considered an authoritative source, I prepared the consultation. I complied with Flickinger's request not to make a specific recommendation concerning Slayton's continued retention in the NASA program. But I made it unmistakably clear, from a medical point of view, what such a heart irregularity could mean.

I pointed out that Deke's fainting episode may have been caused by atrial fibrillation, that individuals who had this condition could form blood clots in the heart that could be most serious (such a clot could go to the brain, causing a stroke, or to the lungs, causing a pulmonary embolus, which could be fatal) and emphasized that when an attack occurred, it limited the heart's ability to pump blood. In reference to flying, I wrote, "Concerning the relationship of this arrhythmia to flying performance, it must be stated unequivocally that the recurrence of such episodes of atrial fibrillation are unpredictable and there are no tests which will enable us to predict when such episodes will occur or how long they will last. During episodes, it is quite clear that such an individual is not at his peak performance level."

There were many false statements about what I recommended and whom I wrote to. It was never true—as was reported—that I had said Slayton's heart problem was of no importance or that I held a board of physicians to make a recommendation on Slayton's case. All of these falsehoods were the work of spin-doctors (the actual written consultation I provided to Bill Douglas is included in appendix A).

Major Slayton's problem relative to space flight was not dissimilar to the plight of the epileptic. Between attacks he could be in excellent health. True, even an epileptic could fly an airplane, provided he didn't have an epileptic convulsion while flying. But that does not mean an epileptic, subject to convulsions, should pilot aircraft or a space vehicle.

This was the blast-off of the Slayton affair. Slayton's understandable ambitions were supported by a cadre of individuals, each pursuing his own agenda. Yes, it was a bumpy ride during the remainder of my participation in the man-in-space project. I was determined to prevent a cover-up and see to it that the nation's effort to send men into space would not be jeopardized. It was a lose-lose situation for me, but I recognized my responsibility and responded accordingly.

7

GETTING READY FOR MERCURY FLIGHTS

medical aspects of

space operations

This is to certify that

LAWRENCE E. LAMB, M. D.

has successfully completed a training course in the

MEDICAL ASPECTS OF SPACE OPERATIONS

designed to qualify him for duty as a

SPACE SURGEON

17 JUNE 1960

L. I. DAVIS
Major General, USAF
Commander

O. K. NIESS
Major General, USAF, MC
Surgeon General, USAF

GEORGE M. KNAUF
Colonel, USAF, MC
Staff Surgeon

AIR

FORCE

MISSILE

TEST

CENTER

Extreme left: Stan White, Lt. Colonel USAF flight surgeon assigned to NASA-Manned Space Craft Center.

PAUL DUDLEY WHITE, M. D.

264 BEACON STREET

BOSTON, MASS.

CONSULTATION BY APPOINTMENT

February 24, 1961

Dr. Lawrence Lamb,
School of Aviation Medicine,
Brooks Air Force Base, Texas.

Dear Larry :-

Thanks very much for your interesting
full report on Mr. Wadsworth. I am in
hearty agreement with your attitude about
his case. *the whole story yet*
I suppose we just cannot tell but
I am going to try to examine some of the
very tall basketball players later on in
the spring or summer after their season is
over.

Will you be so good as to let me
know what disposition may be made of Mr.
Wadsworth's case if you find out?

*With kindest
personal regards.* Sincerely,

PDW:D

Paul D. White

7

⌐ NASA began to prepare for the United States' first manned space flights, in spite of our rather primitive capability. Project Mercury was our fist step in finding out how the hostile environment of space would affect man. By then, we knew the Soviets had survived in space, but we had precious little information from their early flights to guide us. We needed data on how astronauts functioned during weightlessness. *Just how much would the body deteriorate in the absence of gravity? Would the heart and circulatory system function adequately? Would an astronaut be able to do any work while orbiting in the weightless state?* Our ability to monitor astronauts in space was limited. We needed to know what was happening to these early space pioneers and to be able to terminate a flight if an astronaut was in danger. At that date, NASA did not have any centralized monitoring system. The substitute was to ring the globe with a belt of monitoring stations. The Mercury capsule could only transmit about five minutes of data as it passed over each monitoring station. The monitoring area of some stations, such as those across the Southwest United States, would overlap each other, providing frequent sampling. Where larger distances existed, there were periods of time when no data samples could be recorded. The stations extended downrange from Mission Control Center at Cape Canaveral to include the Canary Islands, across Africa, Australia, Hawaii, and the Southwest United States. Also, there were ships in the Indian Ocean that would receive data. The chain would provide a means of intermittent sampling throughout the orbital path.

The crews in the monitoring stations had to be trained for their missions. The space surgeons would not be examining patients resting quietly in an examining room or in a hospital bed. They would be charged with detecting and evaluating changes in active young astronauts exposed to an environment unknown to man. There weren't too many guidelines they could follow. NASA had a two-week course planed to train the medical monitors, and the first week was rocket science, held at Patrick AFB, Florida, amidst the early rockets at the beginning of the space age.

After the meeting in Miami, I went directly to Patrick AFB to participate in the two-week course for the physicians who would be the medical monitors for our first manned space flights: Project Mercury. Each monitoring station around Earth would pick up signals from the astronaut during orbit and transmit the monitor's observations and interpretation to a central monitoring station. There was no way to provide instant information to a central location at the onset of manned space flight. Later, a system was developed to relay real-time in-flight information directly to the Manned Spacecraft Center in Houston.

The two-week course was to bring the medical monitors "up to speed" on the latest information in rocketry and missiles, as applied to the Mercury project: the Mercury capsule and life support system, the communications system, and an overview of the medical aspects of Project Mercury. One week was at Patrick AFB on the Cape, while the second week was at Langley AFB, where the Manned Spacecraft Center was located at that time. Later, all the physicians were expected to have a course in monitoring electrocardiograms. All the individuals who took the course would be designated as *"space surgeons."*

One of the principal duties of the physicians was to interpret the electrocardiogram as it was received at each station to determine the heart rate, any irregularity of the heartbeat, or other changes that might be significant. As the consultant in cardiology to the Mercury project, it was my responsibility to develop and provide the course in electrocardiography. I was one of the newly designated *space surgeons*. The electrocardiogram provided information on the heart rate and regularity and possibly any changes in the heart itself. Blood pressure, respiration and body temperature were also measured. Of course, voice communications between the astronaut and the monitors was very important.

At the beginning of the Mercury project, NASA had little, if any, medical capability and depended heavily on career flight surgeons from the Air Force. That had a lot to do with the conflicts and power plays that occurred. I was quite familiar with the feuds that existed within the Air Force medical group. Long-standing animosities existed between some of the senior medical officers, in part because of the competition for advancement. Part of it was from rivalries that developed between different medical laboratories that were competing for the same mission, as occurred between the School of Aerospace Medicine and the Wright-Patterson Aeromedical Laboratory. The preeminence of the School of Aerospace Medicine at that time engendered no small amount of professional jealousy.

The man-in-space program provided a sudden opportunity for power, recognition, and advancement. Everyone wanted to be a major player and control various parts, or all, of the space program. Large sums of money were involved to support NASA programs at various medical facilities. All of this stimulated a certain amount of destructive competition.

I was suddenly in the midst of a cauldron of multiple turf wars, settling of old scores and new ones, and battles for power. Some individuals who stepped out of the Air Force to serve NASA were no longer under the Air Force's control and some saw an opportunity to exercise power and to exact revenge. This was not something I relished at all, but I would have to deal with it. In truth, some of the feuds within the Air Force medical service eclipsed any problems that existed between top NASA and Air Force officials.

The portion of the course at Patrick AFB was headed by Colonel George Knauf, and much of it had been organized by Lt. Colonel Stan White, previously at the Wright-Patterson laboratory and an arch foe of the School. He was on loan to NASA and in a position to exercise power. Apparently, it was NASA's policy, at least as related to the man-in-space program, that no one would be seen in uniform. I am not sure who, if anyone, within the hierarchy at NASA decided this, but it was clear that at some level NASA didn't want it to be recognized that a large component of the support for the man-in-space effort was really provided by the Department of Defense.

Stan White was an unusual person and very ambitious. He seemed to have a great deal of thrust and spoke in a rather loud voice. He tended to dominate any conversation he was in. He was a bit Napoleonic—in fact, he had some of the same physical characteristics. His black hair was receding, which gave him a large forehead, and he had a large bald spot at the back of his head. He tended to hold his head up with his chin jutted forward, and he had a slightly protuberant abdomen and rounded shoulders.

When we arrived at Patrick AFB the first evening, all the future space surgeons were huddled together and addressed by George Knauf and Stan White. We were told in no uncertain terms that we were there for a very special purpose: that there was a large number of very competent people from the Air Force who had not been invited because there was not going to be any "troublemakers" in the group. We had been selected to support a NASA project and no one was to wear his uniform. Everyone was to be seen in civilian clothes, and, "By God, the Air Force isn't running this program." Those were the welcoming remarks by George Knauf, Colonel USAF, and were indicative of the deep divisions within the Air Force medical service itself.

We took the remarks in stride and were more amused than annoyed by the emotional outburst. Most of the medical monitors had been in the aviation medicine residency program at the School and I had taught them cardiology and electrocardiography. There were also several flight surgeons from the Navy and a lesser number of physicians from the Army. Two Australian physicians in the group added a bit of character and spice to the proceedings.

Driving across the facilities at the Cape was a unique experience. We saw the gantries that had been erected to launch the early missiles. The opportunity to see the development of the early missile program was a fascinating experience. One afternoon, we stood on the top of one of the buildings and watched the first successful firing of an Atlas missile. It went downrange over 5,000 miles and landed precisely on target. The nation's intercontinental ballistic missile capability was being developed. We had just seen the firing of the missile that would orbit the first American astronaut, John Glenn, into space. We had a firsthand look at the Atlas and Polaris missiles and observed a Polaris missile firing as well.

The second week at Langley AFB was spent in more intensive study of the Mercury project, including the capsule and life support system. Al Shepard made a major effort to help with the teaching program. It was a good session, giving each of us a better appreciation for Project Mercury.

When I returned to the School, we started making arrangements to train the physicians who would monitor the Mercury flights. The biomedical engineering section of the School setup a system to telemeter electrocardiograms with the same type of electrical equipment that would be transmitting records from the Mercury spacecraft during flight. Records with different types of abnormalities were put on magnetic tape so they could be played back on monitoring screens.

All seven of the Mercury astronauts came to the School. We recorded their electrocardiograms to show how their records looked while they were doing various breathing exercises, while they were on the tilt-table we used to test for a tendency to faint, and during exercise on the treadmill. All of them exercised until their heart rate reached 180 beats a minute.

The Mercury astronauts were independent and strong-minded: not a bad trait for individuals who would fly solo into space under difficult circumstances. This also made it hard to deal with some of them when their cooperation was needed. I recall Gordon Cooper's reaction to marking his chest for the location of the electrodes. A small spot, the size of the lead in a pencil, was carefully put in place for each of four electrodes. He objected and didn't want it done. John Glenn—somewhat the father figure of the group—persuaded him to cooperate.

This was important because the medical monitors would have to interpret variations of each astronaut's electrocardiogram during flight. How the electrocardiograms looked depended on where the electrodes were placed. There was no substitute in monitoring for the records of each astronaut's own electrocardiograms taken during a variety of stresses. To illustrate how this eventually was used, we recorded Al Shepard's electrocardiogram when his heart was beating at 180 beats per minute. During the first Mercury flight—his sub-orbital flight—his heart rate never exceeded 130 beats a minute. The nature of his electrocardiogram and his heart rate helped the monitors to know that he was within the limits he tolerated—well below his maximum capability.

Each of four groups of physicians stayed for a three-day course and was given didactic training in irregularities of the heart, using material that had been collected from studying the Air Force flying personnel. Mock-up models of the individual monitoring stations were provided so the physicians could practice and become familiar with the variations in each of the Mercury astronauts as demonstrated on the monitoring screen. It was essential that each physician appreciate the changes that would normally be expected with hyperventilation (rapid breathing) or deep breathing maneuvers, simple changes in body position, or stresses that would be expected to occur during flight. The experience at Litton Industries—when the difference in electrocardiograms between lying down and standing up was mistakenly thought to represent heart damage—was proof of how important it was that these variations be understood. Stan White and Bill Douglas also attended the course, along with the medical monitors.

By then, our library of electrocardiograms was proving to be important to the civilian community as well as the Air Force. Dr. Paul Dudley White, who had founded the cardiology service at Harvard, was one of those interested in the data. He was familiar with my earlier work in vectorcardiography (three-dimensional electrocardiography), when I was working with Dr. Pierre Duchosal in Switzerland. He had visited the laboratory and was keenly interested in the three-dimensional models. We even discussed doing such a test for President Eisenhower when he had his heart attack. Dr. White referred some interesting electrocardiograms to me that showed variations in tall, thin people. Eventually, we did a complete study on the electrocardiograms of very tall people with a statistical analysis of the data. Without the development of such a library, information of this sort could not have been provided. Dr. White and I had considerable correspondence about electrocardiograms, and I was impressed by his continued interest in anything new in clinical cardiology. He had long since established himself as the father of clinical cardiology in the United States.

Evidently, because of my recommendation about Deke Slayton's atrial fibrillation, all subsequent annual examinations of the Mercury astronauts were done at the large Air Force hospital at Lackland AFB, a short distance down the road from the Aerospace Medical Center. These arrangements were made by Bill Douglas and Stan White. The Lackland hospital staff was quite competent in clinical medicine, although their main duty was to care for sick people, particularly those sick enough to be hospitalized, rather than the problems related to men flying high-performance aircraft or piloting spacecraft. That didn't really concern me as we had quite enough to do already. However, the wheels were set in motion to produce competition between the medical staffs at the hospital and the School.

Sometimes, competition is healthy. It was understandable that the hospital staff wanted to get a piece of the action in space, and of course there were things they could do—but sometimes, such competition can be destructive. Actually, the hospital had all it could do to fulfill its intended purpose: to provide quality care for sick people in the Air Force, not healthy pilots. One of the main reasons for the School was to deal with the unique problems of the flying personnel. That was defined in the first plan for the School of Aviation Medicine, submitted in 1951, called the Armstrong Plan after General Harry Armstrong, one of the pioneers in aviation medicine and a former surgeon general. It was recognized even then by the original leaders in aviation medicine that such a unique facility, not another hospital, was essential to fill this need.

The Air Force had a knack of constantly reorganizing; the medical service was no exception. Once the new facilities were built at the Aerospace Medical Center, it was decided to form a new administrative headquarters to supervise all the facilities involved in aviation and space medical research as well as the large Air Force hospital at Lackland AFB near the Center. This newly-created administrative monstrosity was called the Aerospace Medical Division. In addition to the School it also supervised the Aeromedical Laboratory at Wright-Patterson AFB in Ohio and the Holloman facility in New Mexico. This was done with the intent to coordinate all the work by the different facilities, but it ended up being a paper-shuffling and planning factory that took up the facilities originally planned for the administration of the School. This made little difference at first, because General Benson was both the first commander of the Division and the commander of the School. But in January 1961, General Benson retired from active duty.

There were not many General Bensons in the Air Force Medical Service, and his departure was not good for the Air Force or the nation. He had been of enormous help to me in launching the various programs I was responsible for. He was my main support in establishing the medical service. When I first arrived at the School, there was essentially nothing you could call a medicine department or consultation service. Now, it was an essential resource for the Air Force and the man-in-space program.

Upon General Benson's retirement, Colonel Robert Blount became commander of the School. He had been General Benson's deputy. His past experience in managing research laboratories, including command of the Wright-Patterson Aeromedical Laboratory, ideally suited him for the position. We had a good working relationship and were good friends.

The new commander for the Aerospace Medical Division was General Theodore C. Bedwell. Under the new organization, he was Colonel Blount's boss. Many different reasons go into the choice of a particular officer for a specific assignment. It was thought by some that the choice of General Bedwell would ensure that the output of the Aerospace Medical Center would be geared to the operational needs of the Air Force in the sense of traditional day-to-day operations. General Bedwell was a genuine product of the military system. His previous assignment had been as the Surgeon for the Strategic Air Command (SAC). In this capacity, he was immediately concerned with the administrative management of the medical support for what was often called the "Bomber Air Force." He was tall and slender.

His thin, straight hair was gray, parted in the center and combed back to either side. He had a neatly trimmed gray mustache and was relatively swarthy complexioned. He had what is called "Good military bearing." In short, he looked like what you might expect a general to look like.

General Bedwell's background included occupational medicine, aviation medicine, and preventive medicine. He was definitely not an outgoing "personality boy." He had difficulty expressing personal warmth—I always thought he was handicapped by an innate sense of shyness. It seemed difficult for him to talk to people in an unguarded and relaxed fashion. These traits made it hard for him to show interest in other people's work. He was no General Benson.

He was also handicapped in supervising the Air Force's medical research facilities by lack of a research background. None of his previous assignments had included any significant aspects of teaching or educational processes: an important mission of the School. He had been asked to undertake a job that did not match his previous training or experience. Much of the research effort was based on advanced technology that was not a part of the medical school curriculum in the student days of General Bedwell. Administration of multi-million dollar laboratories with multi-million dollar annual budgets, plus management of complex diversified advanced research, needed an experienced hand.

Many, myself included, felt General Bedwell had come to his assignment with a chip on his shoulder and a distorted opinion of the School. Those of us who were civilian scientists soon gained the impression that civilian status was equivalent to second-class status. There was a general impression that, unless you were an Air Force officer—and preferably a flight surgeon—you were not part of the club. As one of the civilians, I would have to live with this for the next several years, which made my task harder. His immediate staff also told me the General was particularly annoyed that I saw Vice President Johnson. Perhaps he considered this to be a threat to his position of authority.

In February 1960, the Air Force medical service and commanding generals got a firsthand demonstration of what atrial fibrillation in a pilot could mean. A general officer from SAC had been found to have atrial fibrillation at the time of his annual examination. He was a very capable officer in his early forties, and looked forward to a promising career. He was referred to the School and underwent a series of complex examinations by our team. Other than atrial fibrillation, there were no other significant findings. The general denied having had any symptoms whatsoever and insisted that he had experienced no pain or difficulty or any other indications of heart trouble. I had long since learned to appreciate the importance of the onset of persistent atrial fibrillation. I was strongly suspicious that he had underlying coronary artery disease and possibly had even had an acute heart attack. The complete absence of a history of any symptoms made it difficult to establish the facts. In those days, it was not yet possible to directly examine the coronary arteries or heart muscle involved in heart attacks.

Because of his promising career, and the fact that he was a general officer, there was considerable consternation about my recommendation that he should not be returned to flying status. Despite the grumbling which occurred, it seemed to me that it was very unwise to permit him to continue to fly high-performance aircraft in carrying out his duties in the Strategic Air Command. He was a significant hazard to flying—not only to himself, but also to his flight crew. I stood firm on my recommendation and was supported by the Office of the Surgeon General.

After it became quite clear to the General that he was not going to be returned to flying status, he decided to retire from the Air Force. Flying status in the Air Force had far-reaching significance. In many instances, it was necessary to be on flying status to maintain a command assignment. Without a command assignment, one's career potential for further promotion was essentially nil. In addition to this, there was a certain amount of financial remuneration: flight pay. When the General decided to retire, he told the senior medical officer, who had accompanied him at the time I examined him, that he had experienced previous difficulties. In December, prior to his annual examination, he had experienced an episode of severe pain in the pit of his stomach, loss of consciousness, and an irregular heartbeat. He had been helped into a taxi by a friend and went to a hotel. He had been careful not to bring the incident to the attention of his Air Force physicians.

Approximately one week after the General had admitted the true nature of his illness, which he had so carefully concealed, he dropped dead in his office without warning in the middle of the morning. This was normally the time of day when he would have been flying high-performance aircraft. The reason he was not flying that day was because honest medical opinion had prevailed over the concept of "rank has its privileges (RHIP)."

Incidents such as these, if continued unchecked, could seriously undermine the flying safety of the Air Force. Just one such accident with the loss of a large SAC bomber would amount to a multi-million dollar catastrophe, not to mention the loss of life that could occur. General Curtis E. LeMay, then Vice Chief of Staff of the Air Force, found out about it and was determined there would be no recurrences of this type. He sent out an all-commands letter expressing his displeasure, along with a description of the fatal case. The Surgeon General's Office had vigorously pushed for this action by General LeMay. Such efforts were consistent with the Air Force's long-standing policy regarding atrial fibrillation.

8

BEAT THE SOVIETS:
GO TO THE MOON

January 28, 1961

Dear Mr. Vice President:

Recognizing the need for a Vice President who is fully informed
and adequately prepared with respect to domestic, foreign and
military policies relating to the national security of the United
States, and recognizing also the need for a closer working relationship between the President and Vice President in this vital
area, I would like you to preside over meetings of the National
Security Council in my absence and to maintian close liaison
with the Council and all other departments and agencies affected
with a national security interest.

In addition, I am hereby requesting you to review policies relating
to the national security, consulting with me in order that I might
have the full benefit of your endeavors and of your judgment.

You will need, in fulfillment of this assignment, pertinent information concerning the policies and operations of the departments
and agencies concerned with national security policies, including
the Department of State, the Department of Defense, the Office of
Civil and Defense Mobilization, the National Aeronautics and Space
Administration, the Bureau of the Budget, and the Central Intelligence
Agency.

I will expect the departments and agencies concerned to cooperate
fully with you in providing information in order for you to carry out
the responsibilities outlined above.

Sincerely,

The Honorable Lyndon B. Johnson
The Vice President

THE WHITE HOUSE

WASHINGTON

April 20, 1961

MEMORANDUM FOR

VICE PRESIDENT

In accordance with our conversation I would like
for you as Chairman of the Space Council to be in charge of
making an overall survey of where we stand in space.

1. Do we have a chance of beating the Soviets by
   putting a laboratory in space, or by a trip
   around the moon, or by a rocket to land on the
   moon, or by a rocket to go to the moon and
   back with a man. Is there any other space
   program which promises dramatic results in
   which we could win?

2. How much additional would it cost?

3. Are we working 24 hours a day on existing
   programs. If not, why not? If not, will you
   make recommendations to me as to how
   work can be speeded up.

4. In building large boosters should we put out
   emphasis on nuclear, chemical or liquid fuel,
   or a combination of these three?

5. Are we making maximum effort? Are we
   achieving necessary results?

I have asked Jim Webb, Dr. Weisner, Secretary
McNamara and other responsible officials to cooperate with
you fully. I would appreciate a report on this at the
earliest possible moment.

8

⤚ The parades and ceremonies were over. A youthful, ambitious new President and a new Vice President presided over the nation with its problems and promises. Fortunately, they knew each other well from their days in the United States Senate, when Lyndon Johnson was the Senate Majority Leader and undoubtedly one of the most experienced and powerful leaders in the nation. President Kennedy took steps immediately to ensure that his expertise would be fully utilized in the new administration. On January 28, 1961, he sent the new Vice President a memo outlining the role he wanted him to play in helping to lead the nation. He was to be fully informed and work with the major divisions of the administration, such as the Department of State and Department of Defense.

It is of the utmost importance that the Vice President be able at any moment to deal with the responsibilities of the presidency. In some previous administrations, the Vice President was not well informed. A notable example was what happened to Harry Truman. He had not been informed even about the project to develop an atomic bomb and was suddenly responsible to lead the nation in time of war. Evidently, President Kennedy did not want that to happen again.

Other than obvious common sense in having anyone who might be required to lead the nation to be fully informed, it is possible that John Kennedy was concerned about his own mortality. Although he presented the appearance of robust, youthful health, he had personally faced death more than once. The best-known occasion was when he was the skipper for PT 109 in combat during World War II. Even in his younger years he had been given the last rites during his illnesses. John Kennedy had adrenal insufficiency (also known as Addison's Disease), a severe endocrine disease. In such cases, the small adrenal glands above the kidneys fail to produce enough adrenal cortical hormone, commonly known as cortisone. This hormone is essential to life. He had been receiving hormone replacement for years and was being treated by Dr. Ephraim Shorr, a well-known specialist in such problems. He later referred the Senator to Dr. Janet Travell because of his constant, severe back pain.

Pain was John Kennedy's constant companion. Any objective person in possession of the facts would know that he was a man of infinitive courage and determination. Despite his disability, he provided dynamic leadership with an energetic, optimistic outlook. Although he could not have guessed that he would be struck down by an assassin, he had to have been aware of his own mortality. This could have added to his desire to have the Vice President fully prepared to assume the awesome responsibilities of the presidency at any time.

Vice President Lyndon B. Johnson visited the School again on February 16, 1961. It was one of those warm, sunny Texas afternoons when Lyndon Johnson arrived at the School to get a firsthand look at the progress of aerospace medical research. Unfortunately, at some level within the chain of command, someone invited the local press to cover the Vice President's visit: something they should never have done without clearing it with his office. I was astonished to see the Vice President standing in front of the School's headquarters building, essentially being harassed by a group of reporters. Finally, he tolerated it to the limit of his patience. He explained to them, rather tersely, he had come to the School to learn, not to give interviews or a speech. Up to that point, everywhere he went he looked like a harried fox being pursued by a pack of hungry hounds. After his short statement to the press, he left them standing and loped along at a relatively fast pace toward the building where my office was located.

There had been a lot of changes since Lyndon Johnson was a

Senator: not the least was the Secret Service. I was pleased to see him again, but amused to see the large entourage of military brass following in his wake. In reality, he wanted a medical checkup. As we started down the hall, the military contingent and reporters were brought to an abrupt halt by the Secret Service. They stepped forth and intercepted the invasion of our private conversation. Had it not been for them, no doubt the entire pack would have pursued the Vice President right into my examining room.

Once we were away from everyone else, we talked about how he was doing while I examined him and took another electrocardiogram. When we were through and he was dressed, he pulled out the EKG identification card I had made for him from his wallet. Then came the serious moment.

"Now Doctor, I want a new EKG card. I want the new one to say Vice President on the back."

He paused a moment, looked at the old card. It didn't have my name on it. Then he gave me a firm look and said, *"I want your name on it. And your telephone number, where I can reach you twenty-four hours a day!"* That is how I learned the Vice President intended to be seeing more of me in the future.

It was still not clear what the Vice President wanted. While he was being examined, one of his aides was in the School Commander's (Colonel Blount) office. Colonel Blount asked him what the Vice President wanted. The man simply replied, "The Vice President is getting what he wanted."

The Space Act, passed during the Eisenhower administration, provided for the President to preside over the Space Council: charged with directing the nation's space effort. On April 10, 1961, President Kennedy asked the Congress to amend the act and give the responsibility to the Vice President. This was in recognition of Lyndon Johnson's preeminent role in shaping the space program for many years. In making the request, President Kennedy noted,

As you know, it is now the duty of the President to preside over the meetings of the Council. As has been previously announced, I desire to place the Council under the chairmanship of the Vice President. The

primary effect of the attached amendatory bill, if enacted, will be to make that possible. I believe that the Vice President can contribute importantly to, and give me valuable counsel and assistance with respect to, space programs, and that the chairmanship of the National Aeronautics Space Council will materially enhance his opportunity and capability to render maximum service.

Later, in signing the bill of amendment, President Kennedy stated,

(This)...is a key step towards moving the United States into its proper place in the space race.

...The Vice President brings to the leadership of our space program 30 years experience in constructive action in government. He was the author of the Space Resolution in the Congress, the chairman of the Special Senate Committee which played such an important role in developing space legislation, and chairman of the permanent Committee of Aeronautical and Space Sciences.... Working with the Vice President, I intend that America's space effort shall provide the leadership, resources, and determination necessary to step up our efforts and prevail on the newest of man's physical frontiers.

Once again, on April 12, 1961, the Soviet Union scored a dramatic first in the conquest of space. On that day, Major Yuri Gagarin, the Soviet cosmonaut, became the first man to orbit Earth in a space vehicle. In one dramatic flight, he shattered any reservations about man's ability to survive at least a short duration of weightlessness. The flight constituted a full Earth orbit and proved conclusively the advanced state of Soviet technology in the missile and space field. Worse yet, the Soviet space vehicle that carried Gagarin into space compared to the United States Mercury spacecraft somewhat like a Lincoln Continental to a Model-T Ford.

The Soviet's *Vostok I* had a two-gas system: oxygen and nitrogen. The artificial air within the capsule was essentially the same as the air at sea level. To achieve this, *Vostok I* had to be very heavy—the weight of the Soviet spacecraft was at least three times that of the American Mercury capsule. To lift such a heavy, sophisticated vehicle and hurl it into space at sufficient velocity to orbit the Earth required huge rocket boosters that could deliver a very large payload. The design of Mercury had been restricted specifically because of the limited amount of weight that could be lifted by the American rockets. The ability of the American rockets to provide enough thrust, just to send the small Mercury vehicle into orbit, was marginal. It was not possible to have the luxury of a two-gas system.

The Mercury capsule was designed to create a pressure equivalent to an altitude of approximately 27,000 feet and the gas system had to be 100 percent oxygen: exactly the same as in the space suit used by Litton industry in the high altitude chamber I had studied several years earlier.

It had been clear for some time that the Soviets planned to go to the moon. As early as 1953, A. N. Nesmeyanov, President of the Soviet Academy of Sciences, proclaimed, "*Science has reached a state when it is feasible to send a stratoplane to the moon, to create an artificial satellite of the Earth.*" Their large, powerful rockets were rapidly approaching such capability.

President Kennedy had been in office only a short time, but he understood the need to meet the Soviet threat in space.

The United States still had not accomplished a single space achievement that began to compare to the excitement generated by the Soviet's *Sputnik* success and its subsequent success in orbiting cosmonauts in space. If the United States was going to compete with the Soviets and defend its freedom in space, something had to be done. President Kennedy wanted to do something that would speed up the man-in-space program. He met with Lyndon Johnson and the two discussed the problem. The young President was determined the United States would not stand by idly while the Soviets dominated space. He asked the Vice President, as Chairman of the Space Council, to determine where the United States stood in space and if it were possible to embark on a program to beat the Soviets in space. That was the beginning of the American effort to send a man to the moon. The President memorialized their conversation in a memo to the Vice President on April 20, 1961.

Lyndon Johnson moved swiftly to obtain the best input he

could get. Those who participated included: the Secretary and Deputy Secretary of Defense, General Schriever (AF); Admiral Hayward (Navy); Dr. von Braun (NASA); the Administrator, Deputy Administrator, and other top officials of NASA; the Special Assistant to the President on Science and Technology; representatives of the Director of the Bureau of the Budget; and three outstanding non-government citizens of the general public: Mr. George Brown (Brown & Root, Houston, Texas); Mr. Donald Cook (American Electric Power Services, New York, N. Y.); and Mr. Frank Stanton (Columbia Broadcasting System, New York, N. Y.).

The Vice President pointed out the missile gap, noting the Soviets had developed large rocket engines that enabled them to take the lead in space. He emphasized the need to be successful in space in order to maintain world leadership. He was generally optimistic, even though he recognized the difficulties the United States faced to catch up with the Soviet achievements. Regarding the moon, he stated, "Manned exploration of the moon, for example, is not only an achievement with great propaganda value, but it is essential as an objective whether or not we are first in its accomplishment—and we may be able to be first." His memo ended with the observation, "We are neither making maximum effort nor achieving results necessary if this country is to reach a position of leadership." (See complete memo on page 146).

Once again, Lyndon Johnson was instrumental in setting the nation's agenda for the exploration of space.

A medical conference had been planned for the military component of the NATO alliance to be held in Paris in May of 1961. Surgeon General Oliver K. Niess had decided the Air Force presentation would emphasize our efforts in aerospace medicine. A number of us had been invited to accompany him to the conference at SHAPE headquarters to make presentations.

It was exciting to go to SHAPE headquarters. One of the early speakers was General Lauris Norstad, General Eisenhower's successor as the Commanding General for the NATO alliance. The flags of the different countries that belonged to NATO decked the corners of the stage. The attendees included representatives from Germany, France,

England, and the other NATO nations. The usual interpreter booths, essential to such an international meeting, were busy translating each speaker's remarks into the various languages.

In between the scientific sessions and our own presentations, the group had a chance to enjoy some of the aspects of Paris. Each day we read the headlines across the French papers, to see whether or not America's first astronaut would be launched into space. This was the eve of the sub-orbital shot planned for Commander Alan Shepard. We waited anxiously to see what news, if any, could be gleaned concerning the flight. I could read enough French to understand the news. Always, some new problem arose, most often with the weather.

The Florida cape was used as a launching site, in part because of the limited thrust of the American rockets. The East Coast made it possible to use the Earth's rotation to our advantage. If the West Coast had been used to fire over the Pacific, opposite the rotation of Earth, it would have required a much greater thrust than was possible. The return had to be a splashdown. If the Mercury spacecraft returned to land, the impact would be too great. All the astronauts for the Mercury flights would have to be picked up at sea. The first flight was a major undertaking. The stakes, in terms of our national prestige, were never higher. *Was the system of the free world really inferior to the Soviet totalitarian dictatorship?*

After I made my presentation, there were a few days before the rest of the group would finish. I went to Geneva, Switzerland to see old friends. On the night of May 5, I was dining with my friends Nicholas and Vilma Swiatopolk-Mirski and Aunt Elaine (Madame Teding van Berkhout). Nicholas was a top interpreter for the world's labor center and had escaped from Russia during the war in 1917. We had dinner in a quiet restaurant in the suburbs, at the edge of Lake Geneva.

Things happened in Geneva that I never understood. There were several different factions of Russians living there. Nicholas' family had been part of the government of the Czar. One Russian faction was communist, and other factions claimed to be Russian royalty. Nicholas evidently didn't want me to have contact with one group of Russians who were also dining at the same restaurant. I have no idea how they would have known who I was. When we left, Vilma and Aunt Elaine left by the front door and Nicholas took me through the kitchen and out the back door. As we entered the back yard, one of the Russians he didn't want me to see came up to me. He was an older expatriate. His bald head was fringed with rather long, snow-white hair and he had considerable difficulty with his English, but he managed to convey his message to me, "Your man okay. Flight okay." A Russian gave me the first news of Alan Shepard's successful sub-orbital flight.

Even though Commander Shepard's achievement was a sub-orbital flight—as opposed to the full orbit that Major Gagarin had previously accomplished—it was a significant morale boost for the United States. Certainly, we were behind the Soviets in the man-in-space race, but we were making progress and beginning to learn some of the problems associated with space flight. President Kennedy hailed the flight as a historic milestone and awarded NASA's Distinguished Service Medal to Commander Shepard in a ceremony at the White House.

The first successful sub-orbital flight was also a breakthrough of certain barriers indigenous to large projects. Earlier that year, there had been considerable grumbling about the medical safety of the Mercury project. Many of the comments emanated from the academic or university communities that did not have firsthand knowledge of the Mercury project, and were short in experience on the range of function of normal man. It was akin to my earlier experience in the evaluation of the so-called cardiac problems at Litton Industries in the near-vacuum chamber. Topnotch clinical cardiologists, who were great at taking care of patients, didn't know about the changes in electrocardiograms that occur in healthy people when standing up compared to lying down. Many of the academicians also felt left out of the nation's space program. The biggest single factor that alarmed the university scientists was the medical data that had been obtained from the X-15 flights at Edwards.

The early X-15 was best described as a "real beast." It was the fastest airplane that had ever been designed, and was really a rocket on wheels. While it could be landed, it was not feasible for it to take off like a normal airplane. It had to be carried under the wing of a larger aircraft and dropped into the atmosphere to begin its flight. Its speed was obtained by literally igniting its rockets. The thrust of the plane shoved the pilot back into his seat, creating tremendous pressure against the chest and abdomen, frequently causing the pilot's respiratory rate to increase markedly. Heart rates up to 180 beats-per-minute had been observed on a few occasions. This alarmed a number of the university scientists. Much of their concern, as is often the case, was caused by a lack of complete communication.

It was not surprising that such high heart rates occurred after a rocket thrust associated with the burnout of the fuel tank. As the project progressed, and more experience was gained, the heart rates were not as high. There was considerable discussion about such heart rates and a group from the scientific community planned to approach President Kennedy to insist that the Mercury project be delayed until such matters could be resolved.

Much of our data accumulated from stress testing at the school became useful at this point. Even though there were a limited number of X-15 flights, we had been doing stress studies on as many as three-to-five subjects on a daily basis for several years and had regularly tested air crews as well as the astronauts during heart rates of 180 beats a minute.

The nation's appetite had been whetted by Alan Shepard's successful sub-orbital flight. There were those who began to have hope that the United States would not lag behind the Soviets forever in the man-in-space effort. The challenge of sending a man into space had caught the imagination of the people of the world. It was essential to compete in a meaningful manner with the Soviet achievements if we were to maintain our image in terms of education, technology, and indeed the success of the system of our society.

For this reason, and for other matters of transcendent national importance, President Kennedy decided to depart from tradition and give a special message to Congress. This was in the nature of a second State of the Union address, delivered in person by the President on May 25, 1961. By then, he had received Vice President Johnson's report on what could be done to compete with the Soviets in space. In regards to space, President Kennedy said,

Finally, if we are to win the battle that is now going on around the world between freedom and tyranny, the dramatic achievements in space which occurred in recent weeks should have made clear to us all, as did the Sputnik in 1957, the impact of this adventure on the minds of men everywhere, who are attempting to make a determination on which road they should take. Since early in my term, our efforts in space have been under review. With the advice of the Vice President, who is chairman of the National Space Council, we have examined where we are strong and where we are not, where we may succeed and where we may not. Now it is time to take longer strides—time for a great new American enterprise—time for this nation to take a clearly leading role in space achievement, which in many ways may hold the key to our future on earth.

The young President had become a real space enthusiast and he was determined that during his stewardship of the nation, the United States would not be second in space because of lack of effort. He continued his remarks:

Recognizing the head start obtained by the Soviets with their large rocket engines, which gives them many months of lead time, and recognizing the likelihood that they will exploit this lead for some time to come in still more impressive success, we nevertheless are required to make new efforts on our own. For while we cannot guarantee that we shall one day be first, we can guarantee that any failure to make this effort will make us last. We take an additional risk by making it in full view of the world, but as shown by the feat of Astronaut Shepard, this very risk enhances our stature when we are successful. But this is not merely a race. Space is open to us now; and our eagerness to share its meaning is not governed by the efforts of others. We go into space because whatever mankind must undertake, free men must fully share.

Having made these preliminary remarks, the President unveiled his plans for a national commitment:

First, I believe the nation should commit itself to achieving the goal, before this decade is out, of landing a man on the moon and returning him safely to the earth. No single space project in this period will be more impressive to mankind, or more important for the long-range exploration of space; and none will be so difficult or expensive to accomplish. We propose to accelerate the development of the appropriate lunar spacecraft. We propose to develop alternate liquid and solid fuel boosters, much larger than any now being developed, until certain which is superior—in a real sense, it will not be one man going to the moon—if we make this judgment affirmatively, it will be an entire nation. For all of us must work to put him there....

It is a most important decision that we must make as a nation. But all of you have lived through the last four years and have seen the significance of space and the adventures in space, and no one can predict with certainty what the ultimate meaning will be of mastery of space.

The nation listened to—and was thrilled by—President Kennedy's dramatic appeal for the manned lunar expedition. He had thrown down the gauntlet and challenged the nation to a new and major goal. The effort would accelerate our scientific technology and know-how on a broad basis, affecting education, medicine, and many of the simple facets of our daily lives. The moon goal was about much more than just sending men to the moon. It was the engine that would spur overall scientific achievement. President Kennedy signed the bill, enacted by Congress, for an Expanded Space Program on July 21, 1961—the same date that Captain Virgil Grissom of the Air Force successfully completed Mercury's second sub-orbital flight.

****

April 28, 1961

MEMORANDUM FOR THE PRESIDENT
(Courtesy of the LBJ Library)
Subject: Evaluation of the Space Program

Reference to your memorandum asking certain questions regarding this country's space program.

A detailed survey has not been completed in this time period. The examination will continue. However, what we have obtained so far from knowledgeable and responsible persons makes this summary reply possible.

Among those who have participated in our deliberations have been the Secretary and Deputy Secretary of Defense; General Schriever (AF); Admiral Hayward (Navy); Dr. Von Braun (NASA); the Special Assistants to the President on Science and Technology; representatives of the Director of the Bureau of the Budget; and three outstanding non-Government citizens of the general public; Mr. George Brown (Brown & Root, Houston, Texas); Mr. Donald Cook (American Electric Power Service, New York, N.Y.); Mr. Frank Stanton (Columbia Broadcasting System;, New York, N.Y.)

The following general conclusions can be reported:

a. Largely due to their concentrated efforts and their earlier emphasis upon the development of large rocket engines, the Soviets are ahead of the United States in world prestige attained through impressive technological accomplishments in space.

b. The U.S. has greater resources than the USSR for attaining space leadership but has failed to make the necessary hard decisions and to marshal those resources to achieve such leadership.

c. This country should be realistic and recognize that other nations, regardless of their appreciation of our idealistic values, will tend to align themselves with the country which they believe will be the world

146

leader—the winner in the long run. Dramatic accomplishments in space are being increasingly identified as a major indicator of world leadership.

d. The U.S. can, if it will, firm up its objectives and employ the resources with a reasonable chance of attaining world leadership in space during this decade. This will be difficult but can be made probable even recognizing the head start of the Soviets and the likelihood that they will continue to move forward with impressive successes. In certain areas, such as communications, navigation, weather, and mapping, the U.S. can and should exploit its existing advance position.

e. If we do not make the strong effort now, the time will soon be reached when the margin of control over space and over men's minds through space accomplishments will have swung so far on the Russian side that we will not be able to catch up, let alone assume leadership.

f. Even in these areas in which the Soviets already have the capability to be first and are likely to improve upon such capability, the United States should make aggressive efforts as the technological gains as well as the international rewards are essential steps in eventually gaining leadership. The danger of long lags or outright omissions by this country is substantial in view of the possibility of great technological breakthroughs obtained from space exploration.

g. Manned exploration of the moon, for example, is not only an achievement with great propaganda value, but it is essential as an objective whether or not we are first in its accomplishment—and we may be able to be first. We cannot leapfrog such accomplishments, as they are essential sources of knowledge and experience for even greater successes in space. We cannot expect the Russians to transfer the benefits of their experiences or the advantages of their capabilities to us. We must do these things ourselves.

h. The American public should be given the facts as to how we stand in the space race, told of our determination to lead in that race, and advised of the importance of such leadership to our future.

i. More resources and more effort need to be put into our space program as soon as possible. We should move forward with a bold program, while at the same time taking every practical precaution for the safety of the persons actively participating in space flights.

As for the specific questions posed in your memorandum, the following brief answers develop from the studies made during the past few days. These conclusions are subject to expansion and more detailed examination as our survey continues.

Q.1 - Do we have a chance of beating the Soviets by putting a laboratory in space, or by a trip around the moon, or by a rocket to land on the moon, or by a rocket to go to the moon and back with a man? Is there any other space program which promises dramatic results in which we could win?

A.1 - The Soviets now have a rocket capability for putting a multi-manned laboratory into space and have already crash-landed a rocket on the moon. They also have the booster capability of making a soft landing on the moon with a payload of instruments, although we do not know how much preparation they have made for such a project. As for a manned trip around the moon or a safe landing and return by a man to the moon, neither the U. S. nor the U.S.S.R. has such capability at this time, so far as we know. The Russians have had more experience with large boosters and with flights of dogs and man. Hence they might be conceded a time advantage in circumnavigation of the moon and also in a manned trip to the moon. However, with a strong effort, the United States could conceivably be first in those two accomplishments by 1966 or 1967.

There are a number of programs which the United States could pursue immediately and which promise significant world-wide advantage over the Soviets. Among these are communications satellites, meteorological and weather satellites, and navigation and mapping satellites. These are all areas in which we have already developed some competence. We have such programs and believe that the Soviets do not. Moreover, there are programs which could be made operational and effective within reasonably short periods of time and could, if properly programmed with the interests of other nations, make useful strides toward world leadership.

148

Q.2 - How much additional would it cost?

A.2 - To start upon an accelerated program with the aforementioned objectives clearly in mind, NASA has submitted an analysis indicating that about $500 million would be needed for FY 162 over and above the amount currently requested of the Congress. A program based upon NASA's analysis would, over a ten-year period, average approximately $1 billion a year above the current estimates of the existing NASA program.

While the Department of Defense plans to make a more detailed submission to me within a few days, the Secretary has taken the position that there is a need for a strong effort to develop a large solid-propellant booster and that his Department is interested in undertaking such a project. It was understood that this would be programmed in accord with the existing arrangement for close cooperation with NASA, which Agency is undertaking some research in this field. He estimated they would need to employ approximately $50 million during FY 1962 for this work but that this could be financed through management of funds already requested in the FY 1962 budget. Future defense budgets would include requests for additional funding for this purpose; a preliminary estimate indicates that about $500 million would be needed in total.

Q.3 - Are we working 24 hours a day on existing programs? If not, why not? If not, will you make recommendations to me as to how work can be speeded up?

A.3 - There is not a 24-hour-a-day work schedule on existing NASA space programs except for selected areas in Project Mercury, the Saturn-C-1 booster, the Centaur engines and the final launching phases of most flight missions. They advise that their schedules have been geared to the availability of facilities and financial resources, and that hence their overtime and 3-shift arrangements exists only in those activities in which there are particular bottlenecks or which are holding up operations in other parts of the programs. For example, they have a 3-shift 7-day-week operation in certain work at Cape Canaveral; the contractor for Project Mercury has averaged a 54-hour week and employs two or three shifts in some areas; Saturn C-1 at

Huntsville is working around the clock during critical test periods while the remaining work on this project averages a 47-hour week; the Centaur hydrogen engine is on a 3-shift basis in some portions of the contractor's plants.

This work can be speeded up through firm decisions to go ahead faster if accompanied by additional funds needed for the acceleration.

Q.4 - In building large boosters should we put our emphasis on nuclear, chemical or liquid fuel, or a combination of these three?
A.4 - It was the consensus that liquid, solid and nuclear boosters should all be accelerated. This conclusion is based not only upon the necessity for back-up methods, but also because of the advantages of the different types of boosters for different missions. A program of such emphasis would meet both so-called civilian needs and defense requirements.

Q.5 - Are we making maximum efforts? Are we achieving necessary results?
A.5 - We are neither making maximum effort nor achieving results necessary if this country is to reach a position of leadership.

Signed: Lyndon B. Johnson.

****

9

NASA OR AIR FORCE

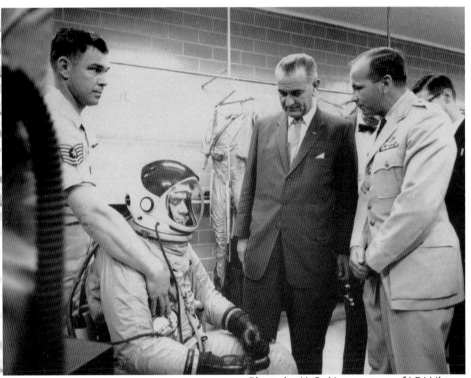

Photo by U. S. Air, courtesy of LBJ Library

Lyndon Johnson at the School of Aerospace Medicine, October 5, 1961. He visits the altitude chambers and talks to Ira Flowers in a pressure suit. Major Fritz Holmstrom, USAF Flight Surgeon is on the Vice President's left.

9

⌒ In September 1961, hurricane Carla sweep out of the Gulf of Mexico onto the beaches of Galveston and charted a path of death and destruction across southern Texas. Forces from the wind of the hurricane were felt as far north as Dallas. In the wake of this huge storm came the Bioastronautics panel of the President's Scientific Advisory Committee, to cut a swath of its own across the space-medical community. University scientists were dissatisfied with NASA's manned space flight program. There were ill feelings between the Department of Defense and NASA, and between NASA and the Atomic Energy Commission, relative to dominance in the nation's space program. As a result, a "Blue Ribbon" committee of the nation's scientists was appointed to review the situation for the President. The group was headed by Dr. Paul Beeson, professor and chairman of the department of medicine from Yale, and similarly prominent individuals from other university medical centers.

The committee toured the nation's facilities that supported the space-medical project, including those of NASA, the Atomic Energy Commission, and those belonging to the Department of Defense. They spent two days at the School, evaluating the physical adequacy of the laboratories and equipment, the nature of existing research programs and the qualifications of the personnel conducting them. The group appeared to be impressed and pleased with most of those aspects of the School.

There were always at least two phases to an interchange of information attendant to such reviews. During the day, there were formal briefings covering scientific areas, and sometimes administrative matters. In the evenings, there were "social hours," where individuals squared off glass-to-glass to get down to some of the unspoken matters. To be successful in this arena, you needed a leather-lined stomach, a strong pair of legs—preferably hollow—and a mind, not numbed by the evening's libations.

During the visit of the President's committee, the first round of "evening fellowship" began at an informal bar under the edge of one of the numerous bridges spanning the San Antonio River, not far from the old Casa Rio Mexican restaurant. Individuals, with glasses in hand, began circling about in quest of a likely situation for the verbal sport. The game for the evening had begun. The Air Force personnel were anxious to impress the visiting dignitaries, and the dignitaries were anxious to probe the Air Force types. In the background, the mariachis strummed their Mexican tunes while the game progressed.

Soon the party boarded two small, flat-bottom boats, converted to miniature floating dining rooms. Mexican food was served for all those who still had room for food, and the game continued. The stakes were high. The recommendation of the committee had every likelihood of significantly influencing the administration's policy concerning whether NASA or the Department of Defense would gain undisputed control of the medical aspects of the man-in-space project—and perhaps, the entire space program itself.

Dr. Jim Hartgering, science adviser from the White House staff, sat next to me, probably not by accident. Finally, he broached the question that must have been uppermost in his mind: not scientific, but political. He asked me what the Vice President's attitude toward the School of Aerospace Medicine was, and whether he was truly a strong supporter of its future.

The survey by the "Beeson Committee" had been authorized by the National Aeronautics and Space Council, headed by Lyndon Johnson. By law, the council had jurisdiction over the space activities of NASA, the Department of Defense, and any such activities occurring in other governmental agencies. The Vice President was, in fact, the space czar for the nation: a fact not lost on Beeson's group.

The difference between the overall capability within the Department of Defense and the limited medical capability of the NASA laboratories was of sufficient magnitude that it was difficult for the committee to frame its final recommendations without creating absolute havoc in the nation's space program. Apparently, a number of revisions were made. The report had to be watered-down and modified numerous times before a final version could be released.

In its final version, the committee pointed out that the largest and best equipped facilities to support a bioastronautics effort belonged to the Air Force, and further, the Air Force laboratories were designed to determine the limit of man's tolerance and to study the matching of men with high-performance machines, as well as develop life support systems for high-altitude flight. The committee indicated their appreciation that the investment in the Air Force laboratories was quite large, and that many Air Force scientists had acquired extensive experience in research and development in the biomedical areas. Cognizance was also taken of facilities of lesser scope, present in the Navy and Army.

The report stated that the Atomic Energy Commission had, by far, the superior program of study in biological hazards associated with radiation, compared to any other in the nation. Predictably, the committee felt that the universities represented a reservoir of talent and knowledge that had not been adequately utilized in support of the manned space program. They did acknowledge that fitting the university research efforts into the space program's requirements posed some problems, since the man-in-space program, particularly in its beginning, was essentially an applied-research effort. Universities excelled in basic research, to understand fundamental causes rather than applying new information in an operational setting.

The committee underscored the lack of development of any competent life-sciences effort within NASA, and the fact that NASA had downgraded its life-sciences input, effective November 1, 1961. No member of the biomedical staff had direct access to the higher administrative and decision making levels of NASA. As a result there was no medical input to the-top level decisions for the nation's man-in-space effort. The program was run by administrators and engineers, without regard to medical considerations.

The Beeson group cited the lack of coordination between NASA and other existing government organizations, particularly within the Department of Defense, and recommended that these problems be corrected. The lack of the Manned Spacecraft Center's interchange with the university community was highlighted. The NASA-MSC Center in Houston was described as being isolated from the national medical-scientific community, which prevented stimulation of the university scientists who might be able to contribute to the space program.

Vice President Johnson came to the School again on the 5th of October, 1961. It was another beautiful day and he was in his best form, radiating enthusiasm and personal charm. He had brought with him a large cadre of reporters and members of the news media. He wanted them to see the Aerospace Medical Center. The Vice President was always at his best when he was showing his friends around, or explaining something to them. He visited the various laboratories, including the altitude chambers and human centrifuge, with the reporters. We had set up the large testing room where many of the specialized examinations for the air crews and the astronauts were done. I had put a subject on the treadmill and another subject on the tilt-table, so that these tests could be demonstrated.

The airman who was the subject for the demonstration on the tilt-table had undergone this test many times before. But the excitement of the moment, the large number of press people arriving, and the impending visit of the Vice President was a bit too much for him. He began to turn a sickly green color. I had learned to recognize these changes on many previous occasions, and knew that at any minute he was apt to spew vomitus over the area. I had the tilt-table returned to a horizontal position with the airman lying flat for the upcoming demonstration. I elected not to tilt the table that day.

As some of the news media arrived, one of the reporters kept elbowing me away from the front so he could get better pictures. Finally, I told him that since I was giving the briefing, maybe I could stay up front. When he recognized this, we both laughed at how things happened in such an environment.

The Vice President arrived, followed by his entourage. We shook hands warmly and he sat down, indicating that the briefing should proceed.

After the briefing and discussion with the press, he added a few points he felt were pertinent. He discussed in an erudite fashion the transmission of electrocardiograms by telephone. His sharp eye had evidently caught the system in one corner of the laboratory. I had not demonstrated this to him before, but it was apparent that he was totally familiar with the procedure. He reminded the group that since he was already present, he wouldn't need to have his electrocardiogram taken by phone, and while he was having an examination, they should continue their tour of the facilities.

Lyndon Johnson obviously was enjoying his role as the chief spokesman for—and acquainting the public with—the nation's space program. After all, he should have, because he was its principal architect in the government circles.

One of the things I noticed about Lyndon Johnson was his ability to change his mood and behavior in a flash. We went into an examining room. The door closed, and the man I had just witnessed in complete charge, full of energy and enthusiasm, became a different person. Suddenly, he was a patient seeing his doctor. He was no longer in charge, but was looking for advice and reassurance. We talked and he complained a bit about how hard it was for him to keep his weight down. He explained that he had just come back from the services for Dag Hammarsjöld—the Secretary General of the United Nations, who had been killed in an airplane cash—and he had had too much to eat on the trip. He was doing what Vice Presidents often do: go to funerals. I was to learn later that he always went to funerals. When one of his friends or someone he thought was important died, Lyndon Johnson went to the services. Often, he would call me later, usually relatively late at night, to talk. I think his own mortality was never far from his mind after his heart attack some years earlier.

October was a month for renewing old acquaintances. Dr. Janet Travell, now President Kennedy's personal physician, had accepted my invitation to visit the School to lecture on the work she had been doing in the musculoskeletal area. By then, the School was sufficiently advanced that it was a pleasure to show its extensive activities to guests.

When I first arrived at the School in 1955, many of my academic friends were horrified and thought I had lost my senses. After I had built my laboratory, started the library of electrocardiograms, developed the consultation service for Air Force flying personnel, and was performing the examinations for the selection of the astronauts, I was asked, "How did you ever get a job like that?" It certainly wasn't because I had any unusual foresight. I just happened to be sitting on the rocket when the fuse was lit—by the Soviets.

Dr. Travell had never been to San Antonio before. Her plane touched down late on the evening of the October 19. I met her at the airport; she had not changed since our earlier meeting in Kansas. She had a natural curiosity about everything and was surprised to see what a large city San Antonio really was.

The next day, we looked at some of the experiments being done at the School. She reviewed the tilt-table studies with particular interest. Later in the morning, we visited my friend Captain James Roman's laboratory at the School, and he demonstrated the in-flight telemetry, with blood pressure readings and the electrocardiogram being received at the ground station laboratory from a pilot flying an F-100 aircraft overhead. Jim was both a pilot and a flight surgeon. Dr. Travell was intrigued with the small electrodes that were firmly attached to the skin, enabling records of such good quality that you could tap the electrode without producing any abnormalities or artifacts in the records. These were the same ones we used to obtain electrocardiograms during treadmill exercise tests and the tilt-table studies.

That afternoon, Dr. Travell gave an outstanding lecture on the problems of musculoskeletal pain to the largest audience that had yet attended any single medical lecture at the School. Every seat in the auditorium was taken and people were standing up in the back. She proved in every way that she was the nation's "First Lady of Medicine." Her presentation was enthusiastically received.

That evening, I gave a reception and dinner honoring Dr. Travell at the San Antonio Country Club for a large number of the staff from the School and the Aerospace Medical Division. It was a pleasant, relaxed, informal occasion. The following morning, before Dr. Travell had to leave, we had an opportunity to visit various parts of the city.

She was amazed to see the carefully-landscaped San Antonio River winding all through the downtown area. We got so interested in seeing the city that she barely made her plane. Dr. Travell was not the type of person to be hurried. Each time something interested her, she stayed long enough to satisfy her curiosity. The door of the plane had to be reopened to get her on board.

A few days after Dr. Travell's visit, I was brought back to reality. One of the senior medical officers from nearby Lackland's Wilford Hall Hospital came to my office and berated me for having invited Dr. Travell to the School. I replied that she was a very capable physician and it was good for the staff to hear her experiences. With some indignation he replied, "Come off it, Larry. You know she's just a goddamned quack."

This was too much for me, and I replied somewhat heatedly that she had far better professional credentials than he had, and that she had graduated number one in her class from Cornell, among such prestigious classmates as Dr. Irving Wright and Dr. Irving Page, both of international stature. She was also an associate professor from Cornell.

In the course of the exchange, the truth came out. He complained that she was a woman, and had taken a place in medical school that some man could have filled. I was shocked. The idea that male doctors would be prejudiced against women had never crossed my mind. Actually, 10 percent of the medical students in my own class were women. We had partners to do our clinical work with patients, and my partner was a very capable woman. It was then that I realized how difficult Dr. Travell's job must be. She was a woman in a man's environment, and she was a civilian occupying a job that the military considered their exclusive domain. The position as physician to the President was usually, but not always, a job for someone from the military services—no woman had ever held that post before.

That October, NASA Headquarters in Washington requested a plan from the School for the continued evaluation of astronaut candidates. I developed the plan with the School's staff and forwarded it as requested. This had a major bearing on events that were to occur in the future. The request was an outgrowth of an effort between the

Department of Defense and NASA to proceed with a mutual effort in the area of space exploration. Major General Victor R. Haugen of Air Force Headquarters and Associate Administrator of NASA Headquarters Dr. Robert C. Seamans, Jr., corresponded particularly in reference to the medical selection of astronauts. Dr. Seamans indicated that, prior to the onset of the Apollo manned flights, NASA intended to solicit the help of the Air Force in the medical evaluations, and would like to "participate with the Air Force in a research program to determine criteria and methods for space crew physical examinations."

Our group had been doing the same examinations for all the pilots entering the test pilot program at Edwards AFB in California for some time. The fact that we had a daily, ongoing program was one of the things that Dr. Dryden, Associate Administrator of NASA, liked about our operation. The final plan was forwarded through channels to General Chuck Roadman, an Air Force medical officer assigned as Director of Life Sciences to NASA Headquarters. I knew Chuck rather well and, in the course of correspondence, I commented on the problems related to medical evaluations, as exemplified by Slayton's atrial fibrillation. I had naturally assumed that as Director of Life Sciences for NASA, he had been informed about it. He had not. Later, as events unfolded, the burning question was, *Who knew what and when did they know it?* This was the first time he had ever been told that one of the Mercury astronauts had a major medical problem. I was shocked that the medical personnel at the Manned Spacecraft Center would have concealed such an important matter from NASA headquarters. Evidently, they did.

Much of the plan from the School was used by NASA Headquarters in preparing NASA's justification to Congress for funding to support its man-in-space program.

NASA needed help, and efforts to establish support from the DOD were being made at the highest levels. Dr. Robert Seamans, Associate Administrator at NASA Headquarters, wrote Secretary John Rubel, Director of Research and Development area for the DOD, on the 14th of December, 1961, and outlined NASA's request for support. The critical part of his letter regarding me was as follows:

...Currently, members of NASA along with personnel of the Air Force and Navy have agreed upon five major aerospace R&D (research and development) areas. We have selected five military scientists who we feel are most competent to assist us in developing this program.

These are:

...Crew medical selection and monitoring:

Dr. Lawrence E. Lamb, USAF School of Aerospace Medicine, Brooks Air Force Base, Texas.

Regarding the ever-present problem of communications and proper channels so dear to the heart of the military, and which got me in so much trouble, Dr. Seamans' letter continued,

It is proposed that direct communication with the five area appointees and the NASA be authorized, with full understanding that the responsible military commands be kept appropriately informed.

I was one of the five named people authorized direct communications. The authorization was forwarded to me through channels from the DOD. This is important in understanding what happened when I actually used direct communications. It upset Surgeon General Niess big time, and he retaliated against me with a letter that could only have been an attempt to damage my reputation and prevent direct communication.

Why were direct communications needed? Simply stated, to get the job done in a timely fashion, without bureaucratic interference. Scientists, including medical personnel, need to have the ability to communicate freely with each other and exchange information, whether it is in industry, an academic setting, or within the halls of government. Bypassing those sacred channels was viewed with horror by administrators who used them to exercise power.

10

OF CHIMPS AND ASTRONAUTS

10

⌒ During the first week of December, 1961, I was called upon to make one of the strangest consultations of my career. I was asked to see an unusual national celebrity: Enos the chimpanzee. This hairy little creature had experienced an irregular heartbeat during his orbital flight. Enos and another chimpanzee, Ham, were orbited to obtain data before sending the first American astronaut into orbit. The original concerns of the potential astronaut candidates were justified; the chimps were going to fly the mission first. The cause of Enos' heart irregularity had to be resolved before giving the final go-ahead for John Glenn's upcoming flight. I flew to the Cape, as requested, to see if this problem could be resolved. Captain Ashton Graybiel, cardiologist from the U. S. Navy School of Aviation Medicine at Pensacola, joined me at the Cape.

We were met by Stan White from NASA for a briefing. He told us that they were very anxious to settle all the questions concerning Enos' irregular heartbeat, so they could get on with Glenn's orbital flight. Stan White claimed a number of people desired to accomplish this before the calendar year of 1961 ended so that in the annals of history, the United States would have successfully orbited a man in the same year as the Soviet Union. The date that had been selected for Glenn's flight was December 20, 1961.

The consultation on "astrochimp" Enos really should have been recorded for posterity. Nothing like it will probably ever occur again. Captain Graybiel and I were seated in a laboratory and the case presentation began. Astrochimp Enos had developed a significant irregularity of the heart during his orbital flight. There was concern that the irregularity might be associated with weightlessness or some other factor related to space flight.

The consultation began with a thorough review by one of the animal psychologists of the psychological factors, which may have contributed to Enos' heart irregularity. Enos' native background was normal for an African-born chimpanzee, unfettered by modern civilization, without any requirement to attend school. His personality had not responded well to civilization, much less to training for orbital flight. Enos did not like school.

It seemed that Enos had a mind of his own. He did not take well to a program where he received a reward of a banana pellet when he pushed the right button or pulled the right lever, but received an electric shock if he didn't. His reaction to shock treatment was particularly bad. In fact, he behaved so badly that the manufacturers of the equipment he was to operate in space seriously regretted the terms of their contract. Enos had the capacity to demolish one performance machine after another. There were bets being placed on what would happen to the equipment that he was to use during his space flight to demonstrate his continued capability. Almost all the scientists who were associated with the project expected he would reduce it to nothing more than a twisted mass of scrap metal.

Enos had other bad habits, such as running off if the opportunity presented itself, and he was not exactly affectionate. He was known to be brutal if an unsuspecting handler dropped his guard. In short, far from being the lovable little chimp that Enos had been portrayed to be by the news media, he would have been more appropriately described as a little monster.

There was real justification for astrochimp Enos' destructive behavior. When the time came to load him into the space vehicle, the physiologist, James Henry, had decided this was the ideal opportunity to find out what happens in space. He had ingeniously constructed instrumentation to do this. One large catheter (tube) had been inserted and passed through a vein, through the right side of the heart, and out into the pulmonary artery to the lungs, to measure the blood pressure in that artery. Another catheter had been inserted into the artery in the leg to provide continuous measurement of the arterial pressure from the left side of the heart. The usual electrocardiograph electrodes were put in place. Finally, a urethral catheter was inserted into the bladder to drain urine. The large urethral catheter was kept in place by a bag on the end of the tube that was filled with dilute salt water after the catheter was in the bladder.

With these few modest attachments, astrochimp Enos began whirling around the Earth. In this state, while orbiting at approximately 18,000 miles per hour, he was expected to carry out his tasks on the machine. The equipment developed a malfunction, delivering electrical shocks regardless of whether his performance was correct or not. Enos soared through the unknowns of space, restrained, catheterized, grabbing levers like crazy, and intermittently getting the hell shocked out of him! Life in the jungle was never like this. In view of the test protocol the medics had devised for Enos, the astronauts had good cause to harbor some suspicions about the NASA medics; and John Glenn was next.

While Enos was rocketing through space, doing his best to master the performance tasks, he started having an irregular heart beat, technically called ventricular premature contractions, and short runs of ventricular tachycardia—the latter can become dangerous. At the end of the flight, he splashed down in the cold Atlantic Ocean. Sitting there, bobbing up and down in his dark little capsule, this evil creature seized the instrumentation attached to him and wrenched it from his body. He pulled loose his venous catheter, stripped off the electrodes, then grabbed the catheter to his bladder with its fully inflated bag—and jerked it manually from its location—an action he had cause to regret for some time thereafter. With real prudence, he refrained from breaking off the catheter to the femoral artery in his leg. Had he done so, he probably would have bled to death. Who says that chimp wasn't smart?

Finally, we got a look at the records that caused all the trouble. It was obvious that the irregular beats were coming from the right side of the lower portion of the heart (right ventricle). This, plus the timing of the irregularities, strongly suggested that they were related to some stimulus occurring intermittently in the right ventricle. From previous experience with cardiac catheterization procedures, I suspected that the catheter Jim Henry had placed in the pulmonary artery to the lungs was the cause of the difficulty—not space flight—nor, for that matter, the chimpanzee's psychological background or possible hypertension.

I took the film with the pressure recording that had been obtained with the catheter, supposedly located in the pulmonary artery. By running the film backward, I located a change in the pressure graph, which demonstrated conclusively that the catheter had slipped back from the pulmonary artery to the lungs into the lower right heart where it tickled the wall of the heart and set off the irregularity.

The consultation visit turned out to be a real success. It was most gratifying to be able to pinpoint the cause of the difficulty as resulting from the instrumentation rather than space flight. We visited Enos to see how he had survived, but kept a respectful distance from his menacing glare. I helped myself to a handful of his banana pellets to try out on the way home. Considering Enos' discretion regarding which catheters he had torn loose from his body, I felt there was just a possibility these banana pellets might be the legendary smart pills.

When we first arrived for the consultation, Stan White began telling us about the crew members chosen for Glenn's upcoming flight. He informed me that the backup pilot would be Deke Slayton. This absolutely astonished me. Until then, I hadn't the slightest idea there was any serious intent to use Slayton as a pilot for such an important mission. I told Stan that I would not recommend Slayton for an orbital flight under any circumstances, nor as a backup for any other astronaut, in view of his documented episodes of atrial fibrillation. He replied that the NASA selection committee determined who would be utilized, and the current plan was to use John Glenn with Deke Slayton as the backup.

The NASA selection committee referred to individuals from the Manned Spacecraft Center. It was clear to me that no one making the decision had any training or experience in cardiology. There was, after all, no one in the medical field at the Manned Spacecraft Center at that time who had the professional qualification to make such a decision regarding a person with atrial fibrillation.

As the debacle unfolded, news stories based on information from NASA's Manned Spacecraft Center reported that there had been a disagreement about whether Slayton was qualified for flying or not. The only disagreement was between representatives from the Manned Spacecraft Center and the many highly qualified heart specialists outside MSC—I learned later—who had expressed an opinion on the case.

At no time in the course of this discussion did Stan White indicate to me that Slayton had experienced any more episodes of atrial fibrillation after I had examined him at the School. I gained the impression that he had not had any further difficulties. These conversations were all held in the presence of Captain Ashton Graybiel. Sometime after we had arrived at the Cape, and the consultation on Enos had begun, Stan White returned to the room and told me that the backup pilot for Glenn's orbital flight would be Scott Carpenter. Was I being tested to see if I would agree that Slayton was qualified to pilot a Mercury flight? If not, who made the sudden change in plans? Stan White? Other than Jim Henry, none of the other individuals making such decisions were present. Or was Stan confused and simply corrected his mistake?

After the consultation was completed, Stan asked me to have a drink with him. We discussed a number of matters, including Air Force and NASA politics. Finally, he got around to asking me about my relationship to Lyndon Johnson. I expressed surprise that he knew I had seen the Vice President at all. He replied with a knowing smile that he made it his business to keep abreast of such things and, after all, if he were going to be run over by a locomotive, he wanted to know who the engineer was. This conversation disturbed me because it implied that a doctor-patient relationship could provide a suitable platform for the exercise of power. I was to remember these remarks later, during the hectic days ahead.

The discovery that Chuck Roadman at NASA headquarters had not been informed about Deke Slayton's medical problem, coupled with the indications from Stan White that the Manned Spacecraft

Center intended to pursue its own independent course, left me with the disquieting feeling that these important decisions would be kept in the hands of headstrong individuals, uncontrolled by NASA's higher headquarters and without regard to national priorities. There was an enormous amount riding on the man-in-space program. The Kennedy administration had made it a national goal of the highest priority and an instrument of foreign policy—the United States simply could not afford anything that would bring discredit to the man-in-space effort. Since I was a consultant in cardiology to NASA for the Mercury project and the NASA-DOD key scientist for crew selection, I knew that whatever happened would be, in part, my responsibility.

There was no way I could recommend Slayton for a solo flight in the Mercury spacecraft. I also knew that if I took steps to stop this, Slayton and his supporters, such as Stan White and Bill Douglas, would become my mortal enemies—although I didn't know then to what lengths they would go. This would also engender problems with some of the partisan top Air Force brass who were especially keen on having the first man to orbit into space be an Air Force pilot. That chance was gone, but when the next flight occurred, the Air Force must be represented. It was a lose-lose-lose situation for me.

Soon, I learned that personnel from the Manned Spacecraft Center had repeatedly sought out other heart specialists in an attempt to find someone—just one competent cardiologist in the country—who would agree that Slayton was qualified to make a Mercury flight. The usual approach was to present a hypothetical case to a prospective consultant to see what type of response he would give if he were confronted with the problem of someone with atrial fibrillation. When an unsatisfactory reply was given, any effort to obtain a consultation from that particular heart specialist was no longer pursued. It also became obvious to me that since my original professional opinion on the matter at the beginning of the problem in September 1959, every effort was made to avoid bringing this matter to my attention.

I pondered my responsibility in such strange circumstances. Obviously, the nation's interest came first and should transcend any personal desire by any one man to make a multimillion-dollar ride into space. I saw no evidence that Chuck Roadman was taking any steps to resolve the situation. Perhaps he couldn't. Having seen the way the information had been concealed and the problem managed for several years, it was apparent that if I were going to do anything to prevent the cover-up, the time for action had arrived. I decided I would not sit by and allow the nation's man-in-space program to be jeopardized without making an effort to expose the truth.

Subsequently, a NASA history commissioned by the Manned Spacecraft Center mistakenly reported that I had written the administrator of NASA, informed him of Slayton's condition, and recommended that he not be used for the Mercury flights.• This was not true. I had already passed the information to General Roadman, who had this responsibility to the director of NASA, then James Webb.

Long ago I had been impressed with the importance of going to the top. The one person who could solve this matter at this late date was President John F. Kennedy, so I wrote to Dr. Travell. I respected her judgment and knew she would consider the problem carefully in light of the administration's goals. As President Kennedy's personal physician, I knew she had firsthand information on the importance of the man-in-space program. It was on this occasion that I was indeed grateful that the White House physician was a real professional and not just a military buddy of the President.

Dr. Travell concluded that I was trying to help and likewise agreed that it was too important not to have presidential scrutiny. Accordingly, she gave the letter to President Kennedy. In this way, the President of the United States first learned that within the bureaucratic morass of the space program there were efforts underway to take an unnecessary gamble that could seriously jeopardize one of the nation's goals of the highest priority.

• As reported in *This New Ocean, A History of Project Mercury* by Loyd S. Swenson, Jr., James M. Grimwood and Charles C. Alexander, published by the Scientific and Technical Information Division Office of Technology Utilization, National Aeronautics and Space Administration, Washington, D.C., 1966.

Later, I was told that President Kennedy had directed that Slayton not be used for an upcoming Mercury flight. If he did give such directions, by the time they reached the point of action, they had been so changed or distorted—or ignored—that they had no effect on the Manned Spacecraft Center's plans. This was my first real introduction to the President's limitations in getting specific objectives accomplished deep within the bureaucracy. Even presidents didn't have to be obeyed. Thus, at the close of December, 1961, the stage was set for the curious saga that followed in the Deke Slayton case.

The group stopped to look at *Friendship Seven* after we had established that astrochimp Enos' problem had nothing to do with space flight. The Mercury spacecraft was being checked out in a large hangar-like room. *Friendship Seven* rose from the center of the room like a giant flask, dominating everything and everybody. The area was congested with activity, as each technician and scientist went about the serious business of checking out every facet of the spacecraft that would orbit America's first astronaut around the world. The stakes were too high to permit any defect, however small, to occur during this monumental event. Every circuit, every switch, every hinge, every bolt, had to be tested and accounted for. Soon, John Glenn's life would depend on how well his spacecraft functioned. The vehicle would be his only protection from the unknowns of the strange vistas of space.

Actually, *Friendship Seven* had arrived at the Cape on April 27, 1961. The detailed systems checkout continued for 167 working days. The pace of the checkout gradually accelerated, and now, time was the enemy. Would the vehicle be ready for a launch date in that calendar year: 1961?

The medical monitors were alerted and gathered for a final briefing before being dispersed to their respective stations around the globe. An air of expectancy developed throughout the space sciences community. A formidable array of talent and capability was mobilized for the effort. A force of more than 19,000 people was at the ready for deployment. This was D-Day in the American conquest of space. At Cape Canaveral, over 2,500 people were to support the launching operation. Another 16,000 were deployed for a worldwide recovery capability—and still, the uncertainty of the launch day remained.

The year of 1961 passed. No American astronaut had yet orbited the Earth. The Soviet Union remained supreme, with a clear first in manned orbital flight: a victory by a very wide margin.

Finally, *Friendship Seven* moved to the launching pad on the 3rd of January, 1962. An impatient America waited on a daily basis for any news of the expected flight. Again, there were new problems uncovered after mating the spacecraft to the Atlas missile. There were problems of stuck or leaky valves, and even a reversal of wiring to Glenn's helmet. Just when one problem was licked, there was always another one. In many ways, it was as difficult as trying to eat spaghetti with greased chopsticks.

The weather was no ally in those troubled days—it was almost as if the gods resented the invasion of their heavens. Winter storm centers gathered and strong winds challenged any man-made object that might be lofted into their grasp. Below lay an angry sea, churning huge waves of cold water, waiting to swallow any surviving small spacecraft that escaped from the heavens. These were the days of trial for John Glenn—the stress of being ever ready, day after day, for the great adventure. Each day he would run along the beach: dissipating his frustrations and maintaining his physical vigor, while communing with his tormentor—Mother Nature. Glenn ran as many as five miles a day along the wet, sandy beaches, as the surf lapped at his feet.

While John Glenn was waiting for a break in the weather, I was called to the Surgeon General's Office. Air Force Chief of Staff General Curtis LeMay wanted to review the possibility of centralizing all the medical records for flying personnel. Surgeon General Niess requested that I discuss such a plan with his staff, as well as plans to implement it at an early date. Centralizing the electrocardiograms from the flying personnel at the School had been such a success that LeMay wanted all their medical records centralized as well.

At the Cape, John Glenn's marathon wait continued. Well over a month had passed since his scheduled rendezvous with history. Time after time, he had climbed in and out of *Friendship Seven*. Day after day, the countdown began: the seconds ticking away before igniting the rocket engines. One day, he almost made it. Lying on his back in his small space cradle, he heard the countdown and waited to feel the crush of gravity as the rocket's thrust would push him away from Earth. His voice was calm and controlled, but inside Mercury, his heart beat faster and faster, his muscles tightened: awaiting the zero hour. Then the counting stopped. All was quiet in the spacecraft.

As the public grew impatient, the popularity of the man-in-space project plummeted. Expressing national frustration, Congressman James Fulton of the House Committee on Science and Astronautics exclaimed, after watching an unsuccessful attempted launching, that the Mercury spacecraft would go down in history as "a Rube Goldberg device on top of a plumber's nightmare." His comment was reminiscent of John Kennedy's first reaction to a miniaturized mockup model of the Mercury capsule when he wondered if James Webb, Administrator of NASA, had "bought it at the five-and-dime store on his way to the White House." The press was anxious for a story, and they worried about Glenn. *What was Glenn thinking about? Had the long ordeal rattled his nerves? Was he now too tired for the upcoming space flight? Should he be replaced at this date with a fresh astronaut?*

11

⮌ I was in the Surgeon General's Office at the actual time of Glenn's launch. I had arrived in Washington on Monday evening, February 19, 1962 and went directly to the hospital at Andrews Air Force Base. Colonel Archie Hoffman was then the hospital commander. He would join me at the Surgeon General's Office the next day to consider expanding the Air Force's central records program.

It was a delight to see Archie again. We had remained good friends through the years. He even changed his lifestyle. One summer, he came to see me for his annual physical examination—he liked to do that because he had borderline high blood pressure. After he calmed down and had a good night's sleep, his pressure would be normal. He had not lost any weight and had continued to smoke constantly. When he got up in the mornings, he had prolonged coughing spells. When I pointed this out to him, he claimed it was because he had not yet had his morning cigarette. His total cholesterol was too high and I was not pleased with his blood pressure.

Archie had two severe shocks on that visit. He wanted to go downtown and buy some clothes. We went to a men's clothing store, and he told the clerk that he wanted some "Ivy League" trousers. The clerk looked at him and told him he couldn't wear them. Archie demanded to know why not and pointed to me and said, "He wears them." The clerk was no diplomat. He told Archie that he was too fat to wear "Ivy League" trousers.

Archie's other shock came when I wrote his wife, Gert, a letter about his health and what he needed to do to avoid a stroke or a heart attack. The wife is one of a doctor's weapons when all else fails with a husband who refuses to do anything about his medical problems. Gert didn't fool around. She told him that if he didn't stay away from the refrigerator, he was going to lose 20 pounds of ugly fat real fast. She also made him start walking every night. She really got him in good shape—Archie was transformed into a trim, neat-looking colonel in good physical shape. Later, I asked him if he was angry about my letter to Gert.

He replied, "Well, I was pretty mad at first, but afterward, I was glad you did it."

On his next visit to San Antonio he asked me to go shopping with him again. He headed straight for the same store we had gone to before. He looked up the same clerk and said, "I want some Ivy League trousers."

Archie and I compared notes on recent events and talked about some of the cardiac problems in the hospital. Then I called Dr. Travell at her White House office. After some discussion, she asked me to take an Air Force vehicle and come to her office.

It was around 6:30 p.m. when I arrived; the White House guards were expecting me. After the identification process was complete, they pointed out the entrance closest to Dr. Travell's office. As I started walking toward the entry, I could see a silver-haired lady in the distance who could be none other than Dr. Travell, coming out to be sure I found my way easily.

Soon we were in the White House basement and entering Dr. Travell's office. We continued a running conversation while she completed the tasks of the day. With her natural instincts as a medical teacher, she kept finding more choice medical articles that she thought I should know about. There were other items that she wanted to study more thoroughly herself. These kept finding their way into her brown attaché case, which, despite its small size, seemed to have an unlimited capacity.

Finally, the day's tasks were complete and a last few items were dropped into her handbag. Then we were ready to leave. We slipped on our coats, took the briefcase, and stepped out into the snow-blanketed winter night.

Safely seated in the back of a White House limousine, we drove to Dr. Travell's Georgetown home. As we approached her house, she leaned forward and pointed out an attractive red brick house next to where she lived. It was the former home of President and Mrs. Kennedy.

Dr. Travell's husband, Jack Powell, was patiently awaiting our arrival. We sat down to a tasty, relaxed dinner and talked about the upcoming flight. Tomorrow was the day. Tomorrow, John Glenn was surely going to blaze a new trail in space—and he did.

At the Cape, John Glenn had long since known that the next day's weather was forecast to be ideal for his space voyage. All the difficulties of the preceding, anxious days appeared to be solved. He must have wondered that night if tomorrow would really be the day; or would some new problem arise to thwart his odyssey in space?

In Washington, while we talked of the upcoming space venture, the hours ticked away toward the new dawn at the Cape. Long before the first rays of the sun caught the water's edge, men at the Cape were everywhere in the cool predawn making last-minute checks before the flight.

A 19,000-man task force had been deployed around the globe. In Kano, Nigeria, an Air Force flight surgeon nervously thumbed through his booklet of electrocardiograms, showing different cardiac irregularities and those from Glenn's stress tests. All the medical monitors were at their stations. In Bermuda, in Zanzibar, on a Navy ship in the Indian Ocean, at Woomera, Australia, on Canton Island and in Hawaii: all were ready. The ships at sea cruised around their prescribed areas and their crews wondered if they would pick up the first American to orbit Earth. The Navy's frogmen rescue team was at the ready. The spotter planes sat waiting to take their positions. The cold, giant Atlas missile, flanked by its supporting gantry and crowned by the tiny Mercury spacecraft at its very top, stood silhouetted against the sky.

The hands of the clock had just marked the beginning of the new day. It was the 20th of February, 1962. At 2:20 a.m., John Glenn sat on the edge of his bunk and ran his hand across his sparse, sandy-blond hair, stood up, stretched, and wondered if this was it. While he showered, then dressed, he contemplated with pleasure the opportunity to have a real man's breakfast, having been on a low-residue diet in preparation for the flight. He made short work of his meal—first, there was coffee and orange juice, then a generous breakfast steak smothered with scrambled eggs and toast.

It was now just after 3:00 a.m., and the familiar figure of Bill Douglas was bending over him, counting his pulse, taking a last minute inventory of his charge. Their conversation was sparse and flat. The two men had come to know each other very well during the preceding years of training, and each had long since taken the other's measure. There was no need for much talk—a communion of thought existed, as often occurs between two individuals at the edge of a crisis. Bill Douglas picked up the electrodes for the electrocardiogram and carefully attached one to the top of the breastbone, then one at the bottom. Two more were attached; one to the right and one to the left side of the chest.

Joe Schmitt, the space version of an astronaut's valet, was waiting on Douglas to finish placing the sensors. It was his job to help Glenn into his 25-pound pressure suit. Finally, it was done. As if the pages of history had suddenly reversed themselves, John Glenn stood there in his silver suit with his helmet under his arm, like "a knight in shining armor" waiting to be hoisted onto his space horse to gallop into the heavens. Then they were in the transfer van, bumping across the terrain, moving slowly toward the launch site.

Launch time was close at hand when John Glenn arrived at the gantry flanking Atlas. Up, up, up he went, until he reached the top of the missile. He wormed himself through the small hatch of the spacecraft and stretched out on the astronaut's couch, just as he had done so many times before. All the checkouts and connections were complete, and the hatch slammed shut, leaving behind an eerie silence. He was alone now. Lying on his back, he could hear the muffled noise of the preparation outside. Time passed and there were more delays. He squirmed about in his suit and restraints, verbally inventorying again the actions he had planned for the flight.

As a grim reminder of Mother Nature's undisputed power, the weather was overcast, a last reluctant maneuver before surrendering the vistas of space to Glenn. Once again, there was mechanical trouble. This time, it was the booster's guidance system—it had to be replaced and checked out. Then the sensor measuring Glenn's respiration chose this particularly inopportune moment to go awry.

The technicians began bolting down the hatch to the spacecraft. As one of the 70 bolts was being secured, they discovered that one was broken. No one wanted a repeat performance of a hatch problem that had plagued Grissom during his previous suborbital flight. The hatch was removed and the bolt replaced. Like a reluctant virgin emitting her final protestations, the skies began to clear as the final stages of securing the hatch progressed. All was ready for the conquest of space.

Finally, the gantry was pulled back from the Atlas and the missile stood, unsheathed, on the pad. As Glenn moved in his couch, he could now feel the entire vehicle sway. He felt the spacecraft shudder and vibrate as liquid oxygen filled the tanks. White plumes of LOX (liquid oxygen) could be seen through his periscope. Using his periscope, he gazed across much of Cape Canaveral—and he waited.

Soon the countdown began and his heart raced faster and faster. Ordinarily, being in superb physical condition, his resting heart rate was in the low 50s—now, it was well over 100 beats per minute.

At the range station, Glenn could hear the Capsule Communicator counting:

Nine... Eight... Seven... Six... Five... Four... Three... Two... One... Zero.

The launch occurred at 9:47 a.m. When the engines started at the count of zero, they shook the spacecraft and Glenn knew the lift-off had begun. The missile was released. It soared upward like a giant bird. John Glenn had adjusted his window mirror so he could watch the ground falling away. The vibration continued as the rocket accelerated towards space. Astronaut Glenn could hear the muffled roar of the engines as he felt pressed into his couch.

After about two minutes the forward thrust decreased abruptly and Glenn eased up a bit from his couch. Soon, the power surge began again as the space vehicle was propelled faster and faster. As the LOX and fuel were consumed, the giant Atlas missile was no longer in its turgid state. It behaved like a flexible springboard, gently bouncing the space capsule at its tip.

Soon the spacecraft and the Atlas missile had reached orbital velocity. It was now over five action-packed minutes since the lift-off had begun. As the engine thrust cut off, Glenn felt like he was tumbling forward. Just then, there was a loud report as the rockets used to separate the capsule from the missile fired. Glenn watched the Atlas missile as it disappeared from sight. The giant rocket had fulfilled its purpose: spewing forth smoke and fumes as its fuel was exhausted, it had carried *Friendship Seven* into orbit. Now, with its fuel spent and in a semi-collapsed state, it was relegated to the graveyard of space.

On the Cape, thousands of onlookers had watched the huge missile and spacecraft gradually diminish in size as they disappeared in the distance. Some wept as this crucial moment passed. At home, in the office, and in the classroom, a whole nation watched and prayed as America launched her first astronaut into orbit.

The physical data was being telemetered to the ground stations. Individual receiving stations from private groups picked up the signal as the vehicle orbited about Earth. Millions of Americans saw John Glenn's electrocardiogram on the television screen as he continued on his orbital path.

Within a short span of time, the spacecraft glided from the day side to the night side of Earth. On the day side, the Earth lay below, drenched in a vivid halo of light, illuminated by light rays striking the particles in the atmosphere. By contrast, the emptiness of deep space was a void of darkness. The horizon itself was vividly marked. Even on the night side, the moonlit Earth was contrasted to the blackness of outer space.

John Glenn found weightlessness to be a pleasant sensation. The discomfort of prolonged constraint was relieved. His now-weightless body no longer sank against the couch. He moved his head from side to side—testing what influence weightlessness had on the balance mechanism in his ears. He checked his visual responses and his control over body movement. Slowly and methodically, he inventoried his body's response to this new experience and was pleasantly surprised to find how easy it really was to do without the burden of gravity. He could set his camera anywhere in the space vehicle and it stayed there, just as if it had been placed on a table.

Over Canton Island, he ate some apple sauce, and found eating in space was really no problem. Then he talked about the possibility of eating a ham sandwich while in flight, and said it should be tried—and it was, by astronauts Gus Grissom and John Young, to the horror of the NASA medics. They had carefully planned a "controlled metabolic study" that depended on following a prescribed diet—one that did not include a ham sandwich.

Far below *Friendship Seven*, Glenn could see the city lights on the night side of Earth, and on the day side he could see the towns, the colors of the desert, and different colors in the water. The brightness of Earth, the darkness of space, and the brilliant blue-and-white of the horizon created a spectacular view that no American had ever experienced.

The first orbit was nearly over. The man and the machine were functioning perfectly. As the spacecraft soared over the monitoring station at Guaymas, Mexico, it was a simple matter to decide to continue on into the second orbit. Jubilation prevailed at Cape Canaveral's Mission Control. At home and in their offices, waiting Americans began to yawn, stretch, and go about their normal daily tasks. The suspense was over and the whole thing was beginning to get a little boring.

Then, John Glenn noted that the attitude (position) of the spacecraft was beginning to drift slowly to the right. It didn't take him long to discover that the stabilizing mechanism was malfunctioning. A similar problem had caused a lot of trouble when astrochimp Enos was in orbit. If the spacecraft drifted, or tumbled through space, the fuel requirement would be increased sharply and the mission would have to be cut short. Glenn had already verified his ability to pilot the spacecraft manually. Now the successful continuation of the mission depended upon his manual control. The value of man as a back-up to the automatic controls was about to be dramatically demonstrated to the world.

The real crisis was yet to surface, but it was not long in coming. As Glenn piloted his space chariot across the heavens over Cape Canaveral, an unwelcome signal was noted at Mission Control. A light indicated that the heat shield of *Friendship Seven* was no longer locked in its proper position. This large, saucer-shaped shield in front of the capsule was the astronaut's protection from a fiery death in space. As the spacecraft loses orbital velocity and enters denser atmosphere, which creates friction, enough heat is generated to incinerate the craft and the astronaut—leaving no trace of man's intrusion. *Was this to be nature's cruel reward for Glenn?* The spacecraft had a collapsible landing bag stored between the heat shield and the main part of the capsule. Its purpose was to help cushion the shock to the Mercury capsule during landing. The signal indicated that the landing bag had been released.

Retrorockets were strapped directly in front of the heat shield. They were used to slow the Mercury capsule so it would lose orbital velocity and start the return to Earth from the pull of gravity. When they fired, they created a backward thrust, like a strong force was pushing against the heat shield in front of the space vehicle. If, in fact, the heat shield was unlocked, only the retrorockets that were external to the heat shield were holding it in place. After they had been fired to slow the spacecraft, the external pack was programmed to be jettisoned. There was the possibility, and hope, that the malfunction was solely in the indicator switch.

There was a hurried conference among an anxious group at Mission Control. *Had Glenn set the deploy switch for the landing bag in the "on" position? Should they relay this information to Glenn? How were they going to get the spacecraft back through the atmosphere with the heat shield unlocked?* While they tackled the more difficult problems, they decided not to tell Glenn immediately of his apparent danger. Instead, using the monitors at the various stations, they would try to find out if the indicator switch was in the correct position.

Over Zanzibar, Glenn went through his checklist with the flight control communicator, indicating, "The rescue aids are normal. Landing bag is off. All other sequence panel items are in normal position." Each monitoring station inquired about the landing bag switch.

While personnel in Mission Control at the Cape continued to fret over the heat shield problem, John Glenn blissfully soared on through space, now coming within range of the Canton station. Glenn scanned the vastness of space, continuously gaining new information about this previously unexplored dimension of the universe.

At Mission Control, an anxious phone call was placed to Maxime A. Faget, back in Houston, who had been the chief designer for the Mercury vehicle. The plan was to leave the retropack, which contained the rockets in front of the heat shield, in place. Hopefully, the mechanism which strapped the retrorockets to the outside of the heat shield would hold it in place until the pressure of the atmosphere during reentry became great enough to hold the heat shield against the spacecraft. Originally, the mission had called for jettisoning the retrorocket pack as soon as it had been fired.

The information received from Max Faget was not entirely reassuring. He thought the plan might work if the retrorockets all fired. It was recognized that the retrorocket assembly would burst into flames and disintegrate when the spacecraft encountered the atmosphere's friction during reentry. If any of the rockets failed to fire, the unused solid rocket fuel would ignite, enveloping *Friendship Seven* in a ball of fire. The anxiety of the team at Mission Control was transmitted to a worldwide audience. An anxious nation waited in strained silence to learn if this was to be a space spectacular or a national tragedy.

John Glenn's space odyssey continued. Over Zanzibar, now in his third orbit around planet Earth, he described his reaction to a storm. "There is quite a big storm area under me. It must extend for—I see lightning flashes as far—way off on the horizon to the right. I also have them almost directly under me here. They show up very brilliantly here on the dark side at night. They're just like firecrackers going off. Over."

Friendship Seven was now over Muchea, Australia: homeward bound. It could be only a short time now until the flight would be all over: an event of history past. John Glenn began to relax and think again of earthly things, unaware of the heat shield problem. No doubt President Kennedy watched the TV screen in the White House and, like millions of Americans, wished with all his heart for a successful conclusion to the flight. He knew well what far-reaching ramifications a space catastrophe would have. It had only been a few months since he had set the national goal of sending a man to the moon. This was to be one factor in mobilizing the nation's resources and talents for a period in history that he hoped would be marked by unprecedented achievement. *Was John Glenn, along with the nation's hopes and aspirations, to be burned to ashes in a fiery furnace at the edge of space?*

The mission profile called for the retrorocket firing sequence to

191

begin over California. The crucial moment was close at hand. Would the retrorockets fire and burn all the solid fuel? John Glenn had now been orbiting through space for more than four and one-half hours.

Thank God! All of the retrorockets fired. There would be no problem of unused rocket fuel when the craft heated up during reentry into the atmosphere. As the retropack blazed, Glenn saw flaming pieces streaming past the spacecraft window. As the pieces bumped against the window he wondered if the heat shield was breaking up. Gradually, the intense external heat penetrated the vehicle. By the time *Friendship Seven* descended to 80,000 feet, John Glenn was hot. He was soaked with sweat. The spacecraft swung and tossed as Glen waited for the chute mechanism to deploy and stabilize the craft.

Just as he reached to deploy the chute at 28,000 feet altitude, out came the drogue chute, ending the troublesome oscillations. Then, at 10,800 feet, the main chute streamed out behind *Friendship Seven*, billowed in the air, and jolted the spacecraft to a slower speed.

At 2:43 p.m. EST, *Friendship Seven* splashed down on the surface of the Atlantic and bobbed like a cork on the water, awaiting the pickup. John Glenn was the first American to orbit through space. The in-flight odyssey had lasted four hours, fifty-five minutes and twenty-three seconds. Soon, he felt a bump as the spacecraft struck the side of the destroyer *Nova*. He was lying in his couch as the side hatch was removed.

Glenn had planned to exit through the bottleneck opening at the top of the spacecraft, but he was hot and very tired. He was content to be helped out through the side. During his flight, he had lost 5 pounds 5 ounces. Most of this was probably from sweating, considering the short period of weightlessness. The heat, plus weightlessness, would have caused him to lose enough body water to make him susceptible to fainting. That response to space flight was why returning astronauts, rescued at sea, had a supporting buddy on each side as they walked across the deck of the ship.

Although Glenn was in excellent condition, his space flight took everything he had and proved how important it was that the man who piloted the Mercury spacecraft be able to function at maximum capacity. There was no room for less-than-maximum physical and mental capability. Even the stouthearted Glenn knew he had been wrung out and had given his all. Glenn's flight served as an important reminder of the absolute necessity to the success of the Mercury mission that the astronaut not be handicapped by any significant medical disorders. John Glenn and the United States had come through. The nation had a new hero—and John Glenn had a new achievement.

As soon as Glenn's flight was over, President Kennedy immediately hailed the successful flight. Standing on the South lawn of the White House, the President said,

I know that I express the great happiness and thanksgiving of all of us that Colonel Glenn has completed his trip, and I know that this is particularly felt by Mrs. Glenn and their two children.

A few days ago, Colonel Glenn came to the White House and visited me. And he is—as are the other astronauts—the kind of American of whom we are most proud. Some years ago, as a Marine pilot, he raced the sun across this country—and lost. And today—he won.

I also want to say a word for all those who participated with Colonel Glenn at Canaveral. They faced many disappointments and delays. The burdens upon them were great. But they kept their heads and they made a judgment, and I think their judgment has been vindicated.

We have a long way to go in the space race. We started late. But this is the new ocean, and I believe the United States must sail on it and be in a position second to none.

Some months ago I said that I hoped every American would serve his country. Today Colonel Glenn served his, and we all express our thanks to him.

Despite John Glenn's success, the United States was still far behind the Soviet Union in manned space flight. Gherman Titov's seventeen-orbit feat on August 7, 1961, greatly surpassed the American achievement. The two space flights were hardly comparable. Glenn had achieved success with the dice loaded against him. Titov had achieved success with the dice loaded for him. The Soviet spacecraft was a real ship: with interior conditions much like a commercial jet aircraft. The cabin pressure was maintained at sea level equivalents. This permitted using the normal ratio of oxygen and nitrogen. There was appreciably more room in the Soviet spacecraft. Since it returned to land, there was no problem with an angry sea submerging the Soviet capsule.

These added features required more weight. The weight of the space load was still a critical factor for the United States. By taking advantage of every possibility, the Atlas could barely launch the Mercury capsule into orbit. The Mercury astronaut was crammed into the space vehicle like the proverbial sardine in a can. Afterward, when Gherman Titov visited the United States and Glenn showed him *Friendship Seven,* he remarked that he wouldn't fly it because it was not a safe vehicle. No matter, part of the gap between Soviet and American achievements had been closed by a man—John Glenn.

Despite the superiority of the Soviet Union's capability in space, Nikita Khrushchev sent a very courteous letter of congratulations to President Kennedy as follows:

Esteemed Mr. President:

On behalf of the people of the Soviet Union and myself personally, I congratulate you and the American people on the successful launching of a space ship with a man on board.

Another step has been made in the exploration of space, and the family of the cosmonauts has this time been joined by a citizen of the United States of America, Lt. Colonel John Glenn.

Successful launchings of space ships, marking the reaching of new heights in science and technology, make us justly proud of the unlimited potentials of human genius to serve the welfare of man.

I should like to hope that the genius of man, who penetrated the depth of the universe, will be able to find a road to an enduring peace and to ensure prosperity to all people on our planet Earth which, in the space age, though it does not seem to be so large, is still dear to all its inhabitants.

If our countries pool their efforts—scientific, technical and material— to explore outer space, this would be very beneficial to the advance of science and would be acclaimed by all people who would like to see scientific achievements benefit man and not to be used for "cold war" purposes and the arms race.

Please convey hearty congratulations and best wishes to astronaut John Glenn.

N. Khrushchev

(Courtesy of LBJ Library)

February 21, 1962

Dear Lyndon:

I greatly appreciate your willingness to meet
and congratulate our first earth-orbiting
astronaut after his history-making flight. It
is most fitting that you, as Chairman of the
Space Council, express to him, on my behalf
and on behalf of the entire nation, how deeply
grateful we are for his courage and his dedication.

I am looking forward to meeting the astronaut
at Cape Canaveral so that I can personally
express my congratulations to him and to all
of the dedicated men and women who have
worked together to produce this superb achievement for their country and for advancing the
knowledge of all mankind.

Sincerely,

Honorable Lyndon B. Johnson
The Vice President
Washington, D. C.

12
ASTRONAUT'S WINGS ARE CLIPPED

12

The day after Glenn's space flight was an important one for me. Dr. Travell invited me to have lunch with her at the White House. After the luncheon, we discussed President Kennedy's back problem. Anything that put a strain on the President's back was likely to cause severe pain. It was necessary to adjust many aspects of his daily life to keep him comfortable. One of his legs was shorter than the other one; if the legs are unequal in length, the pelvis tilts when a person is standing, and the entire spine must curve to maintain balance and keep the head level. The crooked spine can cause back strain. In the President's case, the strain caused muscle pain from his degenerating spine. Later, in her book, *Office Hours: Day and Night,* Dr. Travell explained that Kennedy had so much pain in his left back and leg he could hardly bear weight on his left foot. He also had a stiff right knee from an old football injury, so he could hardly bend his right knee. The taxi driver that brought him to see Dr. Travell helped him down the steps to her office. She relieved his short leg problem in part by increasing the height of the heel of his shoe and putting a small lift inside the shoe for the foot of his short leg. You would not notice any real change in his shoe unless you really examined it closely.

The short leg was not the only problem—I learned this when Dr. Travell showed me his X-rays. One half of his pelvic bone was smaller than the other. Whenever the President was seated, his pelvis was like a lopsided basket, tilted to one side. Again, the tilt would put a strain on his back and cause pain. We went into the Cabinet room and she showed me how she had built up one side of the seat of his chair. That lifted the short side of his pelvis and kept it level—it was like putting a wedge under a short leg of a table. She had done this for all the places where the President would be seated. Dr. Travell had done a remarkable job in helping the President regain his health when he was still a senator, which had a lot to do with why she was given the honor of being the White House physician. When she first started treating him, he arrived at her office on crutches. He had used them so long that there were calluses under each arm. She was practically a magician in dealing with musculoskeletal pain and had done pioneering research in the field. It is not an exaggeration to state that if the Senator's health had not improved under Dr. Travell's care, it is unlikely that he could have considered being President at all.

Dr. Travell was never one to let a potential patient get away without treatment. After showing me the President's problem, she had me stand up to take a good look at me. Next, my shoes were off, and she was doing careful measurements. She announced that one of my legs was too short. Then she put magazines of various thickness under the foot for the short leg until she was satisfied that a perfect level had been achieved. She cut a thick piece of felt and inserted it inside my shoe and gave me instructions to have the heels of all my shoes adjusted.

That was the beginning of getting my muscles tuned-up. On another occasion, she discovered that my mouth did not open enough to put three knuckles between my upper and lower teeth. That would certainly have surprised some of my colleagues. She sprayed my jaw muscles with coolant spray and stretched them until I could insert three knuckles. My neck muscles were too tight. So, my neck was sprayed and my head was rotated and stretched until she was satisfied that they worked properly. I also learned that she had very strong fingers. When she found an area of muscle spasm, she could apply very strong pressure. She taught me a great deal about the management of muscle and skeletal pain over the next several years.

Afterward, while I was still at the White House, we listened to the President's news conference. Of course, one of the main topics of conversation was John Glenn's space flight. The President commented that he had received a message from Chairman Khrushchev of the Soviet Union, who had stated it would be beneficial if the countries worked together in the exploration of space. This was what the President had already suggested many times. He said,

Previous to that, under the previous administration, many suggestions were made for international cooperation. On one occasion, the Vice President, then Senator Johnson, acting on behalf of President Eisenhower, presented a proposal to the United Nations for the peaceful uses of outer space.

One evening during my stay in Washington, immediately after Glenn's successful flight, I had dinner at Dr. Travell's house with a number of her friends. We had a great time discussing some of the effects of weightlessness and some of the problems still to be overcome in the man-in-space effort. Among those present for the evening was Major General Chester "Ted" V. Clifton of the U.S. Army. He was an intelligent man with an agile mind, and was the Army aide to President Kennedy. He was quite familiar with the background of the old NACA (National Advisory Committee for Aeronautics) that became NASA, as well as the German scientist group headed by Wernher von Braun, who had developed missile projects under the auspices of the Army. Thereafter, I communicated with Ted Clifton about the Slayton problem and he relayed the information to the President.

I met President Kennedy one morning while visiting Dr. Travell in her office. The President had been profoundly impressed by the change in public reaction from the long period of waiting while Glenn's capsule sat on the launching pad compared to the wave of enthusiasm that followed his successful flight. In the Kennedy tradition, he asked me many searching questions, including who decided which astronaut would be chosen for an individual space flight. I understood well the nature of his questions, since I knew he was aware of the Slayton problem. I knew he was concerned that each space flight should be equally as successful as John Glenn's.

My remarks were not exactly reassuring on this point, considering the reality of how the decisions were made at the Manned Spacecraft Center in Houston. Already, the buildup for the next space pilot had begun. The Manned Spacecraft Center released a picture of the man to make the next space flight—and President Kennedy did read the newspapers. There were news stories about the man who would follow John Glenn into the annals of history as one of the early space pioneers. The Marines had already had their day, and now the Air Force would follow them on the trail of glory into space. The next man to make an orbital space flight was to be Major Donald K. Slayton.

A few days after I had returned to the School, I was called to Washington again to participate in a briefing on the Air Force's activities in aerospace medicine for John Rubel—Director of Research and Development for the Department of Defense. I was at the Pentagon when I received a call from General Roadman at NASA headquarters. We exchanged a few pleasantries, then he got down to business. He inquired specifically if I was going to "nitpick them" if they orbited Slayton on the upcoming space flight. By then, he was fully informed of my earlier recommendation to Bill Douglas in 1959 concerning Slayton's participation in the program. I told him my role was that of a consultant, I had given them my advice, and I did not believe Slayton should be used for a Mercury flight. I added that if they chose to do this, they were strictly on their own, and I would not back them up if they got into trouble with the flight. I repeated to him the reasons why it was not a good idea to choose Slayton for an upcoming solo-manned space flight. After the briefing, I returned to San Antonio.

At noon the next day, Saturday, March 3, 1962, I received another call from General Roadman. He had been considering my remarks of the previous day concerning Slayton and told me that he had decided to have a meeting in his office with Robert Gilruth, the director of the Manned Spacecraft Center; Stan White, Bill Douglas, and all pertinent personnel involved from the Manned Spacecraft Center. He wanted me to come to his office and confront them with my point of view on the upcoming flight. I declined, pointing out I had already given my professional opinion and an argument over the matter would not be helpful—that my recommendations were based on solid facts which could not be changed by a confrontation.

I had already seen how my statements could be distorted and twisted by those involved. I told General Roadman that I preferred to state all of my professional opinions on matters relative to this important problem in writing, and I would send him a letter immediately, again, specifically stating my recommendations.

Apparently, one of my earlier remarks—that atrial fibrillation, should it occur during flight, could not be covered up—had struck a nerve. Evidently, no one had considered that any such attack would be picked up by receivers from other nations—friendly or unfriendly. All the world would know that the United States had orbited an astronaut with a heart problem. It couldn't be hidden. Observing John Glenn's in-flight electrocardiogram on TV sets throughout the country was an adequate demonstration of my point. I had already reviewed the in-flight records of the two Soviet cosmonauts, Gagarin and Titov, for the intelligence community that tracked the data during those flights—a fact that was top secret information at the time, which I could not disclose. Certainly, the Soviets would obtain similar information from the American flights.

Incredible as it seemed, the purpose of the Mercury project was evidently still lost, or totally ignored, by the decision-makers at the Manned Spacecraft Center. The Mercury project was to determine man's response to space flight: particularly weightlessness. The only way this could be determined was from space flights. This information was critical to develop the capability to send a man to the moon. The goal of the project was not to see if you could hot rod around Earth, or who was the best pilot in the world, but to develop the information essential to future manned space flight. Each flight was an experiment: a rather costly one, representing a multi-million dollar expenditure for the rocket, the vehicle, ships at sea, and over 19,000 people to provide global support. Such an expensive experiment deserved to be planned to provide useful information. This would be impossible if atrial fibrillation occurred during orbit, since it would affect the heart rate, blood pressure, and cause other changes: perhaps even fainting, or worse. It would be impossible to tell whether any changes that occurred were caused by atrial fibrillation or by space flight. Such a poorly designed experiment would have subjected the man-in-space project to worldwide ridicule.

In terms of the astronaut's safety and the success of the mission, it needed to be remembered that John Glenn's heart rate reached maximum levels. He had reached the limit of human endurance, even though he was not handicapped by a cardiac problem.

In my letter to General Roadman on March 5, 1962, I reviewed again the significant points of my earlier consultation in September 1959. I made the point that any attack of atrial fibrillation while in orbit would be known to the world and concluded my comments as follows:

...it is not in the best interest of Donald K. Slayton or the national program of man-in-space flights to utilize him as the pilot for Mercury orbital flights and I am compelled to recommend that his retention in the program should be restricted to a point short of primary control of high-performance aircraft (See Appendix B for the complete text of the letter.)

I knew that submitting my opinion again, in writing, would make it very difficult to distort its meaning. I had no intention of anyone failing to understand exactly what my professional opinion was, and no intention of leaving these matters in the form of verbal communications which could be distorted, as had already occurred.

Many false statements have been published about the Slayton affair, as in the 1966 NASA-sponsored publication *This New Ocean: A History of Project Mercury.* It states that,

He (Douglas) and Slayton visited the Air Force's School of Aviation Medicine in San Antonio, Texas, where a member of the internal medicine staff voiced the same opinion (that the condition was of no consequence and should not influence Slayton's eventual choice as a flight astronaut). Sometime later Douglas learned that this individual wrote to Administrator James E. Webb, making a recommendation that Slayton should not be assigned a flight.•

• *This New Ocean: A History of Project Mercury*, Scientific and Technical Information Division Office of Technology Utilization, National Aeronautics and Space Administration, Washington, D. C., printed by the U. S. Government Printing Office, Washington, D. C. 20402.

Since I was the only one who saw Slayton, I can say unequivocally that the statement is totally false (see actual consultation in Appendix A). At no time did I ever say that it was of no consequence and my written consultation at the time of that visit clearly stated otherwise. At no time did I write James Webb about Astronaut Slayton. On the contrary, I was surprised that General Roadman, in charge of life sciences at NASA headquarters, had not been informed about Slayton's condition. Although the NASA account states the Surgeon General's Office was informed by Dr. Douglas about Slayton's problem, the Surgeon General stated that he had not been informed, which I believe to be true. Evidently, he was first informed after my letter to General Roadman, long after my consultation in September 1959.

In view of General Flickinger's request that none of the records were to be forwarded, and the promise of immunity to the astronauts at the time of selection—if such a promise was ever made by the Surgeon General's office—it is highly unlikely that the Surgeon General was informed at all. The NASA account was also erroneous in stating that Administrator Webb referred the case to a group of three nationally-eminent cardiologists. It was not James Webb's responsibility to order a medical board on an Air Force officer. It was Air Force Secretary Eugene Zuckert who requested the consultation, and the events that happened are detailed in this account. The reason for the misinformation is undoubtedly related to what the historians who wrote the account were told by personnel at the Manned Spacecraft Center. I was never contacted by them to learn the truth. I could easily have shown them the actual documents.

The crisis concerning Slayton as the next astronaut to fly the Mercury spacecraft was reaching epic proportions. The big fight was going on behind closed doors within NASA and within the Air Force. The publicity buildup created in anticipation of his flight—and orchestrated by the Manned Spacecraft Center—had made Slayton's upcoming space flight a front-page news story worldwide. A problem which should have been settled quietly in September, 1959, now involved the highest levels of the government. There remain many confused reports about the incident, concerning what happened in the Surgeon General's Office and within NASA. The irony was that there were six other well-qualified Mercury astronauts. The nation's success in manned space flight did not depend on one man.

There were issues dear to the hearts of some of those involved. The Manned Spacecraft Center was determined to call the shots, very reminiscent of the statement made to the medical monitors when we arrived at Patrick Air Force Base to begin the medical monitoring course, by Colonel George Knauf, an Air Force flight surgeon on loan to NASA, "By God, the Air Force is not running this program." There was the personal involvement with Slayton of individuals at the Manned Spacecraft Center, including physicians, that was getting in the way of responsible, professional judgment.

I always have had a great deal of empathy for Bill Douglas in this critical case, whether what he did was right or wrong. As the personal physician to the Mercury astronauts, he had bonded with them, and evidently that bond with Slayton was especially strong. Male bonding can result in strong emotions. Of course, there was Deke Slayton's personal ambition. Ambition is an admirable trait—unless it overwhelms reality. And there were egos and power struggles. It was all there, a bureaucratic mess and power struggle.

As the issue grew more contentious, I was in Washington, once again, on March the 8th, for the joint planning exercises between NASA and DOD. I was in charge of a committee to study the feasibility of sending astronauts to Mars and the costs involved. That afternoon, General Roadman called and asked me to come to his office at NASA headquarters. We reviewed the problem relative to Slayton again. He discussed his meeting with Robert Gilruth, Bill Douglas, Stan White, and Donald Slayton that had occurred earlier that week. We also discussed the letter I had sent him on the 5th of March. In the course of our discussions, General Roadman told me that Gilruth was very unhappy with my recommendation, and stated that if I had gone to the Vice President and prevented Slayton from making a Mercury space flight, he would see to it that the School would not get any support from NASA for research.

Why were they so concerned about the possibility I might "squeal" to Lyndon Johnson? Because the Vice President, by law, was responsible for the nations space effort as chairman of the National Aeronautics and Space Council. As such, he had authority over all of NASA and all space activities within the government, including those in the Department of Defense. I recalled Stan White's remarks the previous December, asking about my relationship to the Vice President, and had a pretty good idea who had made such a suggestion to Gilruth. The fact was, I had never mentioned the problem to the Vice President and never discussed Air Force or NASA problems with him. That was not why I was seeing him. I recognized the statement attributed to Gilruth was a threat, but I was not one to bow to pressure. The Manned Spacecraft Center could not influence my professional opinion, and my recommendation would stand, unaltered. The Manned Spacecraft Center (MSC) contingent had come face-to-face with an immovable object: ME.

After our discussion, General Roadman took me downstairs and introduced me to Brainerd Holmes, who was in charge of manned space flight activities in NASA headquarters. We again discussed the problem and the impact on the manned space flight program. It was my impression that Holmes clearly understood the situation. He stated that if there was any reasonable doubt, Slayton should not be used for an orbital flight. During several conversations with representatives from NASA headquarters, I never received any indication that any of them had any desire whatsoever to take such an unnecessary risk with the manned space flight project. The big problem was at the Manned Spacecraft Center in Houston, not in Washington D.C.

A major difficulty was in the way NASA was organized. The individual NASA centers were relatively autonomous. Strong-minded individuals heading each center were able to circumvent the wishes of NASA headquarters to a large extent. A similar problem existed in the Air Force medical service. It was not organized like the Navy and Army Medical Corps. The Surgeon General's Office had limited control of what was done in each of the individual commands.

I kept receiving calls from General Roadman about the Surgeon General of the Air Force's opinion concerning Slayton's flying status. Slayton was still an Air Force pilot. One time Slayton was qualified for flying status. Then, he was not qualified for flying status. Confusion ruled the day.

***

Air Force Chief of Staff General Curtis LeMay returned to Washington and had both General Niess and General Roadman over to his house one evening after reviewing the records about the Slayton affair. After the meeting, I received a call—near midnight, Washington time—from General Roadman, and he sounded very excited. Apparently General LeMay was quite distressed after reviewing the records, and had some choice comments about why Slayton was still on flying status after my September, 1959, consultation. General Roadman said it was their opinion that Slayton was not qualified for flying and should not be used for Mercury flights. Evidently, that was General LeMay's feeling.

Not long after that, Air Force Secretary Eugene Zuckert discussed the matter with both General Niess and General LeMay. By that time, the Air Force position presented by General Niess was that Slayton was qualified to make a manned space flight. Supposedly, he had held a board composed of his own medical staff within the Surgeon General's Office that had come to that conclusion. None of these officers were cardiologists. Secretary Zuckert—a former trial judge and wily as a fox—pressed General Niess further and obtained an admission that Slayton was not qualified to fly high performance jet aircraft. From there on, the Secretary bored in unmercifully on the Surgeon General's position. He had acquainted himself with sufficient details on atrial fibrillation to seriously shake the General's confidence. The upshot of this highly-charged exchange was that Secretary Zuckert demanded that a board of three top cardiologists be appointed to review the case. The physicians appointed included Dr. Thomas Mattingly, who had been chief of cardiology at Walter Reed Army Hospital for years. He had attended President Eisenhower during his heart attack. Dr. Mattingly was respected worldwide for his clinical judgment in the cardiovascular field. He was the professional father for the Army's very competent cardiovascular programs and the training of most cardiologists in numerous hospitals throughout the Army. Other members of the board included Dr. Eugene Braunwald, a distinguished cardiologist from the National Heart Institute (later head of cardiology at Harvard) and Dr. Proctor Harvey, a distinguished professor of cardiology from Georgetown University in Washington, D.C. The board was to meet and examine Major Slayton on the 15th of March, 1962.

I was invited to participate in the meeting, but declined. I wanted to avoid any impression that I had influenced the outcome. I had no doubt what such a well-qualified group would recommend.

Despite some variations in the story and the newspaper reports, all three of the cardiologists comprising the "Blue Ribbon Panel" agreed unanimously that Major Slayton should not be used for the upcoming Mercury flights. None of them recommended that his atrial fibrillation should be disregarded. One of the remarkable aspects of the case, considering the potential for publicity and fame, was the relative unanimity of opinion of all the cardiologists asked about the case. Not one, to my knowledge, ever recommended that Major Slayton was medically qualified for a Mercury flight.

After the major news buildup stimulated by NASA, the news of Slayton's removal from the upcoming Mercury flight caused a rash of headlines and publicity across the nation and, indeed, around the world. Some of the Mercury astronauts were unhappy over the publicity that ensued and pointed out that if Slayton had been a pilot in the Air Force when such an event occurred, it would not even have been noticed. That was right. He would simply have been removed from flying status in the first place, but Major Slayton was given special treatment. He was not just a pilot in the Air Force. It was the Manned Spacecraft Center's publicity efforts that caused it to become a national story. Deke Slayton had campaigned like a veteran politician for his "Seat in Space," and wrote letters criticizing the "faint-hearted" men who had thwarted his ambition. It has always been my opinion that the people who really did Deke Slayton—as well as the nation—a disservice, were those who falsely encouraged him to think his medical status was not a problem for the Mercury project.

Slayton's reaction was headlined in the *New York Herald* as *"An Astronaut Blasts Off."* He felt this damaged the space program's prestige. He was quoted as saying, *"I feel the situation developed through ignorance of the problem and resulting panic and can therefore best be resolved through education of responsible personnel."* It was not clear who was to be educated and by whom.

The question that has always remained in my mind is, *Why was there such a major effort assign Slayton to pilot a Mercury flight? Why take a chance with the future of the man-in-space program, considering its high level of national priority? Was it impossible to carry out the Mercury project without sending Slayton on a Mercury flight?* One high-level Air Force officer assigned to NASA involved in the decision even told me that the other Mercury astronauts were not qualified, meaning in terms of capability. That was a real slap in the face to the rest of the Mercury astronauts, and certainly not true. Gilruth could have stopped this entire problem at its inception, but instead, he apparently supported Slayton's ambition, possibly based on what he had been told. That is the old story of being the boss of a big organization—you can't be everywhere and you are fated to depend on others to properly inform you.

For Slayton's part, making a successful flight meant becoming a national and international hero. There were lucrative, even political, opportunities for the future. He might even become a U. S. Senator, or maybe even President. The opportunities were unlimited, if only he could get past the obstacles between him and the fulfillment of his ambitions. John Glenn did become a hero, a U. S. Senator, and was a candidate for the presidency. At the very least, Slayton wanted to be known as the best damned test pilot that ever lived. Before Slayton's cardiac problem surfaced, he was the likely astronaut to make the first space flight, rather than Alan Shepard. Slayton thought and believed he was the best jet jockey of the group. In such a climate, it would not be surprising to be ruled by one's ambitions rather than the nation's needs.

Slayton did want to be first. He was quoted by Joseph Bell, writing for SAGA magazine, as having told him earlier, *"I feel I'm in on the ground floor of something human beings will be concentrating on for the next thousand years—and I hope like hell I'll be the first one to go up."*

There were additional facts that came to light after it was announced that Slayton had been scrubbed from the upcoming flight. During my earlier conversation with Stan White, at the occasion of the consultation on Enos the chimp, I had gained the impression that Major Slayton had not had any recurrence of atrial fibrillation. But, during a news conference, Slayton acknowledged that he had atrial fibrillation as often as once every two weeks, with episodes lasting as long as 18 hours. Some reports stated he had episodes that could last as long as two-and-one-half days (60 hours). For the first time since my original evaluation of him at the School in September 1959, I became aware that he had continued to have frequent attacks. After that, I had little confidence in the veracity of medical information I might get from medical representatives of the Manned Spacecraft Center.

I managed to escape the publicity associated with the scrubbing of Slayton for Mercury flights. Thank God! I referred all reporters, such as William Hines, science writer for Washington's *Evening Star*, to NASA headquarters and told them I was NASA's consultant. I also suggested that it would not help matters to include me in their news stories. My wishes were respected. But there were many false reports claiming I had originally okayed Slayton for the Mercury project. When *Aviation Week* erroneously reported that I had held a board that had recommended Slayton for a manned space flight, some of my well-meaning and concerned friends urged me to write the editor and correct the record. I was in no hurry to do this, and decided the prudent action was to let the fever run its course. My responsibility was to do my part in being certain the individuals who would make the final decisions had the benefit of whatever knowledge I possessed on the subject to prevent a cover-up, uncomplicated by the glare of national publicity: This I did.

Major Slayton was indeed fortunate to be assigned to NASA. He was given an outstanding opportunity that would enable him to advance career-wise to a top management level position in NASA-MSC. He was rewarded by being put in charge of all the astronauts and appointed as the Director of Flight Crew Operations. He may have missed a multi-million dollar ride into space, supported by a task force of over 19,000 people, a ticker tape parade, and a ceremony at the White House, but the nation's space program was far more important than that. He was afforded ample opportunity to continue to make whatever contributions fell within the realm of his ability; and his ability was considerable.

The immediate aftermath of the Slayton affair left many scars and ill feelings. My name was number one on the list of bad guys with Slayton and his supporters. The Slayton affair also increased the hostility of some of the personnel at the Manned Spacecraft Center toward the

School. It was all so unnecessary, so petty, and so detrimental to the nation's man-in-space effort. The Manned Spacecraft Center would have loved to have taken their medical examinations elsewhere, and I was so advised. Some of the NASA personnel were bitter about moving from Langley AFB in Virginia to Houston. They were furious with Lyndon Johnson for that. It was a spring of discontent.

13
PRESIDENT KENNEDY SAYS 'NO GO'

TO

𝕷𝖆𝖜𝖗𝖊𝖓𝖈𝖊 𝕰. 𝕷𝖆𝖒𝖇

The Department of Defense Distinguished Civilian Service Award is presented to Dr. Lawrence E. Lamb, Chief, Internal Medicine and Director, Consultation Services, School of Aerospace Medicine, U. S. Air Force, for his distinguished leadership of Air Force cardiological research and education. Under Dr. Lamb's leadership clinical technological advances have been made which have increased substantially U. S. Air Force medical capabilities, contributed directly to national manned space operations, and broadened medical knowledge to the ultimate benefit of mankind. Among Dr. Lamb's many achievements are the establishment of the Central United States Air Force Electrocardiograph Program, organization of the world's first International Symposium on Cardiology in Aviation, and material extension of the research, consultative and instructional capacity of the School of Aerospace Medicine. These accomplishments reflect great credit upon Dr. Lamb, his profession, and upon the United States, and warrant recognition at the highest level in the Department of Defense.

Robert S. McNamara

Secretary of Defense

MAY 22, 1962

27 June 1962

Lawrence E. Lamb, M. D.
School of Aerospace Medicine
USAF Aerospace Medical Center
Brooks AFB, Texas

Dear Doctor Lamb

Many thanks for your letter of May 29th concerning the Slayton case, which I found on my return from leave just the other day.

Slayton's examination by Doctor White in Boston was arranged by NASA. General Roadman came over and talked to General Niess and me about it after the appointment had been made. General Niess felt that Slayton's examination should be done by the Air Force and should include a period of hospitalization at Lackland, where you might participate if you should feel there was an indication (I imagine you feel that you have examined Slayton quite adequately already).

When Mr. Zuckert first insisted on civilian consultation we tried to get Doctor White as one of the consultant group; but he was not available at the time.

We were able to have Chuck Berry accompany Doctor Douglas and Slayton to Boston. Doctor White's report has not yet reached Roadman's office.

General Niess does not now have the slightest intention of ever approving Major Slayton for orbital flight. He was willing to have him hospitalized at Lackland for a thorough general physical examination for the sake of his own health. The idea of an examination by Doctor White subsequent to the final action of the Board originated in NASA, I believe, among some of the lay officials.

Many thanks for your letter, which attests your continuing interest in correct decisions by this office concerning the flying status of individuals assigned to other services.

Sincerely

R. L. BOHANNON
Major General, USAF, MC
Deputy Surgeon General

13

⤳ In an effort to find out what resources were actually present in the Department of Defense—particularly in the Air Force—to support the man in space program, Dr. Hugh Dryden, Associate Administrator of NASA, undertook a tour of the installations. News of his planned visit to the School was well received. He had many friends in the Air Force who held him in high esteem because of his many outstanding achievements. I was the project officer for his visit on the 19th of April, 1962. We had a relatively strenuous day, visiting most of the laboratory facilities. He was particularly impressed that the School's air crew evaluations were continuous—an ongoing, daily affair—and not something that needed to be cranked up for a special occasion. The examinations, such as those for potential astronauts, were well within the range of the daily activities of the staff.

The visit was not totally without its humorous aspects. We had paused to have lunch at the Officers' Club. In the midst of our discussion, the club officer approached the table and told me that I had a long distance telephone call. My first duty was to Dr. Dryden, so I asked the club officer to tell the caller I was not available at the moment and would return the call later. At this point, Dr. Dryden and I discussed how we had learned not to respond to every long distance telephone call to allow us to carry out our normal duties with some semblance of orderliness. We had just completed congratulating ourselves on the wisdom of our daily management methods when the club officer returned. He was relatively agitated. He interrupted us and said, "Dr. Lamb, it's the Vice President calling, and he wants to know if he can speak to you *now!*"

Naturally, I took the call immediately. Afterwards, both Dr. Dryden and I had a good chuckle about the unexpected call from the Vice President. Dr. Dryden and Vice President Johnson were good friends, and it was an incident both of us could fully appreciate. The Vice President had called to tell me that he planned on visiting the School the following morning.

It was Dr. Dryden who told me how Lyndon Johnson had found out about Slayton's medical problem—from the newspapers—like millions of other individuals. As soon as the Vice President saw the headlines, he called NASA and requested a briefing. Dr. Dryden had briefed him on the problem. Of course he learned about my role in the situation from the briefing and what my recommendations had been. He must have been surprised when that information surfaced. Still, we never discussed it.

While Lyndon Johnson was the extrovert's extrovert, always surrounded by friends, he liked to be able to do some things outside the glare of the public, specifically without press coverage, when he could be himself. He could obtain press coverage any time, but when he wanted to learn something, or had personal matters to attend to, he didn't want it. I was expecting the Vice President at any time on the morning of April 20, 1962, or to receive a phone call telling me when he would arrive. Finally, a secretary came to my office and said there was a Mr. Johnson on the phone and would I speak to him? Apparently, his aide had contacted General Bedwell rather than me. The General had driven to the edge of San Antonio to meet the Vice President and had missed him. The Johnson ranch was only 60 miles from San Antonio, and the Vice President was driving in from the ranch with Mrs. Johnson and others, who planned to do some shopping that day.

Vice President Johnson called me from a roadside stand to confirm his arrangements for coming to the School. When he was annoyed, he often made exaggerated statements for emphasis. He told me he didn't know how to get to the School and the only places he knew in

San Antonio were the Alamo and the Gunter Hotel. Of course, he knew downtown San Antonio very well. I told him I would send a military vehicle to the Alamo to pick him up. He agreed to that, but added, "You tell him to flat get out there right now." By the time he arrived, he was in a good humor and was in the front seat, visiting happily with the driver.

When Vice President Johnson first arrived, we chatted a while and he told me that he was disturbed about his secretary, Mary Margaret Wiley. As he explained, she had been with him for 14 years and was leaving to get married. He had done his best to get her to marry someone in the military so he could have him assigned to Washington, but she was marrying some fellow from Houston, a Jack Valenti. Later, Jack Valenti would become one of his most valued aides. While he was being weighed, he commented on his own military service. He said he was A-plus in everything but military bearing. That thought brought a smile to his face. I gathered he didn't put a lot of store in military bearing.

As I opened the door, General Bedwell was nervously pacing up and down the hall. Lyndon smiled at him, but he wasn't quite through with the question of transportation. He thanked the general for "making Doctor Lamb available" to him. Then he added that he should get a radio installed in his vehicle. The Vice President had a complete examination, including X-Rays. He was nearly too tall for the machine. This was the examination that would also be used for his personal life insurance policy. The X-rays turned out to be quite important.

Earlier that morning I had received some disturbing information that promised to give me a very complicated day. Without any prior arrangements with me, the Information Office for the Aerospace Medical Division had arranged for Roy Neal and his news group to come to the School that same morning to interview me. The news crew was already in Houston and on their way to San Antonio. Now I had the problem of seeing Vice President Johnson at the same time, and I knew he would not want the news media around. Roy Neal's group was interested in the medical examinations done for the astronauts. Finally, I decided to do both things at the same time and not tell either the reporters or the Vice President about each other being there. This was risky business, but I did it.

I made some rapid arrangements for Roy Neal's group to be in the large examining laboratory where the exercise tests and other procedures were done. The doors connected to the rest of the building were locked. Then I sent members of the staff in, one at a time, to be interviewed while I was seeing the Vice President on the other side of those locked doors. One of my colleagues, Lt. Colonel Don Flinn, head of the psychiatry department, was a facile communicator. He kept them occupied for some time, and was followed by others. I was glad to have Don in the act, as it seemed likely I might have needed a psychiatrist myself, before the morning was over.

The Vice President went from one area of the building to the other, intermittently returning to my office to make phone calls. While this was happening, we had our usual patient load of referrals from the flying personnel. These were all military officers. They were all instructed not to comment on the presence of Vice President Johnson. They, in turn, went back and forth through the locked doors—where Roy Neal's group was—to have their tests done. Not one squealed on me, but there was a tense moment at one point. The Vice President was walking down the hall in an examining gown and little else when one of the reporters came out and started toward the men's room. Fortunately, a trusty technician immediately spotted the problem before the reporter saw the Vice President and put him in a bathroom. He held the door on him until the Vice President had passed. Lyndon completed his business and departed, unaware that Roy Neal and his group were in the same building.

I never knew what Roy Neal's group thought of the strange proceedings that morning, but if they ever suspected that they were being kept away from a good news story on the other side of the locked doors, they never showed it.

I had lunch with the news group, and in the afternoon completed my interview with them on camera. In the course of the interview Maurice Levy said to me, "You seem to be preoccupied." I'm sure he had no idea how accurate his diagnosis was.

Sometime after Dr. Dryden's visit to the School of Aerospace Medicine, I received a memorandum he had written to Mr. James E. Webb, Administrator of NASA, on April 30th, 1962. It is important, as it documents the intent of NASA headquarters to promote a cooperative effort with the School in support of the man-in-space effort. As later events proved, it also demonstrated how their intent could be subverted by Manned Spacecraft Center personnel. In reference to the school, Dr. Dryden had written:

The School of Aviation Medicine is an outstanding facility for analyzing the mission requirements with respect to aeromedical factors, for aerospace medical evaluation of individuals to carry out the mission, for medical aspects of indoctrination and training, and for consultation with project flight surgeons in the supervision and monitoring of individuals during the mission. The School has done outstanding work in research and development on instruments and methods for flight monitoring of pilots and astronauts.... The School has supported Project Mercury in all these respects....

NASA has no capacity for clinical medical research and should not develop a competing effort. I recommend that after a preliminary screening of applications for participation in NASA programs as student astronauts, all candidates be given an aerospace medical evaluation by the School of Aerospace Medicine. We have already transferred $500,000 to the School under an existing NASA-DOD agreement for research on aerospace medical aspects of selection. From discussions on this visit, it is believed that the School would be willing to evaluate all screened applicants regardless of their source, military or civilian, if approved by higher authority within the Air Force and the Department of Defense. The resources of the School should also be used for indoctrination and training and for advice and consultation on all aerospace medical aspects of our programs.

It was plain from Dr. Dryden's memo that he believed $500,000 had been transferred to the School. Either Dr. Dryden had been misinformed, or the money had been transferred to NASA's MSC but never released to the School. There was a missing half-million dollars somewhere! *Was Gilruth carrying out his threat to see to it that the School received no money from NASA to support its efforts, if he really had made such a threat?*

I had been appointed as the Technical Area Scientist for air crew selection for the joint NASA-DOD efforts at the highest levels of the

Department of Defense and NASA. The notification of this had gone through channels at the Department of Defense and the Air Force, which authorized direct communications in carrying out these duties. This was not a matter I considered lightly. I knew I had a responsibility to find out about the missing half-million dollars. And I did.

In May of 1962, I joined General Don Wenger, from the Surgeon General's Office, at Myrtle Beach for a "World Wide Air Force Personnel Conference," to talk about aerospace pilot selection. That was when I first met Eugene Zuckert, then secretary of the Air Force. He was an enthusiastic, intelligent individual—clearly a man of action. It was a great morale boost to meet him. One of his first remarks to me was how pleased he was to meet me because I was the only person in the Air Force who had supported his decision relative to Major Slayton. He didn't back away one iota from accepting his responsibility in the final decision that Slayton should not be a pilot for the Mercury project. It was refreshing to see someone at this high level in the Air Force take the overall view of the interests of the nation, as opposed to individual agency rivalry.

Despite the numerous problems I had to deal with on a daily basis, I was rewarded for my efforts. On May 22, 1962, I was invited to the Pentagon for a special ceremony and awarded the Department of Defense Distinguished Civilian Service Award by Secretary Robert McNamara. That was the highest award the Department of Defense could give to a civilian. (See citation)

Just after the Myrtle Beach meeting with Don Wenger, I received a call from General Aubrey Jennings of the Surgeon General's Office— apparently, they had no record of the $500,000 allegedly funded by NASA for the medical evaluation program.

About that time, I learned the Manned Spacecraft Center planned to reopen the case of Deke Slayton. I was told Gilruth had requested that this be done, and Slayton was to be seen by Dr. Paul Dudley White, an eminent cardiologist at Harvard, considered by many to be the father of cardiology in the United States. He had long experience in clinical cardiology and was one of the first to start the ball rolling to prevent heart attacks through diet and exercise. I learned that Bill Douglas and Gilruth had made other efforts to reopen the case. The appointment with Dr. White was scheduled to occur about the time Bill Douglas was being replaced by Dr. Charles Berry as personal physician to the astronauts at the Manned Spacecraft Center. Dr. Berry was also an Air Force flight surgeon on loan to the NASA. I was told both flight surgeons would accompany Slayton to see Dr. White in Boston.

Since I knew how important the man-in-space program and the national goal of sending a man to the moon in that decade was to the administration, I had kept General Ted Clifton, President Kennedy's aide, advised on the situation. I recognized that Ted Clifton was a man you could trust with your wallet. He was bright and mature. There was no possibility that he would misuse any information I gave him, or that he would create any unnecessary or precipitous crisis. He could act effectively as a good filter, knowing which items needed attention and what action to take.

As the Slayton saga unfolded, I wanted to be certain that the White House had more input than my own professional opinion. That is why I recommended to General Clifton that he also review the case with General Tom Mattingly of Walter Reed Army Hospital. I knew General Mattingly was an outstanding cardiologist at the pinnacle of world specialists. He had trained under Dr. Paul White and was a man of unshakable personal integrity. The White House would get nothing but straight answers from him, exactly as he saw the picture, untroubled by NASA or Air Force politics. He was privy also to the details of the Slayton case, having served on the "Blue Ribbon" board requested by Secretary Zuckert.

Soon, I received a call from General Clifton. He told me he had just come from discussing the Slayton problem with President Kennedy, and the President had asked him to call me to say they would proceed to talk to General Mattingly as I had suggested. General Clifton continued that he wanted to emphasize that the President and he both appreciated my help. It was a good shot in the arm for me at the time I was dealing with the animosity that had developed over Slayton's medical status. I was impressed that President Kennedy and General Clifton would take the time to inform me.

225

After conferring with General Mattingly, General Clifton told me President Kennedy had decided to await the outcome of the consultation with Dr. White, and then, if it became necessary, he would personally request that all parties cease and desist from their efforts to use Major Slayton for a Mercury flight—and he would issue a public statement to that effect. The White House also took some damage control measures of their own. General Mattingly was asked to contact Dr. White and brief him on the situation. General Mattingly met Dr. White in New York on the President's behalf. I knew, regardless of what problems I might have because of this episode, that I was helping the President in an area that was vital to the future of manned space flight and the national objective of sending a man to the moon. That was sufficient reward for me.

Dr. White saw Slayton in June of 1962. After a careful and thorough evaluation, characteristic of his lifetime career, he came to conclusions which were essentially the same as those that had been made by all the other cardiologists who had seen Major Slayton. Dr. White concluded that,

These frequent paroxysms of atrial fibrillation are, however, distinctly abnormal and a bar to his inclusion under any heading of perfect health.

He mentioned the possibility of the formation of blood clots (intracardiac thrombosis and embolism) and also stated that the heart can eventually dilate and fail without any other cause and that such cases "are seen by almost all cardiologists of long experience."

Dr. White did not recommend that Slayton's health was no bar to making a Mercury flight as some reported. The truth is, he concluded,

I believe that the hazards from the arrhythmia under these particularly stressful present circumstances are too great both for the individual himself and his family, as well as for the program which is still in its infancy and under study, to recommend that he face the same conditions faced by Glenn and Carpenter (the two previous Mercury flights). (See Appendix C for more details of Dr. White's consultation of June 29, 1962).

The Surgeon General's Office was still waiting to hear the results of Dr. White's consultation when General Bohannon wrote me on June 27, 1962, about the situation. As the letter indicates (see photo of letter) personnel at NASA-MSC tried once more to get the okay for Slayton to be the pilot for a Mercury flight. The consultation with Dr. White was arranged after the board of nationally-recognized cardiologists Secretary Zuckert had requested had already recommended that Slayton should not be cleared to be a pilot for the Mercury flights.

Despite Dr. White's professional evaluation, his remarks were apparently still not understood. Deke Slayton was quoted in NASA's *This New Ocean: A History of Project Mercury* as saying,

"Even Paul Dudley White, Ike's personal physician, gave me a clean bill of health but rendered an operational rather than a diagnostic decision, recommending that the unknown factor in my heart murmur not be added to all the other unknowns for manned space flight".

Didn't Slayton realize that Dr. White actually said, "*These frequent paroxysms of atrial fibrillation are, however, distinctly abnormal and a bar to his inclusion under any heading of perfect health?*" Was he never told what Dr. White advised? Many accounts, and statements by Slayton, said his condition was a heart murmur. He did have a mild, insignificant murmur, but that was not the problem. A heart murmur is a sound created by blood flowing through the heart. Atrial fibrillation is a grossly irregular heartbeat that can result in blood clots in the heart and numerous other complications. Slayton and his cadre of supporters never seemed to grasp that the arrhythmia itself—not just the question of whether there was or was not underlying heart disease—was the problem. It was not just my opinion, but the opinion of all the highly qualified cardiologists in the country who had seen him. But since I was the first to say 'No,'—and didn't mind saying it again and again—and was working for the Air Force, I was considered as Slayton's "enemy." Nothing could have been further from the truth. It was true that I was going to do whatever I could to prevent the nation's man-in-space program from being unnecessarily jeopardized. If that conflicted with Slayton's personal ambition, so be it.

The main difference in medical opinions about Slayton's retention on flying status was really between some flight surgeons assigned to NASA-MSC who were not experienced in taking care of heart patients, along with administrative personnel at MSC, who had never been to medical school, versus the many experienced cardiologists—such as Drs. Mattingly, Proctor Harvey and Eugene Braunwall—who reviewed his case at the request of Secretary Zuckert. The NASA-MSC flight surgeons involved were not trained or experienced in cardiology. Most of them had probably never taken care of patients with atrial fibrillation. In discussing rare complications, Dr. White noted that *"they were seen by almost all cardiologists of long experience."* Put plainly, he was saying politely that flight surgeons were out of their area of expertise and really not qualified to make a professional recommendation regarding the problem. *But they should have been aware of the real mission of Project Mercury: to determine the effects of space flight on normal people—a mission that could not be accomplished during an episode of atrial fibrillation.*

The political axes were out for the man-in-space program. Funding by Congress was always questionable. Sending an astronaut with a heart problem into space for the Mercury project would demonstrate such a low level of scientific competence that the program could have been scrapped all together. There was a danger that no man would land on the moon in the near future—at least from the United States.

After Dr. Paul White's examination, the Manned Spacecraft Center finally announced that Donald Slayton had been permanently removed from consideration for Mercury flights. Eventually, Major Slayton resigned from the Air Force and had an important post as a civilian in the managerial and operational team of the Manned Spacecraft Center.

That was not the end of the story, nor the end of the problems caused by the Slayton affair. He had not relinquished his ambition to journey into space. But as far as Project Mercury was concerned, he would not make a multi-million dollar ride into space.

Some personnel at the Manned Spacecraft Center's top management apparently continued to suffer a bad case of "denial of illness" and couldn't make a distinction between national priorities and personal ambitions. History proved that Deke Slayton was not the only astronaut who could pilot the Mercury capsule. The project went on to a highly successful completion, and provided the first basic information necessary for the future of manned space flight—and to send men to the moon.

14

TESTING THE GEMINI ASTRONAUTS

14

↪ During the turmoil caused by Slayton's medical status, NASA announced it was going to select additional astronauts to prepare for the Gemini project, the next man-in-space project after Mercury. Hopeful candidates began to file their applications with NASA. Dr. Dryden at NASA headquarters had already decided that the School would do the medical examinations in support of the selection process. However, some individuals at NASA-MSC in Houston were determined to control the medical aspects of the astronaut selection process themselves, permitting them to do as they pleased without any outside supervision. Soon, Air Force flight surgeons assigned to the NASA-MSC were dispatched to review the Navy and other facilities to replace the School. But the decision of NASA headquarters prevailed.

Medical personnel from the MSC returned to the School to discuss the scope of the evaluations. This was almost a farce, since the School did such examinations on a daily basis. We had been doing them for approximately three years. The medical examinations for the selection of new astronauts were well within the range and scope of the daily activities of a highly experienced, well-trained professional team. The facilities had been specifically developed for such purposes.

Finally, in a letter of June 19, 1962, Gilruth, director of the Manned Spacecraft Center, formally requested that the School perform the examinations. By then, I knew that the half-million dollars Dr. Dryden had budgeted for such evaluations had gone to MSC, but I decided to say nothing about it until after those important examinations had taken place. Hopefully, the funds for the School would have been released by then.

The MSC medical personnel worked diligently at screening the large number of applicants. All candidates had to have at least a college degree and be a graduate test pilot with demonstrated experience. The experience factor was reviewed carefully, since, in many ways, exposure to new and unusual stresses of the space program would be similar to what test pilots encountered with new aircraft. There were age limitations and even physical limitations dictated by the size of the small space vehicle.

None of the astronauts could be over 6 feet or they would be too tall for the astronaut's couch in the spacecraft. That requirement alone eliminated a few well-qualified individuals. One candidate, who was just barely over 6 feet, spent the day jogging and exercising in hopes that by the end of the day he would be shorter. People usually are taller when they first get up than they are at the end of the day—yet another influence of gravity. The body weight gradually compresses the small disks between the vertebrae, like compressing a pillow. A person can be as much as an inch shorter by bedtime compared to when he first got out of bed.

There were more qualified candidates available than there were for the Mercury selection since the program at the Test Pilot School at Edwards Air Force Base had been expanded. The project would also be different, requiring two-man crews rather than a single pilot. This introduced the need for men who could be team players. We were told the new breed of astronauts would be more intellectually inclined, more thoughtful, and better trained in the scientific disciplines compared to the Mercury astronauts, who emphasized being "macho" and were referred to by some as "airborne hot rodders."

After the initial screening of the applications at MSC, 32 highly qualified young men, age 35 or younger, were chosen by NASA to undergo the evaluation. The potential astronauts came in groups of two and three at a time, on a daily basis. Their eyes were bright with hope, their faces well-scrubbed, and their fingernails clean. Each was the epitome of friendliness, with an outgoing personality. Clearly, each applicant regarded this as one of the most important events of his life.

I had known many of the candidates before, during their previous visits to the School, and sometimes prior to their entrance into the test pilot or space pilot programs. Two of the prospective astronauts, who had just recently completed examinations, came into my outer office and peered around the door at me with mischievous looks on their faces. They wanted to eliminate part of their examination procedures—specifically those which they didn't like and had recently had. This amused me, but since their request was completely legitimate, I discussed their request with the MSC physicians, and they agreed it was not necessary to repeat those tests after such a short time interval.

None of the astronaut candidates were completely without any deviation from perfect health, but as a group they were very healthy. Doctors trained in the different medical specialties made sure they had good eyesight and that their hearing and balance was optimal.

Tolerance to motion was important. All were tested on a device that would whirl the candidate around and around at different angles. On Earth, we are accustomed to motion and the body has adjusted to it. Since gravity gives weight to the body, it has a major influence on position sense and balance. But once an astronaut is weightless, a lot of the stimuli related to balance no longer occurs. How this would affect the astronauts was not certain. During longer flights, the lack of gravity stimulation could cause the astronauts difficulty in maintaining balance when they returned to Earth. That was particularly important at the time of landing in the ocean. Bobbing up and down and sideways in the ocean could certainly induce motion sickness in its own right, but after a period in space, it was likely to be much worse.

Most of the individuals were lean, but some were heavier than they should have been for optimal health. Some—who were evaluated more than once from the time of entering the space pilot program and the time they became astronaut candidates—made a point of losing excess pounds and getting in better shape. In many instances, that resulted in a significant improvement in cholesterol levels.

Not all of the applicants had the best cholesterol levels, but over half of them did have levels below 200. Body weight did not always correlate with cholesterol levels, either. One striking example was a topnotch test pilot I had seen several years earlier. Originally, his cholesterol level was 300, even though he only weighed 155 pounds. We talked, and he began a better diet and a daily exercise program. Two years later, although he still weighed 153 pounds, his cholesterol had decreased to 173. He had not lost much weight in pounds, but his exercise and diet program had increased the size and weight of his muscles while decreasing his body fat. We knew this because we did tests to measure the percent of body fat. Much later, at age 50, he was the command pilot for one of the nation's important space flights.

These were the kind of observations that strengthened my belief that diet and exercise were very important in preventing heart disease. Our studies at the School provided good evidence of what could be accomplished with preventive programs. Today, it is common knowledge that this is the way many people can at least decrease their risk of heart attacks and strokes.

The astronaut and space pilot examinations not only identified the health status of each candidate, but they served to motivate them and teach them how to follow a lifestyle that would keep them in good health. The candidate who lowered his cholesterol to optimal levels from a previous level of 300 was a good example of this.

We also studied the pentathletes in training for the Olympics at Fort Sam Houston, the large Army post in San Antonio. They provided a good indication of what you should expect in subjects in optimal health, which we could compare to the astronaut applicants. On average, they were 10 years younger than the astronaut applicants. Almost all were much leaner and had lower cholesterol levels. Only half of the astronaut candidates had low cholesterol values within the range seen in the pentathletes. Many of the pentathletes were so lean that less than 8 percent of their body weight was fat. You could pick up the skin over their bodies as easily as most people can over the back of their hands.

There were individuals who slipped through MSC's initial screening, even though they had medical problems that precluded them from entering the space program. In one candidate, who appeared quite healthy in all respects, the radiologist noted opaque tracks in the thigh and groin area on his X-rays that should not have been there. Upon investigation, it was discovered he had actually been in treatment for a malignancy and these were the tracks left from injections for chemotherapy. There was always the danger that someone who desperately wanted into the space program would not be entirely truthful about his medical problems.

In another instance, a candidate did enter the program by concealing that he had a family history of psychotic depressions. He developed depressions himself at a later date. Nevertheless, the team of examiners was accustomed to that possibility, because some Air Force personnel also would go to great lengths to cover up medical problems to remain on flying status. A good example was the general who had atrial fibrillation and gave a completely negative history, although he had had a heart attack. A week after admitting it, he dropped dead.

Like the Mercury astronauts, the names of those who entered into the Gemini program would soon become familiar to the American public. Some would be our heroes of tomorrow. Among the individuals in this group to fly the Gemini mission were Ed White and James McDivitt. I had known Ed White from previous examinations. Ed was a topnotch athlete, and particularly interested in the physiology of exercise. We had long discussions about the influence of exercise on the blood flow to the heart muscle. We talked about the advisability and proper use of exercise during the growth phase of children and what was the best program for his son. Ed became the first American to walk in space: called extravehicular activity (EVA).

The School of Aerospace Medicine did not select the astronauts—our function was to provide a competent medical examination and evaluation. The staff did, in each instance, make an assessment of the significance of any observations they had made, but this was simply to provide information. The selection of future astronauts was made by the managerial staff at MSC after interviews and evaluation of the candidates' abilities as pilots and engineers. Shortly after all of these procedures had been completed, NASA announced the addition of nine new astronauts to its program. These men and some of the Mercury astronauts would be the nation's Gemini astronauts.

***

In July, during the course of the astronaut examinations, I was pleasantly surprised to receive a call from Lyndon Johnson. My old friend from Emory University in Atlanta, Dr. Willis Hurst, had come to spend the weekend. I had worked with Willis before I went to Switzerland as a research fellow with the American Heart Association. This provided a unique opportunity to see him again for the first time in many years. He was an outstanding cardiologist and was in the Navy for a two-year tour when Lyndon had his heart attack. Willis had taken care of him at that time. Vice President and Mrs. Johnson invited me to join them for the weekend. This was a welcome break from the intense activities at the School.

It was a short trip across the Texas countryside to the ranch. The long, sloping, peaceful hills, dotted with their live oak trees, looked warm and friendly in the summer sun. I drove along the curved driveway entering the ranch, down the steep grade to ford the river below the dam, as I had done before, and up to the large stone-and-white-frame ranch house. Willis met me halfway across the front lawn and we exchanged enthusiastic greetings. The Vice President was sunning himself beside the swimming pool, beyond the house. His attractive secretary, Marie Fehmer, and Mary Margaret (Wiley) Valenti were alternately floating across the pool and dangling their feet in the water. It didn't take long for me to get into the proper attire for the occasion. Soon, we were all splashing in the pool or sunning ourselves at the water's edge.

Later, Mrs. Johnson joined us and we went for a drive. This was my first opportunity to see the expanse of the Texas Hill Country, beyond the main highway areas. We drove through the ranch and drank in the beauty of watching native deer herds browsing their way along the timberline. Lyndon Johnson was justly proud of the countryside and plainly enjoyed contemplating nature's beauty. Being a Midwest farm boy, it was easy for me to feel at home in the rural surroundings. Despite my subsequent involvement in medicine and the space program, these early origins had caused land to be in my blood. Nothing gave me greater pleasure than the great outdoors in its natural, unspoiled state. We stopped and looked at the prize Hereford cattle that had gathered under the shade of one of the trees. Lyndon had a special horn in his Lincoln Continental to "moo" to the cattle.

After a bountiful lunch, we went to the nearby Granite Shoals Lake, later to become known as Lake Lyndon B. Johnson. The vice President revved up his boat and we spent the afternoon careening across the lake's wide placid surface. The beautiful lake was nestled between large rolling hills of the Texas countryside, and the giant, old live oak trees, with their perpetually green leaves, hung over its banks. Truly, this was a place to enjoy.

In August 1962, the Soviets scored still another advance in their man-in-space effort. They were the first to orbit two cosmonauts in a tandem space flight, demonstrating their ability not only to launch one space vehicle, but another one immediately afterward. This achievement brought a resurgence of national concern. The successful flight also heated up the competition between the Soviet Union and the United States, which was described by noted columnist Marquis Childs as "ruinous rivalry."

There was a drum roll for a military space program. The fear was that while the United States was pursuing the peaceful aspects of space, the Soviets would achieve an insurmountable military advantage. Senators Howard Cannon and Barry Goldwater publicly assaulted the Department of Defense's civilian leaders for not having aggressively established a military space program. Senator Cannon stated that we might well become the best informed nation regarding space while being destroyed by the military capabilities of the Soviets. Of course, both Senator Cannon and Senator Goldwater were generals in the Air Force Reserve.

The Soviets' tandem flight increased fears about the Soviet military's capabilities in space. On August 22, 1962, Washington's *Evening Star* printed a lead editorial pointing out that the United States had no means to knock down orbiting space vehicles that could be used in a nuclear attack. Even if it were possible to strike back at land-based missiles, we had no protection against nuclear weapons in orbiting space vehicles. The point was made that if the United States lost its ability to strike back against a nuclear attack from satellites, the country could be faced with an anguishing decision between "capitulation and annihilation."

Senator Goldwater was quoted in a front page story of *The*

Washington Post that civilian "whiz kids" at the Pentagon were blocking vital military space projects. He argued that only a strong "space deterrent" could maintain the peace.

Most individuals involved in the space age from its beginning recognized back in 1957—when the Soviets first launched *Sputnik I* and *II*—that it would be a long time before the United States was in a truly competitive position. To the credit of the government, there was little attempt to claim that the problem could be remedied with a quick fix. Instead, a planned program to move forward with competence was developed with bipartisan support between a Democratic Congress led by Senate Majority Leader Lyndon Johnson and Republican President Dwight Eisenhower.

As the ability of man and machines to function in space became more apparent, it was increasingly evident that the survival of the free world could well depend upon the United States' success in space. The possibility of orbiting atomic weapons, intercepting and disarming satellites, surveillance and perhaps even the control of tides and weather were all to be of immense importance. Some of the space pilots and I talked about a "death ray" that would be able to zap targets on Earth from space. On the road to these achievements, the successful completion of each step by each nation stood as testimony to its own system of government. The stakes in the race for control of space were far greater than the general public seemed to realize: nothing less than the security and survival of the United States was at risk.

After the medical examinations for the astronaut selection program were done, it seemed like a good time to turn my attention to the problem of the missing half-million dollars that Dr. Dryden believed had been provided to the School. I first brought the matter to the attention of General Roadman at NASA headquarters in a letter of August 31, 1962.

The only indication of a reply to my letter was a call on the 11th of September from Colonel Robards in the Air Force Pentagon Office. Grady Wise, from General Roadman's office, was also on the telephone. I was asked if I had received any communications concerning the funding and implementation of the crew selection proposal. Then I was told the money (the half-million dollars) had been transferred to NASA's MSC at Houston. Grady Wise from NASA headquarters stated that Stan White had removed the item from the Center's budget. Stan could then use the money to fund research elsewhere, although it had been earmarked for the School. The allocation of such funds was largely under Stan White's control. Individuals who controlled such funds could use them for contracts to various groups, such as civilian organizations, and were well-positioned to pass out goodies and exercise control.

In the wake of the flap over the military uses of space, President Kennedy personally toured a portion of the nation's space facilities. He journeyed to Cape Canaveral; the Huntsville, Alabama, facility; the Manned Spacecraft Center in Houston; Rice University; and the McDonnell Aircraft Corporation in St. Louis, Missouri, where the Mercury capsule had been built. At the onset of his trip, while visiting the Launch Operations Center at Cape Canaveral, he stated,

I don't think that we can exaggerate the great advantage which the Soviet Union secured in the fifties by being first in space. They were able to give prestige to their system. They were able to give force to their argument that they were an advancing society and that we were on the decline.

But I believe that we are an advancing society, and I believe that we are on the rise, and I believe that their system is as old as time. As long as the decision has been made that our great system and others will be judged at least in one degree by how we do in the field of space, we might as well be first; and, therefore, this country, both political parties, have determined that the United States shall be first. We started behind. We have a long way to go, but with your effort and the commitment and effort of all of our fellow Americans, we shall be first.

Later, at Rice University he stated,

Those who came before us made certain that this country rode the first waves of the industrial revolutions, the first waves of modern invention, and the first waves of nuclear power, and this generation does not intend to flounder in the backwash of the coming age of space. We mean to be a part of it—we mean to lead it. For the eyes of the world now look into

241

space, to the moon and to the planets beyond, and we have vowed that we shall not see it governed by a hostile flag of conquest, but by a banner of freedom and peace. We have vowed that we shall not see space filled with weapons of mass destruction, but with instruments of knowledge and understanding.

We choose to go to moon in this decade and do the other things, not because they are easy, but because they are hard, because that goal will serve to organize and measure the best of our energies and skills, because that challenge is one that we are willing to accept, one we are unwilling to postpone, and one which we intend to win, and the others, too.

The President journeyed to NASA's Manned Spacecraft Center in Houston. There, his guide for part of his tour was Donald K. Slayton.

He completed his tour at McDonnell Aircraft Corporation in St. Louis on the 12th of September, 1962, with these remarks,

I can imagine no action, no adventure which is more essential and more exciting than to be involved in the most important and significant adventure that any man has been able to participate in the history of the world. And it's going to take place in this decade.

At this time, the Air Force increased its insistence for a military role in space. At the Air Force Association's annual meeting in Las Vegas, the Association warned:

Space must be used to press our deterrent capability, to protect the future against the agonies and miseries of war, and thus to provide the climate required for the growth of freedom.

Timed with a spate of announcements, the Air Force issued invitations to the aerospace industry for formal proposals to study a manned space station, the beginning of an effort to obtain a "manned orbital laboratory (MOL)."

President Kennedy went to the Air Force Association's 16th National Convention in Las Vegas, Nevada, and told them,

The Air Force has a great role to play in the future in the struggle against insurrection and guerilla war, in the maintenance of our strategic force and strength, in the increasing responsibilities and burdens which will be placed upon the Air Force in the field of space, to make sure that space is maintained for peaceful purposes, and that no nation secure a position in space which can threaten the security of the United States and the free world.

15

WHO TALKED TO THE MEDIA?

was important in obtaining public support for the man-in-space program. Of course, I agreed.

I was impressed by the relationship between Vice President Johnson and Sargent Shriver. Obviously, Lyndon Johnson thought very highly of the Director of the Peace Corps. At lunch, he said the only thing he had against Shriver was that he had stolen his able aide and right-hand man, Bill Moyers, when he had left the Senate to become Vice President. This was all in good humor, as Bill Moyers was also at the luncheon. He spoke in glowing terms of Sargent Shriver's achievements, as well as the goals of the Peace Corps.

The Vice President enjoyed some light humor about Sargent Shriver's relationship to the Kennedy family. He invited the guests to ask Shriver as many questions as they liked: He said, "If he was able to hold his own and debate with the rest of the Kennedy clan, he could handle any questions they wanted to ask him." Lyndon Johnson gave the unmistakable impression of a man who was thoroughly enjoying himself: proud of the accomplishments of the members of the administration and anxious to have other people also appreciate their achievements.

Although Lyndon Johnson was often portrayed as chafing in his role as Vice President, I never got that impression. Rather, I saw him as relishing his role as elder statesman to the younger men who comprised the Kennedy administration, and enjoying the young Kennedy administration's enthusiasm without being subjected to all the hassles attendant to the presidency or being Senate Majority Leader. In the days and years that followed, it is easy to forget that Lyndon Johnson had suffered a major, life-threatening heart attack. That did affect what he wanted to do with the rest of his life. On more than one occasion, he said to me that he hoped to see the government progress to the point he could return to his beloved ranch and spend a few years on the Pedernales (river) before he died; the reality of his own mortality was clearly on his mind.

As the others were leaving, Lyndon asked me to stay for the weekend, and I did. Again, I was impressed with the simple sincerity of the Johnson household. Mrs. Johnson personally planned the household activities. The following morning, I noted she was in the upstairs bedrooms making beds, like many other housewives. She was always gracious and friendly, never too busy to sit down for a chat or to show some kindness to a guest or member of the household. We sat on the edge of the bed and discussed "Lyndon's diet," just as I had discussed diet with many other wives.

The man-in-space program soon got a good shot in the arm. Navy Commander Walter Schirra's six-orbit flight on the 3rd of October, 1962, was a stunning success. Everything went exactly as planned, with the splashdown of the vehicle right on target. All of this brought a wave of relief across the nation. There had been problems with both of the previous orbital flights. The usual congratulatory telephone call was forthcoming from President Kennedy to the Commander. On October 15, he issued a statement of commendation—another important day in the history of our country.

On that date, I was in Washington and was invited to the welcoming ceremony for Prime Minister Ben Bella of Algeria, held on the White House lawn. It was a first, since before then, the President had always gone to Andrews AFB to greet visiting heads of state. Thereafter, these dignitaries would stay at nearby Blair House and be driven to the White House lawn for the welcoming ceremony.

It was a very picturesque scene. Stretching beyond the White House and across the ravine, one could see the Washington Monument. Cannons were lined up in the ravine for the appropriate salute. The customary flag-bearing honor guard stood on the White House lawn. A black limousine rolled down the driveway, stopped, and Prime Minister Ben Bella stepped forth. He was greeted by President Kennedy and they walked to the microphones to express mutual cordialities. Then, as cannons boomed in the distance, the two world leaders reviewed the troops. I saw President Kennedy pass through the White House more than once that day, in conjunction with the ceremonies and meetings. I was surprised to find out later this was the day he first learned for certain about the installation of the Soviet missiles in Cuba. In retrospect, I wondered at his air of calm and poise in dealing with a dignitary and Chief of State from another country while being faced with such a momentous crisis. I had returned to San Antonio by the time it was possible to announce the Cuban Missile Crisis. Brooks AFB, where the School was located, to explain how he had obtained the material for his series. It would be necessary to clarify this matter if individuals at MSC elected to use the stories as a political weapon against the School. No doubt Warren Burkett was amused with my interest in how he put together a news story. He replied in part as follows:

Naturally we assumed that such an occasion as the selection of the new team of astronauts would not go unphotographed. We contacted Public Affairs Offices, Astronaut Affairs Offices, and others at Manned Spacecraft Center and I learned that this was true. Through our normal contacts with Colonel Powers, Mr. Chop, and the local astronauts we learned that the photographs were not of the type that could be considered offensive. Prints of these photographs were made for our examination, and in consultation with the Houston MSC Public Affairs Office, we selected the pictures that would best illustrate the procedures involved. Some were new and had never been published before. The NASA-MSC newspaper published a suitable Schirra photograph only a week before the series opened. Others showed the specific tests so well we did not mind prior publication.

The Houston Public Affairs Office saw each of the photographs and assisted in identification. So much has been published about the NASA astronauts and about the Air Force crews that we did not need to look any further than our files and NASA's for such things as age, height, weight, families, etc. Naturally we are grateful to NASA-Houston for supplying us with this background of biography and photographs; this is the function of any competent Information Service.

Mr. Burkett specifically indicated why he did not need any material from the School as he continued his explanation.

I selected appropriate anecdotes and situations to add something concrete, specific, and illuminating at what I considered proper points in the stories. The physicians at MSC (Air Force flight surgeons assigned to the Manned Spacecraft Center) were in many ways the source of some of the better ones. It really became a matter of throwing away appropriate material because I could not possibly use all that was available.

As your speech in Washington made clear, the interest lay in the implications that your examinations had for the average man. I wanted to satisfy myself that a statistically significant number of people had gone through the examination first.

Warren Burkett then described the various brochures, including the Apollo Project proposal, which he had reviewed prior to his interview with me. He stated that he had read both the Senate and the House Appropriations Hearing transcripts and a book called *America On the Moon,* written by Jay Holmes, who was an information consultant for NASA. He had reviewed documents written by the astronauts, Dr. Charles Berry, Dr. William Douglas, Robert Gilruth, Walter Williams, Brainerd Holmes, and James E. Webb. He had also followed and kept track of key speeches made by NASA personnel. He did express his disappointment that individuals were not well informed on the profession of writing. His letter continued:

Later, in Los Angeles, Dr. Berry told me about some agreement whereby NASA would release any photographs or intimate personal details.

Your people kept your end of the agreement very well, and so did NASA in releasing the pictures and other data. (See Appendix D for the entire letter from Warren Burkett.)

This illuminating letter from Warren Burkett strongly suggested that some individuals at MSC were trying to sabotage the decision to do the astronaut selection examinations at the School. But they had neglected to find out that a major source of the information had come from the MSC itself. In fact, in some instances the individuals who were complaining the loudest were the actual sources of the information!

I was relieved that none of the School staff had done anything they should not have. They were topnotch professionals. I wondered why, if Robert Gilruth was so livid about the stories, he didn't find out what his own organization was doing. Surely he realized that such favorable stories about the man-in-space project were essential for continued support for it—including funding by Congress. This was something Lyndon Johnson used very effectively. Since the struggle between NASA and the Department of Defense for control of the space program was hot and heavy, Gilruth may not have wanted the public to know how much support came from the Air Force.

I was certain that the complaints by the NASA-Air Force group at the Manned Spacecraft Center had been duly relayed to the Surgeon General's Office. They had been. By then, I was familiar with the steady barrage of distortions emanating from MSC in an attempt to undermine the School's medical evaluations program so they could get control of it. And there was the "get even" approach over Slayton not being allowed to pilot a Mercury flight. This was just one more example. There wasn't too much I could do about it, but I was determined not to allow such a malignant effort to poison the attitudes of the new astronauts against me, my professional colleagues, or the School. To thwart that effort, I forwarded a copy of Warren Burkett's entire letter to each of the astronauts who had been examined at the School.

A number of the astronauts wrote to me after having read Burkett's letter. In no instance did any of them express any irritation with the articles. Their letters gave the lie to the statement that "All the astronauts in the group were very upset." Astronaut Ed White, the first American to walk in space, wrote,

I appreciate your letter concerning the articles that appeared in the Houston Chronicle. Actually, Mr. Burkett handled the articles in rather good taste as far as I could see. It is quite interesting to learn about all the sources of information that a newspaperman uses to put together a story such as this.

How are your physical training programs coming? Are you running the daily mile much faster than initially? Our physical training is left almost exclusively to the individual so that it becomes difficult to find enough time for a good daily routine. Nevertheless, I have been able to remain in good condition, perhaps better than when I was at Brooks last summer. At any rate, I look forward to improving on the 26-minute record on the treadmill, unless you have already improved on it.

Please give my regards to the other members of your very competent staff.

Astronaut Charles Conrad, Jr., wrote, in part,

I, personally, found nothing wrong with articles in The Houston Chronicle.....

Astronaut Frank Borman wrote, in part,

I was not offended by any of the articles. As a matter of fact, I thought several of them were good. Even if I had found the articles distasteful, I would never have been concerned that the information had been "leaked" by members of your staff. Their obvious competence and professional stature place them in a class by themselves.

The reaction from the Test Pilot School at Edwards AFB was entirely different from the loud screams from a few individuals at MSC. The news stories of the examination procedures and their purpose, which included the space pilots, were well received, and there were no problems or adverse criticism from that source.

I wondered why such a petty fuss would come from MSC. There was the Deke Slayton affair, the missing half-million dollars and, above all, the desire of some flight surgeons at NASA to gain complete control of the medical evaluations for the selection of the astronauts and independence from the Air Force. I suspected Stan White, who had been in charge of the medical aspects of the Mercury astronaut selection and gave the contract to the Lovelace Clinic, wanted to regain control of the process by eliminating the School and contracting out the examinations, or assigning them to an Air Force facility that would do his bidding. By controlling the budget for the examinations, he could maintain absolute control of a contractor's decisions. He had apparently gained support for this from other individuals at MSC.

At that particular time, the School staff was providing pre- and post-flight backup in a number of important areas for the medical program for manned space flights. We had just completed a major effort in supporting the selection of the next group of astronauts. It was disheartening that the thanks the staff received was an unnecessary hassle over the *Houston Chronicle* stories. It was particularly disappointing in view of the fact that the so-called "objectionable" parts of the stories were from material obtained from NASA's MSC personnel. None of these events did much to maintain the morale of the team of fine scientists at the School.

But they were motivated to support the man-in-space program. That was more important than the petty snipping by a few bad apples.

16
THE CASE OF THE CURIOUS LETTERS

OFFICE OF THE ADMINISTRATOR

December 13, 1962

Dr. Lawrence E. Lamb
School of Aerospace Medicine
Aerospace Medical Division (AFSC)
United States Air Force
Brooks Air Force Base, Texas

Dear Dr. Lamb,

I thank you for your letter of November 5th
which brought to my attention a situation with which
I was not familiar. Mr. Webb, Bob Seamans, and I
have discussed the matter and we are taking steps
to see that funds are allocated to support the work
of the School of Aerospace Medicine in research on
aeromedical evaluation and astronaut selection
problems.

With respect to the last paragraph of your
letter, a letter of appreciation to those responsible for assisting us in astronaut selection was
forwarded to the Secretary of the Air Force on
October 8, 1962. I regret that a copy of this
letter was not sent directly to the School of Aerospace Medicine. For your information a copy is
attached.

With best personal regards,

Sincerely yours,

Hugh L. Dryden

Hugh L. Dryden
Deputy Administrator

THE VICE PRESIDENT

WASHINGTON

January 14, 1963

Dear Larry:

The glasses arrived in fine shape, and
I've already put them to good use.

But I would like to ask you for another
pair. Could you see that the maker of
these two pair fixes another just like
them? This time, however, I'd like
for the bifocals to extend all the way
across the lens -- the reading part
still to remain at the bottom.

Many thanks for all the assistance to
me -- and to my near and dear.

Sincerely,

Lyndon B. Johnson

disregard
Bird talked
to you, I
have already
used the new
ones.

Dr. Lawrence E. Lamb
Chief, Clinical Sciences Division
School of Aerospace Medicine
Brooks Air Force Base, Texas

16

↜ The question of the missing half-million dollars was still unresolved. I had written General Roadman, Director of Life Sciences for NASA, to try to solve the problem. No matter what I did, nothing worked. It was fairly obvious there was an effort to cover-up what had happened. I was mindful of my responsibility as technical area scientist for crew selection and evaluation and as a consultant to NASA, and I was certain the matter had been covered up from Dr. Dryden. Since I had been authorized direct communications, I knew it was my responsibility to use the authorization. Accordingly, on November 5, 1962, I wrote to Dr. Dryden as follows:

I thought it might be appropriate for me to drop you a note to clarify a point concerning funding in support of aeromedical evaluation work done at the School of Aerospace Medicine. According to your report to Mr. Webb after various visits to the laboratories, you stated that $500,000 had been allocated for the School of Aerospace Medicine to continue work in this area. I know that this is what you were told, however, this is in error in that no money was ever actually funded for the School, and we have never received any money whatever to support this area of work, to in turn support aeromedical selection type problems and monitoring for NASA. I have been told that this was because there was no money available, however, I am aware that other contracts have been released *from NASA, including over $200,000 to the Lovelace Clinic to prepare a review of the status of aviation medicine.*

I believe you must know that we did the aeromedical evaluations for the last group of astronaut candidates from which the nine subjects were chosen for NASA. I believe this examination went very well. We have received no official comment as yet from NASA. Despite the months which had elapsed since the aeromedical evaluations of astronaut candidates for NASA's Manned Spacecraft Center, there hsd been no acknowledgment of this service. Naturally, it was important to the team of scientists at the School to receive at least a thank-you for the long extra hours and effort that they had expended.

The flap about the *Houston Chronicle* stories created by NASA's MSC developed just after my letter to Dr. Dryden. An Air Force colonel assigned to the Pentagon visited the School at that time and told me that General Niess, the Air Force Surgeon General, was very unhappy with me, and was concerned about my relationship with NASA.

He said General Niess was particularly angry that I had written to Dr. Dryden. This surprised me, as I believed General Niess had signed off on the original authorization from the Department of Defense for direct communications. He could have forgotten, or simply not have been aware of what he had signed. The Surgeon General was ultimately responsible to the Department of Defense and its decisions. In fact, the authorization had been approved down the whole, long chain of command before it ever reached me.

The real problem was that my role in the Slayton affair was embarrassing to the Surgeon General—and it should have been. He was undoubtedly embarrassed when Secretary Zuckert challenged him about the Air Force's position on Slayton's atrial fibrillation and why Slayton was even still on flying status. In addition, there was the steady barrage of criticism that originated from NASA-Air Force flight surgeons who resented the fact that the School controlled the medical evaluations and medical recommendations regarding the selection of the astronauts.

On September 11, 1962, I received a telephone call that explained what had happened to the $500,000 NASA had allocated for the School. Grady Wise, of General Roadman's office at NASA headquarters, told me the entire sum had been transferred to NASA-MSC in Houston, and Stan White had removed the funding for the School. I also learned Stan funded a $200,000 contract to the Lovelace Clinic to review the status of aerospace medicine: not exactly a high priority project in support of the man-in-space project. The Lovelace Clinic had received a contract to do the medical examinations for the selection of the Mercury astronauts when Stan White was at the Wright-Patterson Air Force laboratory. The facts spoke for themselves regarding Stan White's agenda.

Apparently, the problem was Stan White. Of course, Slayton's supporters felt it was my fault he wasn't allowed to make a Mercury flight, and they were mostly right on that score. I stopped the cover-up and made sure the opinions of the best cardiologists in the country were involved in the decision, and that NASA headquarters knew about it. I didn't make the decision, but I made sure the individuals who should have, and did make the decisions, had the facts. Despite all the trouble it caused me, I have never regretted my decision or the steps I took to prevent an unnecessary risk to the man-in-space project.

It was commonly stated that Slayton was like a son to Gilruth. With the input from Stan White, Bill Douglas and Deke Slayton, a great deal of animosity toward the School and me was generated at the management level of MSC.

My contact with Lyndon Johnson also rubbed salt in the wound with some individuals within the Air Force. I was told by General Bedwell's administrative officer that the General was very annoyed that I saw the Vice President. This was a matter of professional jealousy and channels. To some, access meant power, and the situation was very disturbing to those who depended mostly on access rather than ability for the power they had.

At that time, I had not yet received Warren Burkett's letter regarding his series on the astronaut examinations. I had no way of knowing what the Surgeon General's Office was being told. No doubt Stan was angry, having been fingered siphoning off the money for the School.

Not long after that, I received a nice letter from Dr. Dryden,

her boat would slam across each wake. Finally, Lady Bird stood up, shook her finger at him and yelled, "Lyndon, you stop that!"

He did. Immediately.

Rumbles began to reach me that high-ranking medical officers in the Air Force were concerned about my opportunities for regular contact with high-level government officials: particularly Lyndon Johnson. Evidently, some career physicians in uniform felt they should have been fulfilling this function as a physician, or at the very least should have stood by—as my supervisor—while I performed any medical duties that needed to be done, then watched my hurried exit.

Lyndon Johnson knew what he wanted and went to whoever could provide it. I don't think "going through channels" ever interested him. I was told that General Bedwell was most upset when the Vice President's helicopter would land near the building where my office was located and he would see me board the helicopter and disappear. His staff told me he wanted to know what transpired when I was with the Vice President or his party, and I didn't pass on information. From my point of view, Lyndon Johnson was a patient and a friend. I had no reason to report to anyone about seeing him, or his activities. He was entitled to his privacy.

From the time the Vice President wanted to be able to reach me, "Twenty-four hours a day," I had always told the base Air Police where I could be reached—day and night. I learned that General Bedwell had given them orders that he was to be informed whenever I got a call from the Vice President or the White House. This infuriated me, since he had no right to intrude in such matters. The solution was simple. I just switched support to the Army's military police at Brooke Army Medical Center, near my home.

Sometimes, Lyndon didn't help matters. One morning, I had just gone to the grocery store, and he called my home. I wasn't there, so he called General Bedwell at his home and inquired where I was. Of course, he didn't know. Lyndon must have enjoyed himself as he tersely said, "Well, **FIND** him!" and slammed down the phone. When I got home there was a frantic call from General Bedwell. All Lyndon wanted was to invite me to come to the ranch.

General Bedwell had spent his career in the Air Force—he was strictly military and channels-oriented. I don't believe he had ever worked with civilian scientists before. The Aerospace Medical Center with its large cadre of civilian scientists was a far cry from the strict military environment he was used to at buttoned-down SAC headquarters.

I am sure that my own tendency to move ahead with considerable energy on whatever needed to be done was frustrating to him and was perceived as a threat. When he first arrived at the Aerospace Medical Center, he stopped by for a briefing on the consultation service, which I had developed for the Air Force. He was upset because he had been told that we held boards (hearings) on officers referred for medical evaluation with the officer present.

I explained to him that nothing like that had ever happened. The story was totally false; it would have been impossible. The officers had long since returned to their posts of duty by the time all their medical records were available for members of the staff to discuss their cases relative to their flying status. All the various departments: psychiatry, surgery, ophthalmology, internal medicine, aviation medicine and others—worked together in a harmonious and professional manner to provide the best input on each case. Everyone had an opportunity to express his professional view, which was included as part of the consultation. All the consultations were signed by the commander of the School. We did not hold boards. We didn't vote on who could be returned to flying status. We had clinical conferences to exchange information: a rather normal function in any medical group. To put it mildly, General Bedwell was not one of my most enthusiastic supporters.

Some of the senior Air Force medical officers, apparently including General Niess, were suspicious that I was talking to the Vice President about matters involving the School and the space program. That assumption was a serious miscalculation on their part. At no time had I ever discussed what we were doing at the School, or the NASA program, or any of the difficulties that arose between the agencies. My role was to provide medical support as desired, and as a friend, which I was. I knew the Vice President already had enough to be concerned about. I enjoyed the Johnson's for themselves. One reason we were able to maintain a good relationship was that I didn't discuss such matters.

Lyndon Johnson came to the ranch to relax and get some relief from problems, not to have new ones added to his plate.

In the course of time I did learn that the Vice President was one of my most enthusiastic supporters. In a letter to Conway Craig, publisher of the *San Antonio Express News,* on other matters he wrote, "And I am delighted you are preparing a piece on Dr. Lamb, who deserves attention—I'll be looking forward to reading it."

About this time, there were other events, far beyond me, that were having their effect. The Air Force in particular was agitating for a military role in space. Senator Barry Goldwater, a general in the Air Force Reserve, was a severe critic of the administration's reluctance to support such a role. A number of my military colleagues were not pleased with the Kennedy administration, or with Lyndon Johnson.

In the aftermath of the flap over the *Houston Chronicle* stories, I had dropped a note to Air Force Deputy Surgeon General Richard Bohannon. He was a fine individual with a good professional background. His quiet, sensible approach was a good influence. He was not one to be bothered with professional jealousies. I had commented to him, in regards to MSC, that I thought it was time for more cooperation and less retaliation. I was pleased to receive his nice letter of January 2, 1963:

Many thanks for your letter of December the 19th and the photostat of Dr. Dryden's letter to you. General Niess and I have discussed the SAM-NASA relationships you outlined so comprehensively. He tells me he believes the whole matter, including the fund allocation by NASA is now largely water under the bridge.

We both agree that we should all look forward to more cooperation and less retaliation in 1963. You may be assured that your standing here with us has not been undercut, and that we are devoting our thoughts and energies towards facilitating the vital undertakings of your department in aerospace medicine.

Best wishes for a happy and productive new year.
Sincerely,
s/R. L. Bohannon, Major General, USAF, MC
Deputy Surgeon General

I had no idea what machinations were occurring in the surgeon general's office, or what motivated them, but whatever they were, they resulted in a most unusual letter to me from General Niess. I do know that General Roadman of NASA headquarters had been in contact with General Niess. The Niess letter of January 22, 1963, was unusual, as copies of it were distributed to General Schriever, Commanding General of the Air Force Systems Command (the command over the Aerospace Medical Division); his Command Surgeon, General Strickland; General Roadman of NASA; Colonel Talbot of NASA; Colonel Frese of the Department of Defense; General Bedwell of the Aerospace Medical Division; Colonel Ellingson, the Commander of the School of Aerospace Medicine; Colonel Burris at the Executive Office Building and military aide to Vice President Johnson; and Dr. Travell at the White House. It was basically a letter of reprimand circulated with what could only be interpreted as a malicious effort. It was as follows:

Dear Larry,

1. Copies of your recent correspondence with Dr. Hugh Dryden have been forwarded to me by Headquarters NASA.

2. I understand your devotion to your job, to the SAM and to the Air Force, and I appreciate your outstanding contributions to Air Force medicine, and the National Space effort. You are an internationally recognized cardiologist and have brought great credit to Air Force Medicine. Your work is one of the great advances in medicine and must be pursued and developed even further. I am one of your most enthusiastic and ardent supporters.

3. I know that you acted with enthusiasm and in good faith; however, your letter to Dr. Dryden is clearly out of line. It is preposterous and damages Air Force and NASA relationships which are so vital to our country. You have written previous letters which have not had the beneficial effect which you believed to be true.

4. It is true that anyone may write letters as a private citizen, but your responsibility to the School and to the Air Force is not negated by leaving your office and going to your home. You remain a responsible Air Force Scientist whether you are on or off an Air Force Base.

5. Furthermore, you are not the Commandant of the School or the

Commander of the Aerospace Medical Division. You have no authority or moral right to act independently. Attempts to do so lead only to disappointments and create additional obstacles.

6. I ask you to discontinue your out of channel correspondence. Such efforts appear immature, are damaging and bring discredit to the Air Force.

7. I realize and appreciate the care and advice which you have given to very important people in the government. These relationships and this service should continue.

8. So there will be no misunderstanding of position or intent, I am sending copies of the letter as indicated.

9. I will give you my continued support but ask that you channel your efforts properly.

Most Sincerely yours
s/ Ollie
O.K. Niess
Major General, USAF, MC
Surgeon General

I recognized that there was something very strange about the Niess letter in view of General Bohannon's letter from the same office that I had just received regarding my letter to Dr. Dryden. It was also apparent that General Niess, perhaps others now at NASA, didn't know, or had forgotten, that I had been authorized direct communication by the Department of Defense (in terms of channels, well above the level of the Surgeon General's Office, that was part of Headquarters USAF, which in turn was under the DOD). The Surgeon General had no authority to countermand a directive from the DOD. Air Force Headquarters had endorsed this authorization. Finally, there were certainly no provisions for direct communication between the Surgeon General and the Vice President's office. General Niess was actually the one who had written out of channels.

If the General's only concern had been my letter to Dr. Dryden and my communications, he could easily have picked up the phone and asked me about it. Such a telephone call would obviously not have served the purpose he intended. Rather, he chose to write such a letter and circulate it as he did, even to my friends, to discredit me. Contrary to the statement in his letter, he did want to prevent my continuing relationship with high-level government personnel, including Lyndon Johnson and the White House. That is exactly why he circulated it. Cloaking his knife-in-the-back in complimentary phrases didn't hide his real intent.

I discussed the matter with a competent attorney. He read the letter through, and reviewed the pertinent documents. In his opinion, the letter constituted a case of libel, and if I wished to prefer charges against General Niess, he would proceed as I might indicate.

Colonel Ellingson, the Commander of the School of Aerospace Medicine, was very annoyed with the Niess letter. No one had discussed it with him either, although he was my immediate supervisor. He knew that I was authorized direct communication.

Another curious event transpired in the wake of the letter—a request from General Niess. It was unbelievable. Colonel Ellingson was in Washington and he called me long distance. He told me this was very strange, but General Niess wanted me to get Vice President Johnson to serve on an Advisory Committee for a planned International Cardiology Foundation. General Niess planned to accept a post as executive director to this foundation at the time of his upcoming retirement. What gall! I refused to do this and replied that I felt it was inappropriate since I was not in the habit of discussing extraneous matters with the Vice President, or asking personal favors for myself or my friends, and I did not intend do so then. Both Colonel Ellingson and I were aghast that General Niess would make such a personal request at all—particularly in view of his letter, a copy of which was sent to the Vice President's office.

I did not reply to General Niess' letter. It seemed the most appropriate thing to do was to ignore it for the moment. If anything further were to be done about it, it would best be handled in some other manner than by written communications. Naturally, I wondered if the letter had reached the Vice President, and hoped that, if it had, it had not disturbed him.

In February of that year, 1963, the School was holding another one of its annual Lectures in Aerospace Medicine. The keynote speaker was Deputy Surgeon General Bohannon. He lost no time in coming to my office to have a personal discussion about the Niess letter.

He told me he had been unaware of the letter that General Niess circulated until after it had been released. I told General Bohannon that I had already sought legal advice and had been advised that the letter constituted libel. I did tell him that it was not my intention to reply to General Niess' letter, but if General Niess were to write a letter of apology to the same individuals, I would consider not pursuing the matter further.

Actually, I had no real intention of filing charges against General Niess, since it would not have been in the best interests of the nation to bring out in a public hearing all of the many personnel problems related to the man-in-space program at that time. It could only have made a difficult situation impossible.

Dr. Travell told me that just as she had received the letter from General Niess, she received a telephone call from General Bohannon. He called to assure her that General Niess' letter did not reflect any lack of support for my efforts and, further, that my standing was very high in the Office of the Surgeon General. She told him she was glad to hear that.

All of this raised serious questions about how such a letter came about. I discussed the letter briefly with my friend General Don Wenger, then in the Office of the Surgeon General. He said he knew about the contents of the letter prior to its mailing, but was not aware of the distribution list that was attached. And he had not been aware of the previous authorization for direct communications. All of this suggested the possibility that someone other than General Niess had written the letter. Be that as it may, General Niess signed it and the body of the letter indicated that he had to know about the distribution list if he read the letter.

The competition between the Air Force and NASA was becoming a public issue. Air Force representatives emphasized the importance of planning for the upcoming Manned Orbital Laboratory. Jonathan Spivak, a noted columnist, reported that both the Air Force and NASA were lobbying vigorously for the job. The Air Force wanted to accomplish the task with their Titan III rocket and NASA insisted that they could use their C-1 Saturn rocket. The big picture, behind the things I was being buffeted by, was the power struggle between

NASA and the Air Force for the man-in-space mission.

Soon, there was another letter from General Niess, dated February 7, 1963, and circulated to the same list of people, as follows:

Dear Larry:

General Bohannon has just returned from Brooks with glowing reports of the activities of the School. He explained also that my recent letter to you had caused you considerable concern and that you felt it was too severe and that I had intended to damage your reputation. I would like to assure you that this was not the intent in any way at all. It is my desire to get your activities back in proper channels so that the relationship of the Air Force Medical Service with other agencies would be proper and so that we can continue on with the efforts so vital to our country.

I have always held you in the highest esteem and am interested in your progression and in your career. If you have gained any other impression I am truly sorry.

My sincerest regards and best wishes.

Sincerely yours,

s/O.K. Niess

Evidently, General Niess still did not understand that I was authorized direct communications by the Department of Defense and USAF headquarters in relation to my responsibilities.

Shortly after Niess letter number two, the first letter arrived though channels with vituperative endorsements along the way. Colonel Ellingson was so annoyed he never showed it to me. I was somewhat amused to know that the adverse endorsements were by the same people who had endorsed the original memorandum authorizing direct communications. It was a good indication of how well they really did their job and what little purpose "channels" served. I suspect many of those involved didn't read half the things they signed.

There was a thaw in General Niess' relationship with me. In a letter of May 20, 1963, he wrote me a friendly letter to congratulate me on being elected to Fellowship in the Aerospace Medical Association, signed, "Ollie." (See picture of letter)

This was truly, as President Kennedy said, "the winter of discontent." There was much sniping at Vice President Johnson. William S. White headlined the event as a "New 'Get Johnson' Drive Opens." He commented in Washington's *Evening Star:*

The most virulent sniping campaign against Vice President Johnson since he agreed to take second place in 1960—thus making possible the election of the Kennedy-Johnson ticket by holding the moderate South—has now been opened by ultra liberals in both parties....

In part, they are going after Mr. Johnson because they dare not attack President Kennedy.

20 May 1963

)r. Lawrence Lamb
JSAF School of Aerospace Medicine
Aerospace Medical Center
Brooks AFB, Texas

Dear Larry

I was most happy to be in attendance at Los Angeles when
you were elected to Fellowship in the Aerospace Medical
Association.

Your long and dedicated efforts in the science of medicine
during your illustrious Air Force career merits this coveted
recognition.

On behalf of all your U. S. Air Force Medical Service colleagues,
I want to congratulate you and to wish you well in all your
future endeavors.

Sincerely

). K. NIESS
Major General, USAF, MC
Surgeon General

17

MERCURY MISSION
ACCOMPLISHED

17

 I saw Vice President Johnson on the 14th of February, 1963, in Dr. Travell's office in the White House. By that time, I had secured his chest X-rays from before his heart attack when he was Senate Majority Leader, more than six years earlier. There had been some question regarding his heart size on his current X-rays, but there had been no change at all. His life insurance premiums had been greatly increased because in those days it was believed that individuals who had had a heart attack had only two-to-four years to live. Fortunately, this grim outlook was changed about the time of President Eisenhower's attack during his first term in office.

Dr. Paul White had meticulously collected information on patients who had had heart attacks since his early case reports in the 1920s—many of them with long-term survival. He released his data just before President Eisenhower ran for a second term. By 1963, insurance statistics supported the belief that an individual who had no changes six years after a heart attack had the same life expectancy as a similar individual who had never had one. Accordingly, Lyndon's life insurance premiums were decreased. This was a major shot in the arm for him, because it was such an objective indication that the threat of such a short life span was not justified. In the light of events that followed, it was a fortunate turn of events, since it limited—but did not eliminate—his worry about his health.

Failure to understand the changes in life insurance statistics led to some distorted statements by the news media. After President Johnson left office, Walter Cronkite quoted him as saying he had never wanted to be President. This comment was ridiculed by the media, but his statement had not been understood. It is true that when he had his first heart attack, he didn't think he would live. Mrs. Johnson and their two small daughters came to his bedside to tell him good-bye. After his recovery, he used to say, "I had as bad a heart attack as a man could have and live." No doubt he had wanted to be President, but when you have an illness that may shorten your life to two or four years, that changes your priorities. As time went on, and he had done so well medically, his reaction was much like that of the typical patient. When asked about his heart attack, his response was, "What heart attack?"

The Niess letters didn't change my long-standing friendship with Dr. Travell. Genuine friendships are not affected by such efforts. Vice President Johnson was in his usual good spirits when I met him in her White House office, despite the many problems he was dealing with. He made no comment in reference to the Niess letters and neither did I. Actually, we never discussed the matter at any time in the years that followed. That was characteristic of our relationship.

He had not left the White House more than 10 minutes before I received a call from Walter Jenkins in his office. He called to say that the Vice President had asked him to get in touch with me and find out if I was still having "any problems with that Air Surgeon." I assured him that I didn't think so, since General Niess had written a letter of apology. Walter was quick to tell me, "The Vice President didn't consider it much of an apology."

It was apparent from his tone that the Niess letter had not been well received in that office. During the conversation, Walter requested all documents pertaining to my dealings with NASA and the Air Force relative to the space program. It was no longer possible to keep these problems out of the Vice President's office. Ironic as it may seem, despite the many times I had had the opportunity to speak to the Vice President and members of his staff about the situation—and didn't—it was the Niess out-of-channels letter that brought these matters to their attention. The Niess letter had just the opposite effect from what he had hoped to accomplish, and I kept the Vice President's office informed thereafter.

The competitive efforts between NASA and the DOD continued unabated. News stories appeared across the country reporting that NASA had made an effort to recruit Major Robert White, then the pilot of the famous X-15 aircraft, and Colonel Charles E. Yeager, the first man to break the sound barrier, away from the Air Force. According to the stories, both of these officers spurned the NASA offers.

After the Vice President's staff had the opportunity to review the file they had requested, Walter Jenkins wrote me as follows:

Dear Larry:

I read your letter of February 20 very carefully and took the liberty of showing it to the Vice President. We are pleased to have all the valuable and helpful background information about you and your wonderful work.

In the last paragraph of your letter, you indicated concern as to whether the Vice President is satisfied. I can assure you that he is. He is well aware of the meticulous care you devote to each task. I am inclined to the belief that after talking with several people that the Niess incident has now been sufficiently corrected and is best left alone. I believe that most people here think that the letter to you is unfair and I doubt that much can be gained from carrying the matter any further.

Nevertheless, it is excellent to have the splendid documented brief and it is a good addition to our file.

Best personal regards,
Sincerely,
s/Walter Jenkins
Administrative Assistant to the Vice President

I never knew—and didn't ask—what Walter Jenkins meant by "the Niess incident has now been sufficiently corrected." And I have no idea who he talked to, but evidently something was said at fairly high levels. The events surrounding the Niess letter never seemed to have had any influence on the attitude of the Vice President or his staff. At the time, the episode did bother me more than it should have. I didn't adequately consider that in his long political career Lyndon Johnson had dealt with innumerable smear tactics and would recognize one when he saw it. Had I thought about it, I would have realized that Lyndon Johnson was not one to be overly concerned about military channels, anyway. Finally, I filed the matter away as an unhappy incident to be remembered, but deserving of little else.

The turmoil of 1963 seemed endless. The press seemed to be spoiling for anything it could find to complain about. This reached such proportions that humor columnist Art Buchwald wrote a satire on restricting the press from attending parties and functions at the White House. Buchwald described the White House staff and the women reporters as being "eyelash to eyelash" and this clash between the news media and the White House had narrowly been averted "when Mrs. Kennedy blinked."

It was Easter, and I was again invited to the LBJ ranch. Everyone was in good spirits and enjoying a respite from the winter's difficulties. I enjoyed boating on the lake with the Vice President and his secretary, Marie Fehmer. He loved riding across that lake. I was amused to watch his feeble efforts to curtail his calorie intake. When the cook passed the biscuits around the table, he refused them. She returned and he refused them again. But when she got to the door, he called after her, "Come back here; I can't refuse those biscuits a third time."

Often, when he was at the ranch and had enjoyed a full day, he would visit Cousin Oriole a short distance down the ranch road. She lived in a small house that he had provided for her. She was quite elderly and needed someone to look after her, so he did. It might have been close to midnight when he paid her a visit with some of us. He thought nothing of pounding on the door and calling her until she opened it. We would go in and he would visit. Cousin Oriole kept pictures of his previous years. I laughed when he picked up one from his youth, when he was quite skinny. He looked at it a minute and said, "Now, there is a real virgin for you."

His concern for Cousin Oriole was typical of his basic kindness and willingness to help those in need.

***

The Soviet firsts in space continued unabated. In April, they launched a lunar spacecraft—a major step toward a lunar landing. It looked like they would be first on the moon. The Soviet achievements had been so spectacular that this new development occasioned little surprise and produced little shock. The official position of NASA Headquarters was that such an event was to be expected and was a natural outgrowth of a planned lunar landing project. Far from being disturbed by the event, the Congress of the United States was more interested in continuing its efforts to cut NASA's budget. Brainerd Holmes of NASA was quoted as acknowledging that the Apollo project was not going as fast as it could if more money were available, but he was further quoted as saying:

"In my judgment we are going at a reasonable and proper pace... I think it would be a foolish thing to squander money on an all-out crash program, just as I think it would be a foolish thing to risk life in order to get there first."

NASA's budget for Apollo faced serious threats. If the advocates for a military space program obtained approval and had a large budget, that might decrease the funds available for the NASA projects. The other risk was from those interested in social programs, such as education. Those advocates, including Senator J. W. Fulbright, thought it would be better to spend more money on education and social projects on Earth than on space projects. That was one of the reasons why NASA could not afford to make any colossal mistakes, such as sending an astronaut into space with atrial fibrillation or spending a lot of money on a flight that provided no useful information. Those just waiting to throttle the moon project—and NASA—would take full advantage of any misstep.

The Mercury project built to its final climax. On May the 16th, Major Gordon Cooper became the sixth of the Mercury astronauts to pilot the Mercury capsule into space. His was the longest space flight in the Mercury series. Essentially, all the automatic controls of the spacecraft failed. It was a great opportunity to see again why man was needed, even if everything was push-button controlled. Cooper overcame a really bad situation and completed the flight with manual control. He brought the Mercury capsule down right next to the ship that was going to pick him up. If he had been any closer, he would have landed on the deck. Major Cooper was justifiably pleased with his flight, and the nation cheered. In presenting the Distinguished Service Medal to Major Cooper, President Kennedy commented:

I hope that we will be encouraged to continue with this program. I know that a good many people say, 'Why go to the moon?' just as many people said to Lindbergh, 'Why go to Paris?' Lindbergh said, 'It is not so much a matter of logic as it is a feeling.'

I think the United States has committed itself to this great adventure in the sixties. I think that before the end of the sixties we will send a man to the moon, an American, and I think in so doing it is not merely that we are interested in making this particular journey but we are interested demonstrating a dominance of this new sea, and making sure that in this new, great, adventurous period the Americans are playing their great role, as they have in the past.

In the glow of these successful achievements and their status as national heroes, the Mercury astronauts lost no time in trying to influence the course of events to their liking. Behind the scenes, while Gordon Cooper was receiving his well deserved awards and acclaim, the Mercury astronauts began maneuvering for a seventh Mercury space flight. This was at the same time that NASA headquarters was trying to get approval for their upcoming budget; which seemed like an important enough responsibility. Alan Shepard, the first astronaut to be lobbed into space, had not made an orbital flight; and a seventh flight would provide that opportunity.

The astronauts' efforts to obtain a seventh Mercury flight reached President Kennedy. He indicated unequivocally that the decision would be left to NASA, and he meant specifically James Webb and his staff. News accounts stated that the astronauts had given President Kennedy "a hard sales pitch" for an additional Mercury flight, apparently at a party that had been given in their honor. James Webb, NASA's administrator, led the opposition and was said to feel that the 10-to-12 million dollars that the astronauts wanted the nation to spend couldn't be justified for the limited additional information that might be gained. Webb was pointing toward the big picture: obtaining an adequate NASA budget from Congress to support the moon project. He eventually prevailed. Despite all the rhetoric questioning the need to fund a NASA program for the peaceful conquest of space, the entire appropriation was recommended by the House-Senate committee.

With the budget limitations, the Air Force's cherished hopes to develop the X-20 rocket plane for the Dyna-Soar project—the forerunner to the space shuttle—were dashed. Secretary McNamara put the ax to it. I had a personal interest in this development because the individuals who were slated to be the Dyna-Soar crews were the first Air Force space pilots to be examined by the Consultation Services at the School, August 3, 1959.

In May, 1963, I had a pleasant interlude from my usual activities. Dr. Travell came to lecture at the School. Over the weekend, we had an opportunity to wend our way to the New Braunfels area. This quaint little German town, just north of San Antonio, was bursting with its late spring and early summer floral display. We drove to Landa Park and paused for a good swim in a large area of the river that had been dammed. The huge natural swimming pool was flanked on both sides by the ubiquitous giant live oak trees. The water was cold and invigorating, and we made the most of it.

After the swim we went for a walk in the sun to warm up a bit. We passed the water lilies and saw the children playing in the swings. Finally, the temptation was too much. To my astonishment, Dr. Travell spied a large tree and climbed it. She scampered up the trunk with the agility of an 8 year old. After reaching a suitable height in the branches of the tree, she enjoyed looking down impishly at my surprised face and amusing herself with my concern for her safety. Having proved she could handle tree-climbing without difficulty, she consented to come down and we continued our trip. We drove north along the river, forded it at interims across low-water bridges, and sped up the hills to rattle across cattle guards that bridged the roads. Just before Dr. Travell's arrival, I had received a telephone call from Edwards AFB. One of my test pilot friends—I'll call him Smitty—was having major problems with his arm and neck muscles.

He was one of the outstanding pilots at the Edwards Flight Test Center and a fine individual. Since Dr. Travell was a leading authority on musculoskeletal problems, I suggested that he come to the School so she could give us an expert consultation. He arrived that evening, almost unable to move his head and arm from the muscle soreness. He had been disabled for several weeks. Serious questions had been raised about whether he was able to continue in his flying duties. He was in his usual mischievous good humor, despite his pain and discomfort.

General Benson, had remained in San Antonio after his retirement as the first Commander of the Aerospace Medical Division and the School of Aerospace Medicine. I saw him and his wife, Dawn, often. Dr. Travell, Smitty and I stopped by their house for some refreshments and appetizers before the evening meal. Then, all of us drove together to the old Grey Moss Inn west of San Antonio. This was a favorite spot of mine because of its relaxed countryside atmosphere. It was located far off the main highway, and one needed to know the road exactly in order to get there. The natural stone house had been an old stagecoach stop. It was surrounded by outdoor tables and nestled under giant oak trees—a wonderful place for charcoal grilled steaks and all the trimmings. We had a very good time. We were in especially high spirits. Everyone laughed and joked. Poor Smitty joined us in our merrymaking, despite his pain.

The next day, Dr. Travell demonstrated to the staff and resident students why she had achieved such a standing in the field of musculoskeletal disorders. After her lecture she demonstrated the application of her teachings on Smitty. Finally, with the use of coolant sprays, injections, and stretching, she was able to markedly relieve his muscle spasms and stiffness. He required several subsequent treatments, but this was the beginning, and a major step toward his almost immediate and complete recovery. This led to his early return to flying status and participation in important high-performance aircraft testing programs.

I had agreed previously to give a lecture at the U.S. Air Force Test Pilot School at Edwards AFB, California, that month. Smitty and I flew back to Edwards together. That also gave me an opportunity to continue the treatment program for him that Dr. Travell had outlined and demonstrated to me. My two days at Edwards were one of the most pleasant of my visits to Air Force installations. It was a unique facility.

I had the pleasure of meeting Colonel Chuck Yeager. He personally toured me around the School to show me the majority of the support areas for the test pilots and space pilots. He impressed me as being a very bright and able individual. It was clear that his excellent reputation was based on more than having broken the sound barrier. I got a look at all the different types of aircraft that were used in the training program. Colonel Yeager reviewed the history of the Test Pilot School and its development, plus a number of their projects. He then went over the curriculum plans for the future in some detail and explained their efforts to accelerate the training program in a way to increase the nation's output of qualified individuals to enter into space programs at an early age. Certainly, there was no one better qualified to assess how much flight training and previous experience pilots might require to prepare them for such a program than Chuck Yeager.

Before *Sputnik*, the Test Pilot School at Edwards Air Force Base had suffered the fate of peacetime neglect. The Air Force was looking forward to the missile age, not new aircraft. The need for test pilots to test new aircraft was minimal. Other than the new X-15, there was not much activity. That was one reason why the number of test pilots available for the selection of the Mercury astronauts was limited. It took Chuck Yeager to rejuvenate the program. Under his guidance, the Test Pilot School was turning out highly trained professionals for both the Air Force and the space program.

The space pilots were their usual gregarious selves. Having been through the examination procedures at the School of Aerospace Medicine, they were eager for me to experience what they did. I was offered a ride in the F-104 Starfighter jet aircraft. Up to that time my jet experience had been the same as that of most civilians, namely on commercial airlines. None of my other military aircraft flying had been in high-performance aircraft. This seemed like an excellent opportunity, and I was mindful that this was no time to chicken out. I was going to fly with Bob McIntosh, formerly a member of the famed Thunderbird aerobatic flying team. The F-104 was a real hot aircraft with two seats. It was the same jet that later achieved some notoriety because of the number of German pilots who were involved in fatal accidents while flying it. The Germans called it the "widow maker."

The next morning, I eyed the Starfighter with some circumspection. It looked like some form of missile with little stubby wings on the side and a somewhat long, droopy snout. I slipped into the flying suit, including the flying boots, with what could best be described as spurs. The "spurs" were the heel attachments that were pinned to the sockets under the seat to be used for automatic seat ejection. My helmet and oxygen mask were in place, seat belt strapped, then we taxied out to the runway. After a momentary pause, we began moving. The speed with which we covered the runway was like nothing I had ever experienced before. Man! We were flying low! I was pressed back into my seat from the powerful forward thrust of the aircraft. We literally leaped off the runway and began our ever-circling flight upward.

We climbed nearly as high as the capabilities of he aircraft would permit. At the same time, we watched the test pilot trainees flying other aircraft nearby. One of their tasks was to fly the aircraft to its limits of altitude until it stalled out and dropped. As it fell, they recovered control of the aircraft. Far below us, stretched as far as the eye could see, were the dry lake beds of Edwards. Their packed sand provided a natural landing area of sufficient size to support the aircraft testing programs that had been going on for years at Edwards. Beneath us, down on the dry lake bed, we watched a simulated X-15 landing.

In the course of the flight, I had the opportunity to maneuver the aircraft and fly it through several barrel rolls. We broke the sound barrier and achieved a speed of Mach 2—twice the speed of sound.

Because of the rapid changes in ascent and descent, I had begun to have some trouble with my eardrums, which I could not adequately control. As we descended rapidly, the increased pressure pushed my eardrums in. The pain became so excruciating that my body was drenched in sweat. I tolerated it to the point that I felt there was a real danger that I would become a safety hazard. Finally, I told Bob McIntosh that I was having trouble with my ears. He immediately ascended to higher altitude and enabled me to unblock my ears. After a few more turns around the field, we descended more slowly, completing the flight. The pressure had been sufficiently great that there was some external bleeding from both ears. Other than this one slight complication, the flight was an enjoyable experience and very informative.

I checked out how much effort was needed to manage the controls. It did not require brute force, but skill. This was important in evaluating how much physical effort Smitty would need to make in piloting aircraft of this type. Clearly, it was not a job that required one to be a weightlifter.

My ear problem was just one example of the problems that can occur in high-performance flight and altitude exposure. A minor version of this happens to many passengers during commercial flights. We are all exposed to atmospheric pressure: at sea level, 15 pounds per square inch or 760 mm. Hg. all over our bodies, including the external surface of the eardrum. There is a tube in the back of the mouth that opens to the inside of the eardrum, also exposing it to atmospheric pressure. The trouble begins when the pressure on the inside and outside of the eardrum is unequal.

That usually happens because air flow through the tube to the inside of the eardrum is not adequate. As you ascend to altitude, the pressure on the outside of the eardrum decreases. If it decreases faster than the pressure on the inside the eardrum, it bulges outward. The opposite occurs as you descend. If the pressure outside the eardrum increases too fast, it is pushed in. This affects a person's hearing and can be painful. To alleviate the condition, people open their mouths, chew gum and do other things to try to increase the air flow through the tube in the back of the mouth to the inside of the eardrum. When they are successful, the eardrum pops back to its normal position and hearing is suddenly improved.

Since these pressure dynamics occur even in commercial flights, a person with throat and sinus infections should not fly. Pressure changes may push infected material from the throat into the middle ear chamber, causing a middle ear infection.

My problem began as atmospheric pressure increased during descent. We descended so rapidly that the pressure outside the eardrum was much greater than the presssure inside. As a result, my eardrums were pushed into the ear with so much force that bleeding occurred. The pilot ascended to higher altitude, then descended more slowly, providing time for the pressure to equalize on both sides of the eardrum. It was not a serious problem and left no long term effects. Some people have anatomical variations that make it more difficult to change the pressure inside the ear. They are the most likely to have trouble, even with commercial flights.

My efforts on behalf of the flying personnel had not gone unnoticed. The following day, when I was introduced to give my lecture to the class, Major McIntosh made the point that I had probably done more to maintain a large number of people on flying status than any other physician associated with the Air Force. After my trip to Edwards Flight Test Center, Smitty wrote a nice thank-you letter to Dr. Travell. In part, he wrote,

Larry and I flew back to California together, where he was royally welcomed. He enjoyed a flight in the F-104 "Starfighter" at twice the speed of sound. Thanks to you I now hold one 'claim to fame being treated simultaneously by the President's and Vice President's physicians.

18

CEASE FIRE

18

↝ There were many changes in the wind that summer of 1963. Stan White's long tour with the NASA's MSC ended. He was reassigned to the Aerospace Medical Division Headquarters at Brooks AFB, directly across the street from my office. I suspected that the trouble had simply moved from MSC to General Bedwell's office. Chuck Berry announced his intention to resign from the Air Force and accept a Civil Service appointment with NASA's MSC, insuring his continued affiliation with the space program. He had replaced Bill Douglas as the astronauts' physician.

Once again, it was necessary for NASA to augment its group of astronauts. After Gemini came Apollo. The days of space crews were at hand. The development of new rockets had made it possible to have large space vehicles to accommodate a space crew rather than the single-manned flights of Mercury or the two-man flights of Gemini. It was time to plan for additions to the astronaut pool. Again, there were the questions of turf and problems between the School and the MSC medics. The NASA's MSC medical personnel put on a sober face and paid all of the formal calls, beginning with General Bedwell, then to the School and finally to my office to complete the negotiations. The School was where the action was. I should have put a sign on my desk using Harry Truman's saying, "The buck stops here."

Despite various minutiae, the ultimate result was an agreement to do the examinations essentially as they had been done before. During the course of these examinations, and finally the transmission of the reports to Houston, I had several occasions to talk to Chuck Berry. I suggested to him that perhaps things could be handled better between the two groups. Many of the problems were openly discussed and I had every reason to expect a major improvement in relationships. That proved to be the case.

After the changes in personnel at MSC, it was like the end of hostilities. Chuck Berry and I returned to our previous friendly relationship. This change, whether it was related or not, all occurred in the aftermath of Stan White's departure from NASA's MSC. It had been a long and difficult time, but the prospects of peace promised that the efforts of both groups could be expended in a more productive manner in the mutual goal of supporting the nation's effort for the manned space program.

Things got worse with the Aerospace Medical Division headquarters. Stan White was named as the project officer for the Manned Orbiting Laboratory (MOL) a planned Air Force space station. The concept of a project officer was a good one. It provided for one person to be in charge and to utilize personnel and resources across the board. But it also provided the platform for empire-building. Stan White had the authority to appoint various individuals for different aspects of the project. His arrangements were designed to limit the input from the School and shift authority to individuals at the Air Force's Wilford Hall hospital, down the road at Lackland AFB.

On one of the junkets to the West Coast he exposed his hand. Colonel Robert Johnson, from the School, was one of those chosen to work with Stan. He called me the morning after he got back and asked me if I had "done anything to Stan White." He then related Stan's remarks about me and the School. Colonel Johnson considered the remarks so destructive that he and Dr. Paul Stevens, who was also at the meeting, prepared an official memorandum about the incident. While Stan saved the most scathing attack for me, I was not his sole target.

One of the amusing comments that Colonel Johnson and Dr. Stevens reported was Stan White's statement that most qualified cardiologists placed Dr. Lamb in the category with Dr. Paul D. White—behind the times and somewhat out of the picture in current achievement and efforts in cardiology. Colonel Johnson noted that he hardly considered comparison to Dr. White as derogatory—in fact, quite the opposite! Evidently, Dr. Paul Dudley White's approval rating by Stan White had sunk from the leading authority to evaluate Deke Slayton's problem to an old has-been after he also failed to recommend that Slayton could pilot a Mercury flight.

Ordinarily I would have simply ignored it and considered the source and the evening's libations, but the attack on the School was sufficiently destructive that Colonel Ellingson, the School commander, needed to know. After reading Bob Johnson's report, he called Stan to his office. Colonel Ellingson told me that Stan repeated his charges and expanded his criticisms to include most of the School's activities, including the teaching program—all this without the influence of any beverages. This resulted in a face-to-face confrontation of Stan White by Colonel Ellingson; General Bedwell; John Pickering, director of research for the Division; Colonel Johnson and myself. Stan was the soul of sweetness and told me afterward that he had never said any of those things.

Considering Stan's track record over the years, I recognized his fingerprints. It was Stan who first wanted to know about my association with Lyndon Johnson when I did the consultation on Enos the chimp. It was Stan, at that meeting, who concealed from me the fact that Slayton had continued to have frequent attacks of atrial fibrillation. After that, it was Robert Gilruth, his boss, who I was told made the threat about funds for the School if I had told the Vice President about the Slayton problem. It was Stan White who deleted the funds from NASA Headquarters intended for the School and gave contracts to other areas—and now it was MOL. In the last analysis it made no difference, as the MOL project—his new area of influence—was canceled.

I understood Stan's motives. It wasn't just his personal animosity toward me, as his efforts were directed at the School in its entirety. He was affiliated with Wright-Patterson Aeromedical Laboratory in years past and had been in charge of the medical evaluation for the selection of the Mercury astronauts at Wright-Patterson and the contract to the Lovelace Clinic. After the direct face-to-face confrontation, he did not create any new problems for me—at least that I knew about.

The time had come for General Niess to retire. I took the occasion to write him a personal letter to thank him for the many things he had done to support my efforts. Although I didn't appreciate his out-of-channels correspondence to my friends, otherwise it had been a good relationship. I preferred to think of the good days rather than the few bad days. He was pleased to get my letter and wrote back,

Dear Larry:

I am most pleased to receive your kind, interesting, and purposeful letter relating to the advances and research work in the electrocardiographic field.

You have always had my eager support in your important and meaningful endeavors for I felt that your dedicated work added much to the science of medicine. Your studies in syncope and cardiovascular physiology have brought great prestige to the U. S. Air Force Medical Service and world renown to yourself. As I read your most edifying letter, I could not help but reflect upon the number of successful research programs you have implemented and consummated during your tenure at the School of Aerospace Medicine. The excellent cooperation and teamwork which I have personally received from you will always be most memorable and reassuring as I take leave of the Air Force for civilian endeavors.

I am deeply touched and most appreciative of your continued loyalty, support, and good wishes. May you continue in your dedicated work to bring greater glory to the Air Force and yourself.

Sincerely,

s/ Ollie

O.K. Niess

Major General, USAF, Surgeon General

In this way, our correspondence ended on a good note as our paths parted.

By September 1963, there were rumbles of problems with the ill-fated Apollo Moon Project. Originally, the first manned orbital space flight using the Apollo vehicle was scheduled for March, 1965. The project was badly behind schedule. The news media suggested that a significant portion of the delay could be attributed to managerial problems within NASA. These suspicions were triggered in part by the unexpected resignation of Brainerd Holmes, NASA's Director for Project Apollo. Apparently, Holmes had difficulties related to a lack of central control by NASA Headquarters over its relatively independent, strong-minded centers. News accounts described the directors of these centers as being "strong-willed individuals," and that the centers "tended to assume the status of semiautonomous states." I was in complete agreement with those observations.

The Centers that were involved in support of the Apollo project were: the Manned Spacecraft Center at Houston under Robert Gilruth; the Launch Operations Center at Cape Canaveral, Florida; and the Marshall Space Flight Center in Huntsville, Alabama. It was reported that Holmes had been unable to maintain the managerial authority necessary to accomplish his responsibilities as project director. The Manned Spacecraft Center was particularly cited for "bickering" with the Cape Canaveral facility over the launching of the manned space flights. John W. Finney, columnist for the *New York Times*, reported that some Congressmen felt that NASA had not learned very much from looking at the Polaris missile, atomic submarine, and intercontinental missile programs, and that the success of those complex programs had been the direct result of establishing "firm control and clear responsibility exercised by one person." Some columnists took a dim view of these developments and felt it might delay a successful moon landing for the United States by President Kennedy's stated goal of 1970.

There had been talk of an American-Soviet joint effort to land men on the moon. Robert Gilruth, Director of the Manned Spacecraft Center and head of his "autonomous state," had publicly stated that joint cooperation with the Soviets was "incredible." President Kennedy thought otherwise. He announced that the United States was willing to join a Soviet-American moon mission. In addressing the United Nations on September 20, 1963, President Kennedy said in regard to space:

...There is room for new cooperation, for further joint efforts in the regulation and exploration of space. I include among these possibilities a joint expedition to the moon. Space offers no problems of sovereignty; ...Why, therefore, should man's first flight to the moon be a matter of

national competition? Why should the United States and the Soviet Union, in preparing for such expeditions, become involved in immense duplications of research construction, and expenditure? Surely we should explore whether the scientists and astronauts of our two countries—indeed of all the world—cannot work together in the conquest of space, sending someday in this decade to the moon not the representatives of a single nation, but representatives of all our countries.

One of the major national security concerns was the danger of nuclear weapons in space. Satellites loaded with a nuclear bomb could not be shot down and could bomb American cities. Drew Pearson noted in *The Washington Post*, October 7, 1963, that the Soviets were able to arm their large satellites with rockets. He noted that Air Force generals were disturbed by Premier Khrushchev's speech listing space ships as part of their military arsenal. The danger, as the generals saw it, was the Soviets could launch rockets from space against American cities from satellites. Such a formidable weapon would be more dangerous than missiles in Cuba.

This was part of the justification for the Air Force's demand for a larger role in space: the conflict concerning whether the United States should spend more money on a military space program and less on a scientific, nonmilitary, space program.

Neither the United States nor the Soviets wanted a nuclear war launched from space. The United States' vigorous efforts to develop a space capability had at least provided the possibility of also being able to launch a nuclear war from space. While the Americans could not launch as large a space ship as the Soviets, they now had the capability of launching vehicles large enough to pose a threat.

As a result, Secretary of State Dean Rusk and Soviet Foreign Minister Gromyko began to negotiate a treaty against the use of nuclear weapons in space. An agreement was reached between Great Britain, the Soviets and the United States to ban nuclear weapons from space.

With Project Mercury now officially ended and the eyes of the nation turning toward Gemini and Apollo, it was a fitting time to pay tribute to the nation's first space team. Accordingly, on October 10, 1963, the President presented the Collier Trophy to the Mercury astronauts. Donald K. Slayton stepped forth at the ceremony on behalf of the astronauts to receive the award from the President.

Amidst the din of confusion over the space program in the United States, Soviet optimism reached a new high. Cosmonaut Gagarin predicted while in Mexico City that the Soviets would land a man on the moon in 1964, and the Soviets' orbiting romantic couple— Cosmonaut Nikolaye and Cosmonette Tereshkova—made plans to embark on a matrimonial orbit.

Consistent with the improvement in relations between the School and NASA's MSC, a thank-you note to General Bedwell for the School's efforts appropriately came from Robert Gilruth. Despite having set up the first course and trained the medical monitors in electrocardiographic monitoring for the Mercury project, and despite all the other inputs for the previous selection programs for NASA, this was the first time the School had ever received a letter of thanks from Gilruth's office. The School did receive such a letter from Mr. Webb, Administrator of NASA, after I had suggested it to General Roadman at NASA Headquarters. I regarded Gilruth's letter as a good sign of improving relations and hoped this meant the cold war that existed during Stan White's entire tour with NASA was over. Part of Gilruth's letter concerning the examinations was as follows:

I would like to express my appreciation and satisfaction with the conduct of the medical examination of the NASA applicants this year. Dr. Berry and his staff have been most complimentary of the work of Dr. Lamb and the officers and men of the Clinical Sciences Division. They reflect much credit on themselves and on the School of Aerospace Medicine by their energetic, knowledgeable and courteous endeavor to conduct the most searching and complete examination possible. The examinees themselves have uniformly expressed the opinion that their contacts with the personnel involved were most pleasant, that the examination was the most thorough they had ever received, and that it was a very valuable educational experience for themselves.

...It is my hope that this pleasant relationship will be continued.
Sincerely
Robert R. Gilruth, Director

The letter from Dr. Gilruth was a piece of good news I could send on to Walter Jenkins, and I did. He was pleased and wrote back on October 28, 1962 as follows:

Dear Larry:

That was an encouraging letter from Dr. Gilruth. It looks as if strained relations have healed and that progress toward a closer relationship in your work is also being achieved.

Ed Welsh (Executive Secretary for the National Aeronautics and Space Council) tells me that Secretary Zuckert told him just last week that the Slayton decision was the only right one that could have been made under the circumstances.

The President interrupted his busy schedule to hold a news conference on the 31st of October, 1963. Premier Khrushchev had just made a public statement which led to wide spread speculation that the Soviet Union had pulled out of the moon race. President Kennedy was asked whether he thought this was really true and he replied:

In my opinion the space program we have is essential to the security of the United States, because as I have said many times before, it is not a question of going to the moon. It is a question of having the competence to master this environment. And I would not make any bets at all upon Soviet intentions. I think that our experience has been that we wait for deeds, unless we have a system of verification, we have no idea whether the Soviet Union is going to make a race for the moon or whether it is going to attempt an even greater program.

I think we ought to stay with our program. I think that is the best answer to Mr. Khrushchev.

19

THE DAY BEFORE DALLAS

Vice President Lyndon and Lady Bird Johnson walking on the platform in front of the Aerospace Medical Center Headquarters before President Kennedy gave the dedication speech, November 21, 1963, the day before the assassination in Dallas, Texas.

LBJ Library Photo by Cecil Stoughton

First Lady Jacqueline Kennedy and Vice President Lyndon Johnson visiting before President Kennedy speaks, November 21, 1963.

President Kennedy at the podium in front of dignitaries to give his last official address as President, devoted to the nation's man-in-space program.

LBJ Library Photo by Cecil Stoughton

After the President's speech. Lady Bird Johnson on the left with Lyndon Johnson, the President with his back to the camera and First Lady Jacqueline Kennedy are leaving the area to visit the Center's facilities.

President Kennedy visits an altitude chamber to observe a study in progress supporting space research.

19

By 1963, it had been eight years since I had arrived at what was then a primitive School of Aviation Medicine to develop a medical program to support the Air Force flying personnel. Despite the conflicts, they had been exciting years. When I had arrived in 1955, the Air Force had no special facility to support the air crews. I had been part of developing a first class facility to support the men who flew the hottest aircraft in the world and those who would be the first men in history to land on the moon. The Aerospace Medical Center at Brooks Air Force Base had grown to meet the challenge, and the man who had been instrumental in pushing needed funding through congress was Vice President Lyndon B. Johnson. He was instrumental in obtaining the funding for the first increment of buildings in 1952 and defended the funding in Congress. That enabled ground to be broken for the new Center in May 1959, before *Sputnik I* was launched on October 4, 1957. I first saw Lyndon Johnson as a patient when he was Senate Majority Leader, November 14, 1959. He had come to dedicate the first buildings at the Center. I knew he was proud of the School's achievements. Now, the Center was twice as large and it was time to dedicate the new buildings. I thought President Kennedy should see the Center and dedicate the new facilities. The right person to invite the President was naturally Lyndon Johnson. He, more than anyone else at the highest level of the government, had firsthand knowledge of the School's contributions to the nation's space program. The Center was the product of his foresight for the nation's future requirements when space flight was still little more than an interesting fantasy in the minds of many. If anyone were to invite President Kennedy to visit the Aerospace Medical Center, it should be the Vice President. I was young and very enthusiastic and with that thought in mind, I wrote to him, March 26, 1963, as follows:

I read the newspaper version of your comments at the Sixth Annual Goddard Memorial Dinner. As you have stated previously, one of the ways which we can bring public focus to the scientific efforts of the nation in the space program is by emphasizing our institutions and achievements.

Toward this end, if it is possible, a visit from the President to the School of Aerospace Medicine at the time of the dedication of all the new buildings this fall would be a real shot in the arm. Not only would this help draw the nation's attention to the efforts directed toward man-in-space, but I am certain that the President would enjoy seeing the facilities and learning firsthand of the achievements which have been made.

We here are all cognizant of the vital role you have played in the development of the School of Aerospace Medicine which has enabled our scientists to make their many contributions to the nation's space effort. In view of your firsthand knowledge of the installation you would be the ideal person to invite the President. I hope you think this is a good idea and that it will be feasible.

Some time ago I discussed this with Mr. Craig and he has probably already mentioned this to you. I have also suggested this to General Bedwell in the past and he is interested and would like to see it accomplished. My understanding is that an official inquiry has been sent to Secretary Zuckert and he has indicated that he thought it would be a good idea but was not optimistic that the President would have time to accept the invitation.

I can't think of anything that would do the place more good than to have you come down here and introduce the President at the dedication ceremonies. It will be a beautiful campus by then and the nation's major Aerospace Medicine facility.

Hoping my letter finds you in good health and good spirits, With every good wish.

Soon, I received a reply, dated March 29, 1963:

Dear Larry:
Thank you for your letter of March 26. Your pride in the School of Aerospace Medicine is certainly warranted, and my high evaluation of it is contributed to significantly by your presence there.

As for the President's participation in the dedication of the new buildings next fall, I am sure it would do a lot for morale and give due recognition to the fine School. As I understand it, an invitation has already gone through Secretary Zuckert or at least an inquiry has been made through the official channels. So far as I am concerned, it would seem best to see what develops in that way. When the occasion arises, I will talk with the Secretary and see how he is progressing on the project.

Personal regards.
Sincerely,
s/ LBJ

The plans for President Kennedy to dedicate the new buildings for the Aerospace Medical Center were underway. Conway Craig—a San Antonio civic leader and President of the Express Publishing Company—discussed the possibility with me on several occasions. We joined forces to do what we could to bring this about. Leslie Carpenter, a member of the vice president's staff, wrote to Mr. Craig, August 30, 1963, about the plan as follows:

Dear Mr. Craig:
I have talked to the Vice President a number of times about your interest in having him and the President visit San Antonio together for the dedication.

The possibility that it will happen is still active, but there will be a lull. The Vice President leaves Monday for his Scandinavian trip. Nothing will—or can—happen on it until his return September 19.

I hope it will come to a head shortly after that, but at the moment, I cannot be sure. But please know that I am doing everything I can.

Best regards.
Sincerely,
s/Les
Leslie Carpenter

These letters document that the trip to Texas was not a spur of the moment event. The official reason for President Kennedy's subsequent trip was to dedicate the new buildings at the Aerospace Medical Center.

No one could have guessed in the spring of 1963 what horrendous changes would occur. It was a very contentious year and the upcoming presidential election had a lot to do with it. The late summer saw a rise in anti-Johnson sentiment. He had crusaded vigorously for civil rights, and I had heard him say on many occasions in a private setting that if he ever had an opportunity to help the Negroes, he would spare no effort. His outspoken stand on the civil rights issue was soon cited by columnists to cast doubts about the Vice President's future. Columnist Ted Lewis, for one, asked why President Kennedy was planning on keeping Lyndon Johnson as his running mate for the upcoming elections, since he had been identified with such a strong civil rights stand that he had "surrendered" the influence he had exercised in holding the South for the Democratic ticket in 1960. The political season was upon the country. That—superimposed on worldwide problems such as the Cuban situation and Vietnam—resulted in a very onerous year.

There was a groundswell of Goldwater popularity in Texas. Columnist Gladen Hill, writing for the *New York Times*, described the situation as one of "revolution." Hill emphasized that Texas was emerging as a two-party state, and its 24 electoral votes could not be counted upon as a sure thing for any prospective candidate.

With the upcoming election, President Kennedy began making visits beyond the suburbs of Washington and Hyannis Port, to Wisconsin, Minnesota, North Dakota, Wyoming, Montana, Washington, Utah, Oregon, and Nevada. He dedicated a dam and reservoir at Whiskeytown, California. At each stop of this great sweep of the Midwest and far West—dedicating buildings and dams—he reminded the people of the things that his administration had done for them. President Kennedy had already begun his campaign for the 1964 election.

By the middle of October, the Goldwater bandwagon was becoming a national express. Columnist Eric Sevareid referred to it as the "Growing Goldwater Phenomenon," and he likened Senator Goldwater's appeal to the American voter to that of Dwight Eisenhower, based on Goldwater's "simple, homespun sincerity and charm."

The itineraries of candidates for the highest office in the land stepped up sharply in November. The plans for President Kennedy's upcoming visit to dedicate the new additions to the Aerospace Medical Center became more certain. All of us began to look forward to that historic day. At first, it was thought the dedication day would be on Friday the 22nd, and an air of uncertainty still hung over the plans for the President's and Vice President's arrival. The day was fast approaching when the President's tour would take him to the heart of the Goldwater groundswell. The trip that had been planned for months was next. The overriding political concern behind the Texas trip was the outcome of the 1964 presidential election. Columnist Ted Lewis wrote that, "Kennedy considers a 1964 *victory* in Texas almost required if he is to win a second term."

Later, John Connally wrote in *Life*, November 24, 1967, that President Kennedy had wanted to visit Texas for over a year and a half and had wanted him, as governor, to arrange it. There were undoubtedly many reasons, not just one, why the President wanted to make such a trip. It was common to have an official reason so that part of the travel expenses could be paid by the government rather than being charged to the President's political party. Going to Texas to dedicate the new buildings at the Aerospace Medical Center served that purpose.

The President had already heard a lot about the School from Dr. Travell, as she had visited me on several occasions. No doubt Vice President Johnson had also told him about it. The rest of the tour, after the dedication, was political—to raise funds and court potential voters. It was not a spur of the moment trip for political expediency that had just developed, as many news stories at the time suggested. Dedicating the new facilities at the Air Force's Aerospace Medical Center at Brooks Air Force Base provided an official reason to visit Texas. The President had become a passionate enthusiast about the nation's space program and had made it a top national priority. With this visit he could also promote the man-in-space project. It was a win-win situation. As events unfolded, this would be the occasion for his last official address as President and the rest of the Texas trip would be political.

San Antonio began to prepare for President Kennedy's visit. The press speculated for days about his imminent arrival. The date was set for the 21st of November, 1963. A great wave of enthusiasm engulfed the Alamo City and a fiesta atmosphere prevailed. San Antonio's long, winding streets from the airport, all through the downtown area, and along the presidential route, were draped with red, white and blue banners. The great crossroad of Mexican and Anglo-American influences prepared to show its warm hospitality and give an enthusiastic greeting to its youthful President and the Vice President.

Brooks Air Force Base prepared for its day in the sun, when President Kennedy would dedicate the new additions to the Center. A cherished hope in the hearts of many of us was close at hand. The complex of brick buildings seated upon the rolling hills never looked better. Banners draped the front of the division headquarters, and its parking area—somewhat like a large bowl—was cleared to make room for the capacity crowd. The platform for the visiting dignitaries was erected, connected directly to the ground floor of the Aerospace Medical Division headquarters building. Banks of microphones and loud speakers were put in place.

It was a brilliant, sunny morning and good humor prevailed upon the campus. A large crowd of friends of the School gathered for the occasion.

The day of the week was Thursday, and Vice President Johnson had landed ahead of the presidential party at the International Airport. No one who appreciated the traditions of presidential and vice presidential travel expected them to arrive together. It had long been a national tradition that the President and Vice President did not travel on the same airplane.

Lyndon Johnson was in a relaxed and pleasant mood. While waiting, he took advantage of the airport facilities to get his hair cut. The attention of almost everyone, for the moment, was directed to the impending visit of President Kennedy. The Vice President was able to move about with a relative degree of freedom he would not long enjoy.

Mrs. Kennedy was also scheduled to arrive for the Texas visit. She was quoted as saying that of all the stops she would make, the one she was really looking forward to was the opportunity to relax at the LBJ ranch. Mrs. Johnson was well-known for her Texas menus, enjoyed by dignitaries around the world. She planned to serve deer sausage, home-cured bacon, homemade peach preserves, hominy grits, fried chicken, pecan pie and corn bread. A warm and friendly reception was planned for the Kennedy's. It had all the features of an old-fashioned Sunday visit between good neighbors in the tradition of western hospitality.

Finally, to the delight of an enthusiastic throng, the long-awaited airplane appeared in the distance. Air Force One circled the field, winged down slowly, and touched its wheels to the runway. President and Mrs. Kennedy had landed in San Antonio. After descending from the plane, they stopped and greeted members in a party of well-wishers. Congressman Henry B. Gonzales was close by, and when the occasion was appropriate, Mrs. Kennedy made a big hit with the Mexican-American population with her fluent Spanish.

The caravan moved slowly out of the airport to begin the route through the Alamo City, down long, winding Broadway Street. Overhead the red, white, and blue banners flapped in the breeze, and for miles along the route people clogged the city streets. At main intersections the crowds were so heavy that the motorcade was slowed, and still Broadway stretched on for miles. Confetti drifted down from the upper stories of taller buildings. This was a hero's welcome. San Antonio was expressing pride in her national leaders and saying thank-you to President Kennedy and Vice President Johnson for their visit. The motorcade gradually wended its way through the center of town, passing near the old Gunter Hotel. Crowds gathered on the Spanish balconies along the way. Finally, the caravan moved past the major downtown area and sped on to Brooks.

At last, the presidential motorcade approached the entrance. President and Mrs. Kennedy were in the back seat of a white convertible. Their hair was wind-tossed and their smiles radiant. The convertible moved around the circle behind the headquarters. There was a momentary hush while everyone waited expectantly. Soon the doors behind the platform swung open. President and Mrs. Kennedy walked out across the platform, accompanied by Vice President and Mrs. Johnson, Governor and Mrs. Connally, and others.

As Vice President Johnson walked across the speaker's platform, I wondered what he was thinking about. No doubt he had a sense of real pride in having President Kennedy see the magnificent facilities of the Center. After all, they were the fruit of his pioneering efforts over the previous 10 years. They stood as proof of his visionary effort in getting the nation moving along the road to space.

The moment everyone had been awaiting arrived. President Kennedy rose and stood behind the podium. His hair billowed in the wind and the bright Texas sun caught the red highlights in it. He was deeply tanned and portrayed the very picture of vitality. His address was directed toward the future: the space age. He chose the occasion to again justify the nation's goal to put a man on the moon and emphasized its importance to health and medicine. The President said:

I have come to Texas today to salute an outstanding group of pioneers—the men who man the Brooks Air Force Base School of Aerospace Medicine and the Aerospace Medical Center. It is fitting that San Antonio should be the site of this Center and this School as we gather to dedicate this complex of buildings. For this city has long been the home of the pioneers in the air; it was here that Sidney Brooks, whose memory we honor today, was born and raised. It was here that Charles Lindbergh and Claire Chennault and a host of others who in World War One and World War Two and Korea, and even today, have helped demonstrate American mastery of the sky, trained at Kelly Field and Randolph Field, which form a major part of aviation history.

President Kennedy always emphasized the point that developing the means to send a man to the moon and return him would stimulate progress in many other areas that benefit mankind. He made this point again, saying:

Many Americans make the mistake of assuming that space research has no value here on Earth. Nothing could be further from the truth. Just as the wartime development of radar gave us the transistor and all that it made possible so research in space medicine holds the promise of substantial benefit to those of us who are earthbound.

After citing numerous examples of how the space program would benefit the health of those on Earth, the President concluded:

We have a long way to go; many weeks and months and years of long tedious work lie ahead. There will be setbacks and frustrations and disappointments. There will be, as there always are, pressures in this country to do less in this area as in so many others, and temptations to do something else that is perhaps easier. But this research here must go on, this space effort must go on, the conquest of space must and will go ahead. That much we know—that much we can say with confidence and conviction.

(See page 330 for the complete text of President Kennedy's address.)

Following his address, the President visited one of the research buildings to see a project involving the study of four airmen in a space cabin environment. Afterward, the crowd watched as the President's convertible moved slowly around the rest of the circular drive. President Kennedy and Vice President Johnson drove on to Kelly Air Force Base to begin what was billed as the political phase of the trip. The President's tour had started with an auspicious beginning. It was plain to all that President and Mrs. Kennedy were warmly and graciously welcomed.

The President's visit was the ultimate in recognizing how far the nation's efforts in space had come. It was also a tribute to Lyndon Johnson's crusade, beginning in the early 1950s, to develop such a capability.

The following morning was Friday, the 22nd of November. The presidential caravan was beginning to mobilize in Fort Worth. Up to that point, there had been nothing to mar the traditional hospitality of a generous state. That day, he would go to Dallas to test the political climate and address the people.

Dallas had prepared an enthusiastic visit for President and Mrs. Kennedy. Swarms of well-wishers had gathered along the route for hours, waiting for the presidential motorcade to pass. The friendly, spontaneous crowd cheered the President and First Lady as they entered the city. This had all the earmarks of one of the warmest, friendliest receptions that the President had received on his tour throughout the United States. No one could have guessed that a madman would instantly change this enthusiastic celebration into a national tragedy, and make it a very difficult time for all.

I was exceptionally fortunate to be able to participate in the monumental achievement of the century: sending men to the moon and back. However, it had its gut-wrenching side as well, bringing me face to face with national tragedies. One of those occurred on the 22nd of November, 1963. It was high noon and I was sitting at my desk at home, reviewing the research I was involved in to evaluate how weightlessness would affect men during prolonged space flight. I had just seen President Kennedy the day before at the Aerospace Medical Center in San Antonio, and was still thinking about what a glorious, red, white and blue day it had been. A vigorous John Kennedy stood at the podium restating the nation's commitment to send a man to the moon and back before 1970. His last official address as president was an eloquent restatement of his belief in the exploration of space.

The house was quiet except for the strains of classical music on the radio in the background. Suddenly, the music stopped—diverting my attention. There was an electrifying announcement: PRESIDENT KENNEDY AND GOVERNOR CONNALLY HAVE BEEN SHOT during their motorcade route through Dallas. The extent of their injuries was not known.

At first, I thought it couldn't be real. But the announcer continued to give more details and I was forced to accept reality. I hoped that neither President Kennedy nor Governor Connally was seriously injured. I sat in stunned silence at my desk waiting for more news. The announcer reported that the President had been taken to Parkland

Hospital. After an eternity, the second shock came. President Kennedy was dead and Governor Connally was in serious condition.

I wondered where Vice President Johnson was and how he was surviving the tragedy. Soon, my phone rang. A pilot at nearby Kelly Air Force Base was calling to tell me that an F-100 jet was standing by in case I needed to leave. No one knew exactly what the assassination meant or if the United States was in imminent danger of a nuclear attack. It had not been that long since the Cuban missile crisis threatened to start the world's first nuclear holocaust. For the moment, all I could do was watch the TV reports and wait.

Later that evening, Dr. Travell called, and we talked about the tragedy. I knew how much she cared for President Kennedy and what a blow this had to be. I marveled at her self-control. She told me that President Kennedy had not followed the advice of the Secret Service. He had been advised to use the bulletproof bubble for his convertible for protection, but he had refused to do so.

It was a beautiful, sunny day and the President enjoyed responding to the crowd from an open car. The friendly atmosphere had given no hint of any danger. Then suddenly, like a bolt of lightening, the assassin struck, changing a triumphal tour into a national tragedy.

****

ADDRESS BY
THE PRESIDENT OF THE UNITED STATES
at
DEDICATION CEREMONY
BROOKS AIR FORACE BASE, TEXAS
November 21, 1963

Mr. Secretary, Governor, Mr. Vice President, Senator, Members of the Congress, members of the military, ladies and gentlemen.

For more than three years, I have spoken about the New Frontier. This is not a partisan term, and it is not the exclusive property of Republicans or Democrats. It refers instead to this nation's place in history, to the fact that we do stand on the edge of a great new era, filled by both crisis and opportunity, an era to be characterized by achievements and challenge. It is an era which calls for action, and the best efforts for all those who would test the unknown and the uncertain of every phase of human endeavor. It is a time for pathfinders and pioneers.

I have come to Texas today to salute an outstanding group of pioneers—the men who man the Brooks Air Force Base School of Aerospace Medicine and the Aerospace Medical Center. It is fitting that San Antonio should be the site of this Center and this School as we gather to dedicate this complex of buildings. For this city has long been the home of pioneers in the air; It was here that Sidney Brooks, whose memory we honor today, was born and raised. It was here that Charles Lindbergh and Claire Chennault and a host of others who in World War I and World War II and Korea, and even today, have helped demonstrate American mastery of the sky, trained at Kelly Field and Randolph Field, which form a major part of aviation history. And in the new frontier of outer space, while headlines may be made by others in other places, history is being made every day by the men and women of the Aerospace Medical Center without whom there would be no history.

Many Americans make the mistake of assuming that space research has no value here on earth. Nothing could be further from the truth. Just as the wartime development of radar gave us the transistor and all that it made possible, so research in space medicine holds the promise of substantial benefit to those of us who are earthbound. For our effort in space is not as some have suggested, a competitor for the natural resources that we need to develop the earth, it is a working partner and a co-producer of these resources. And nothing makes this clearer than the fact that medicine in space is going to make our lives healthier, and happier here on earth. I give you three examples.

First, medical space research may open up new understanding of man's relation to his environment. Examination of the astronauts' physical and mental and emotional reactions can teach us more about the differences between normal and abnormal, about the causes and effects of disorientation, in metabolism which could result in extending the life span. When you study effects on our astronauts of exhaust gases which can contaminate their environment, and seek ways to alter these gases to reduce their toxicity, you are working on problems similar to those we face in our great urban centers which themselves are being corrupted by gases and which must be cleared.

Second, medical space research may revolutionize the technology and the technique of modern medicine. Whatever new devices are created, for example, to monitor our astronauts—to measure their heart activity, their breathing, their brain waves, and their eye motions at great distances and under difficult conditions, will also represent a major advance in general medical instrumentation. Heart patients may even be able to wear a light monitor which will sound a warning if their activity exceeds certain limits. An instrument recently developed to record automatically the impact of acceleration upon an astronaut's eyes, will also be of help for small children who are suffering miserably from eye defects, but are unable to describe their impairment. And also by the use of instruments similar to those used in Project Mercury, this Nation's private as well as public nursing services are being improved, enabling one nurse now to give more critically ill patients greater attention than they ever could in the past.

Third, medical research may lead to new safeguards against hazards common to many environments. Specifically, our astronauts will need fundamentally new devices to protect them from the ill effects of radiation, which can have a profound influence upon medicine and man's relation to our present environment.

Here at this center we have the laboratories, the talent, the resources to give new impetus to vital research in the life sciences. I am not suggesting that the entire space program is justified alone by what is done in medicine. The space program stands on its own as a contributor to national strength. And last Saturday at Cape Canaveral I saw our new Saturn C-1 rocket booster which, with its payload when it rises in December of this year, will be for the first time the largest booster in the world carrying into space the largest payload that any country has ever sent into space. That's what I consider.

I think the United States should be a leader. A country as rich and powerful as this, which bears so many burdens and responsibilities, which has so many opportunities, should be second to none. And in December, while I do not regard our mastery of space as anywhere near complete, while I recognize that there are still areas where we are behind, at least in one area—in the size of the booster—this year I hope the United States will be ahead. I'm for it.

We have a long way to go; many weeks, and months and years of long tedious work lie ahead. There will be setbacks and frustrations and disappointments. There will be, as there always are, pressures in this country to do less in this area as in so many others, and temptations to do something else, that is perhaps easier. But this research here must go on, this space effort must go on, the conquest of space must and will go ahead. That much we know—that much we can say with confidence and conviction.

Frank O'Connor, the Irish writer, tells in one of his books how, as a boy, he and his friends would make their way across the countryside, and when they came to an orchard wall that seemed too high, and too doubtful to try, and too difficult to permit their voyage to continue, they took off their hats and tossed them over the wall and then they had no choice but to follow them.

This nation has tossed its cap over the wall of space—and we have no choice but to follow it. Whatever the difficulties, they will be overcome; whatever the hazards, they must be guarded against. With the vital help of this Aerospace Medical Center, with the help of all those who labor in the space endeavor, with the help and support of all Americans, we will climb this wall with safety and with speed—and we shall then explore the wonders on the other side.

* *

20

A SCARE ABOUT WEIGHTLESSNESS: MOON MISSION IN DOUBT

Following our examination which included a complete history, physical examination, electrocardiogram, x-rays and laboratory tests we have arrived at the following conclusions:

1. Your general health is good.

2. You have made an excellent recovery from your heart attack of nine years ago.

3. Small kidney stones have been present for many years. They are causing you no difficulty at the present time.

4. There is no evidence indicating that your sustained vigorous mental and physical activities of the last eight and one half years have adversely influenced your health in any way.

5. From a medical point of view you can continue to live an active life in the profession of your choice.

6. General health measures should be continued. We are pleased that you have set Sunday aside for relaxation and contemplation as a break from your busy routine.

Dr. James Cain

Dr. J. Willis Hurst

Dr. Lawrence Lamb

George G. Burkley, RAdm, MC USN

Dr. Janet Travell

Left: James Webb, administrator of NASA and President Johnson in the Oval office of the White House.

20

President Kennedy often made the point that going to the moon was not an end in itself. It was the vehicle that would drive a new era of national achievement. Kennedy was a great spokesman for the space program. Even his last official address as President cited his commitment to the moon project and its overall impact. His strongest partner in the conquest of space was Lyndon B. Johnson. The Vice President was dedicated to making the nation first in space and meeting the national goal of a lunar landing. The space program lost a champion when Kennedy was assassinated, but the national effort was not diminished.

There were many obstacles yet to be overcome and questions to be answered before the goal of landing on the moon could be realized. At the time of President Kennedy's death, it wasn't even clear that man could survive in the space environment long enough to go to the moon and back.

An international space sciences meeting was held in Florence, Italy, the early part of May, 1964. The Soviets were expected to present the results of their extensive studies of manned space flight. This would provide the free world its first real opportunity to hear the conclusions of the Soviet scientists and their comments about the future of manned space flight. Soon, the impressions that were gained by the American scientists attending the meeting were to relay shock waves throughout the aerospace medical community of the United States. The Soviets reported having serious reservations about the length of time man might be able to survive in space. Specifically, the senior Soviet space medical scientist, Dr. Vasily V. Parin, expressed doubts that man could survive beyond seven days. The Soviet studies were interpreted to mean that man experienced progressive deterioration in the weightless environment.

The Soviets had launched Valery Bykovsk into space on June 14, 1963, and the space flight lasted for 119 hours and 6 minutes. Two days after his launch, June the 16th, they launched Valentina Tereshkova, the first woman to make a space flight, and her flight lasted 70 hours and 5 minutes. The Soviets reported that the cosmonauts were unable to stand upright or walk in the post-flight period and showed residual effects of space flight on the heart and circulation for as long as 10 days afterward. Some support for the Soviet observations were suggested from the shorter American flights. Both Commander Walter Schirra and—to a greater extent—Gordon Cooper, had experienced changes in blood pressure and heart rate (in Cooper's case, on the longest Mercury flight: dizziness, unsteadiness, and faintness) in the post-flight period. Parin was also concerned that the calcium losses noted during space flight were dangerous. The Soviet scientists, however, were careful to point out that all the changes they had noted in the post-flight period were temporary and reversible.

These reports unleashed a storm of controversy about the American space program. *If it could not be predicted that man could safely endure the space environment beyond a week's time, why were we planning a mission to the moon—that took longer? Surely, such plans were premature.* There were others who were cynical enough to suggest that the Soviets might have been dragging a "red herring" across the path of planned American space flights. Many of the decisions that had to be made at the highest levels about the moon mission were to be made by individuals who were not knowledgeable in biological or medical sciences. They were very concerned by the reports from the European meeting.

This was when the years of extensive studies by the team at the School paid off. Ever since the National Academy of Sciences meeting in June 1958, our group had been carefully planning, launching, and finally implementing a full-blown research project on bed rest and inactivity as the way to study some of the problems expected from weightlessness during space flight. We reasoned that when a person was lying flat in bed, perpendicular to the earth's gravity field, gravity would have very little effect upon the blood pressure and circulation, then when a person stood up, he would be susceptible to fainting. We had already gained over a year's experience with such studies, and a carefully planned program for the next two years was under way.

When a person is standing upright, the blood pressure in the arteries and the veins at the level of the heel is about 90 mm Hg higher than it is at heart level. If the blood pressure at heart level (close to the level when it is taken with an arm cuff while seated) is 110/70, it would be 200/160 at the ankle while standing. This difference is caused by the force of gravity . In the gravity-free state, these differences in pressure do not occur and its absence affects circulatory function. Gravity creates water pressure in a water tower in the same way: by the tower's height. If the tower were to fall over on its side, parallel to the earth's surface, there would be little or no water pressure. The increased pressure in the leg veins from gravity causes fluid from the blood to flow out of blood vessels into the tissues of the lower body. That is why people often have mild swelling of the feet and ankles in the evening, and by morning it is gone.

The accumulation of fluid in the muscles and other tissues in the legs actually apply pressure to the blood vessels, particularly the veins. This prevents the thin-walled veins from stretching and allowing a lot of blood to pool in the legs when you are standing. When you are walking, the rhythmic contraction of the muscles in the legs repeatedly squeezes the veins, "milking" the blood toward the heart.

If a person lies down, the pressure in the blood vessels to the lower body falls to about the same as at heart level—like the water tower lying on its side—and the fluid that has accumulated in the tissues is drawn back into the blood vessels. That increases the amount of blood in the vessels. Through a series of complex actions, while lying down, the kidneys are stimulated to eliminate water. That is why a person may eliminate a lot of urine when first put to bed rest. The same circumstances occur when you remove the influence of gravity in space flight. It is common for a healthy, young person to lose 5 pounds of fluid with just one day of bed rest. This is an example of how the body adjusts to its environment—in this case, to bed rest.

As the excess fluid is eliminated at bed rest, water is drained out of the muscles and they shrink. A few days later, the bones begin to lose calcium. This is why bed rest is bad for patients who have osteoporosis (dissolving bones) which is common in older women. When a person gets up, after several days of bed rest, he is apt to faint if he stands still. The loss of water decreases the amount of blood in the body. The tissues in the legs have lost a lot of fluid and cannot exert as much pressure against the veins. The veins stretch and that allows blood to pool in the leg veins. As a result there is not enough blood pumped to the brain and that causes a person to faint.

In the practice of medicine, having a person sit on the side of the bed and dangle his feet helps to refill the leg tissues with fluid. The muscles and other tissues then support the veins, avoiding excess pooling of blood in the legs. The gradual resumption of being upright and walking is really adapting the body again to the effects of the force of vertical gravity from head to toe, as opposed to the force of gravity being perpendicular to the spine while at bed rest.

We tried exercises and all manner of procedures to avoid these changes at bed rest. Finally, Dr. Paul Stevens, a bright, young doctor on our team, devised a method that helped. His brainchild was to encase the lower body in an airtight box. The box was connected to a mechanism to create a vacuum. When a vacuum was created in the box, it sucked blood and fluid into the lower body. An adaptation of his device was used in longer space flight to help prevent the tendency to faint on reentry after prolonged exposure to weightlessness.

The other measure that helps is the pressure suit. We studied men with and without a pressure suit for the lower body after bed rest. They would faint after bed rest when tilted feet-down on the tilt-table—or even while standing—without the suit, but not if they were wearing it. The pressure suit squeezed the lower body causing pressure against the veins to prevent pooling of blood in the legs. The suit pressure did the same thing muscles full of water normally do.

Because of the tendency to faint after space flight, someone was on each side of a returning astronaut as he walked across the deck of the ship that picked him up at sea. The problem is minor with a flight that lasts only a few hours. Glenn's weakness after his Mercury flight was mostly due to heat exposure, causing him to sweat and lose a lot of body water.

We studied other problems besides weightlessness. There were many factors involved. One of these was the simple inability to move about normally. Neither the Mercury spacecraft nor the planned Gemini spacecraft provided much room for the astronaut to move about. In addition to weightlessness, there was the problem of immobility or restriction of movement limiting activity.

Our group studied the effects of immobility alone by strapping subjects in overstuffed chairs during the daytime and not allowing them to move. They were allowed their eight hours of sleep in bed at night. These subjects did have head-to-toe gravity affecting their blood pressure and other circulatory functions. But, since they were sitting, gravity's effects were not as great as occurs when standing. It was like having a shorter water tower. Immobilization alone led to loss of function and a susceptibility to fainting when standing perfectly still in the upright position. The deterioration was not as rapid as seen at total bed rest, but it was a very definite factor. Such marked inactivity had exactly the opposite effects of a physical fitness program, as might be used for topnotch athletes.

We also studied subjects confined to a small chamber with not much more space than the Mercury and Gemini spacecraft provided. They showed a significant deterioration in exercise capacity and other circulatory functions, even though they were not weightless or at bed rest. Despite the larger size of the Soviet vehicles, the cosmonauts were strapped in their seats through most of their flights, not dissimilar to the immobility from confining healthy young men to chair rest. When larger spacecraft were developed, exercise routines were added to space flights.

By the time the Soviets expressed their concern about weightlessness, we had done bed rest studies lasting well over two weeks in over 72 subjects, and had studied ways to prevent deterioration. This wealth of information was already available when the Soviets suggested that prolonged manned space flight would be dangerous. The results of these studies were given to a staff writer for *The Journal of the American Medical Association*. They were published in May at about the same time the flap about the Soviet experiences was making headlines. Our reports did much to allay the apprehensions of our engineering and medical colleagues.

About this same time, I received a telephone call from Dr. Willis Hurst of Emory University. He called to set up a meeting with the physicians who had been involved in the care of President Johnson. He wanted to know if I could come forthwith to the White House. Willis was careful to explain that there was no immediate problem and it was strictly a routine matter. President and Mrs. Johnson wanted to know the exact status of the President's health, and how it would affect his ability to continue to carry out his duties as President. They wanted this information prior to making a final decision concerning whether he should seek the presidency in the 1964 election.

No one would have guessed that President Johnson seriously considered not running for election in view of his dynamic leadership after President Kennedy's assassination. But I had heard him say, privately, many times that he hoped he would be able to come back to Texas and "spend some time on the Pedernales" (the river in front of his ranch home) before he died. I think the good news regarding his life insurance had also helped relieve some of his concern about his future. He was really considering just one elected term. I doubt he ever seriously considered serving two terms in the White House, even though he would have been eligible to do so because of the short time he had filled out President Kennedy's term. He knew he was not immortal. That may have been a factor in his successful effort to pass so much legislation during his term, such as securing voting rights for African Americans. The President was well aware of how President Roosevelt's health had deteriorated and resulted in his death only a few months after he was reelected to a fourth term.

All of us were cognizant of the problems attendant to having a number of different physicians show up simultaneously at the White House. There was Dr. Hurst, Dr. James Cain of the Mayo Clinic, Dr. Janet Travell and Admiral George Burkley of the White House, and myself. This could easily have given rise to false rumors and national apprehension. Lesser provocation had been known to cause the stock market to go into wild gyrations. Accordingly, all of us appeared as inconspicuously as possible. I went directly to Dr. Travell's house and, that evening, by limousine to the White House. Even Dr. Travell's husband, Jack Powell, was not aware of what was going on. We told him Dr. Travell was going to accompany me to the airport: that I had just been going through town.

Those of us from out of town stayed in the White House overnight, out of sight, so we would not be seen by the press. This gave Willis and me a chance to renew our friendship and discuss areas of mutual interest. Willis was, as ever, an energetic, extremely capable and intense physician, properly seasoned with the right amount of kindness and interest in others.

I was happy to see the President and to be of any help possible to him. We reviewed his records and did a physical examination. Then we met and each of us expressed our views on his status. In such situations, there is always the danger that an important person may not be given all the facts. Most physicians want to please their patients, and the patient may be given a false sense of security. You didn't fool Lyndon Johnson with that approach, anyway. He was far too smart for that. For years, I had always told him how things really were. When he was overweight, I told him he was, and that he needed to get rid of some pounds. I didn't pat him on the back and tell him, "You are doing great." That was probably one of the reasons we got along well. His staff said, after one of his previous examinations, that he told them, "That little doctor just gave me hell." If you knew Lyndon Johnson, you knew he was pleased.

Through the years I had learned to recognize which role we were playing by how he addressed me. On friendly ranch visits, I was "Larry." When he became serious or he wanted to talk about his health, I became, "Now, Doctor." And sometimes, when I was gone, I became, "That damned little doctor."

The President was fine. It was true that he was a little heavier and his cholesterol level was a little higher than we would have liked. But considering everything, he was doing well despite the nature of his demanding job. We all agreed that there were no health reasons to prevent him from serving a full term. We signed a statement to that effect which would be available for him in the heat of the campaign, should it be needed. Later, Mrs. Johnson wrote about our conference and their thoughts about whether President Johnson should seek election or not in her book, *A White House Diary*. It was an important time of decision for them.

Slowly, plans for the upcoming Gemini mission were unveiled. Astronauts John Young and Virgil Grissom would be the first American space "twins." Soon after this came another announcement of the first relatively long flight—a four-day orbital mission—by astronauts Ed White and James McDivitt. And there was going to be a surprise with that flight.

Earlier that winter, Dr. W. Randolph "Randy" Lovelace was appointed Director of Life Sciences for NASA headquarters, replacing General Roadman of the Air Force. This was an exceptionally good appointment, considering his many years in aerospace medicine and the effective leadership he had demonstrated. He was also a well-qualified and well-recognized surgeon. The results of our studies on bed rest, its influence on how much water the body lost, and other complex factors had reached Dr. Lovelace. He had carefully reviewed our reports before he went to the Soviet Union.

Shortly after his return, he called me from his Washington office. We had a very pleasant discussion about the inactivity studies that had been done at the School. He told me a bit about what he had learned in his conversations with the Soviet scientists, including Dr. Parin. He told me that the Soviet scientists had essentially agreed with the observations our group had made and also recognized that inactivity was a major consideration in manned space flight. They, too, had observed the loss of body fluid and were working hard on problems related to inactivity and exercise. Randy commented that the results of the studies that he had received from the School—and, most importantly, the time he had received them—helped him a great deal in his discussions with a number of professional groups in the United States as well. Here he had reference to the earlier anxiety precipitated by the Soviet statements in Italy. This was the beginning of a recurrent friendly exchange of information between Randy and myself.

At one point he called me at my office: apparently completely frustrated with the difficulties associated with carrying out his duties as Director for Life Sciences. He told me he wanted to quit and go back to Albuquerque to do some "cutting and sewing." He wanted to recommend me to replace him and said I was the only person he knew who could handle the job. It was a high compliment coming from Randy Lovelace, but I was never interested in an administrative position. I only accepted the one I held at the School because it was the only way I could accomplish my first love, the projects we were doing, without too much interference. We talked, and I urged him to stay. I was glad to see that he did, until his untimely death in an airplane accident in Colorado sometime later. I was glad that we had had this opportunity during the early years of the space program to become friends.

Earlier in May, at my invitation, Dr. Chuck Berry and members of his professional staff from NASA's Manned Spacecraft Center came to the School to visit our laboratories. We reviewed extensively the results of our studies on bed rest and inactivity. The exchange of scientific information between the School and NASA had developed very well. Some of the earlier causes for hostility seemed to have run their natural course, promising for the first time a continuation of a good working relationship in a team effort. The flow of scientific articles covering the experiments that our group had carried out had begun. The accounts in the *Journal of the American Medical Association* were followed soon by additional reports in the *Aerospace Medical Journal*. The laboratory had achieved one of its highest levels of productivity.

In the fall of 1964, the Soviets proved again that they were first in space. Three Russians soared into orbit in a new, sophisticated spacecraft. The team, including one physician, clearly demonstrated that the Soviet Union was fast approaching the capability to launch teams into space and perhaps go to the moon. James Webb of NASA commented upon the occasion as follows:

There should no longer be any doubt about the Soviet Union's intentions concerning space. The recent orbiting of the three-man Voskhod spacecraft for a 24-hour period was a significant achievement. But more than that, it was a clear indication that their vigorous manned space flight program is continuing unabated.

The Soviet's *Voskhod* was a sophisticated three-man spacecraft utilizing an Earth-like atmosphere with a two-gas mixture of oxygen and nitrogen. Although the "strong man" Premier Khrushchev had, as columnist Jerry Greene said, *"kissed the cosmonauts goodbye,"* a new Soviet government greeted the space crew upon its return. The forceful little Soviet Premier had suddenly left the center stage of history, and with him—at least for a time—went the Soviet manned space spectaculars. Why? Only the Soviet regime knew. But, somewhere, a three-manned Soviet space ship waited to journey again on its conquest of the cosmos and, somewhere, Soviet cosmonauts waited for another adventure in space.

While Soviet cosmonauts would again orbit Earth, and while a Soviet cosmonaut was the first to walk in space, the dizzy string of Soviet successes appeared to have slowed down. The moon remained a distant and unconquered planet, its virginal territories unsullied by man. It would be 1967 before the United States would orbit its first three-man Apollo crew. No one could foresee then the tragedy that would further postpone the American conquest of deep space.

It was Saturday, the 7th of November, 1964. The presidential election was over and I hoped that any "General Goldwater fever" that had affected some of my high-level Air Force colleagues' thinking would subside. With the long, grueling campaign over, the President came to the School to have some dental work done. The pilot and Secret Service arrived the day before, Friday, and chose where to land the presidential helicopter. They swept the area for security purposes. His visit was somewhat different from the days when he had previously visited the School. Security was especially tight in the wake of President Kennedy's assassination.

That Saturday morning, I arrived early. Troops ringed the building where we did all of our examinations and where my office was located. Extreme care was exercised about who would pass. Of course, I already knew many of the Secret Service members guarding the President, but I was struck by the fact that even those I had never seen before knew who I was on sight. Evidently, they had photos of me. I was greeted and passed through the tight ring of security.

The presidential helicopter settled gently on the green lawn. Soon,

President Johnson was walking toward the building. There was a, "Hi, Larry," and a handshake. I escorted him to the dental area. To me, it was somewhat like old home week. A number of his personal friends whom I had come to know in earlier years were along. The President planned to go on to John Connally's ranch after his visit. Admiral George Burkley from the White House physician's staff was with the President as well. I marveled at how, after an exhausting campaign, the President was able to catnap—even while his dental work was being done. He was completely relaxed. After his dental work, I saw him for a medical checkup, and he was fine.

During December, a large group of influential American citizens were making a tour of the space activities of the nation. It included top level business executives who had been invited by *Life* and *Time* to make this trip. Jerome S. Hardy, publisher of *Life,* and James Webb, Administrator for NASA, accompanied the party. San Antonio was blessed with one of its sun-splashed December days to welcome the group. I was impressed with the searching interest of these bright, able people, taking valuable time from their busy occupations to learn for themselves the state of the nation's space effort. I was especially pleased with Mr. Webb's spontaneous enthusiasm and his warm and friendly manner as he accompanied them on their tour. This was my first opportunity to meet him in person and it was easy for me to understand why he had been selected for such an important post. The staff responded well to our visitors and the visitors responded well to the staff. Later, I was pleased to receive a letter from Mr. Hardy in which he wrote,

In retrospect, the members of LIFE's Executive Space Tour realize even more keenly how privileged they were to spend a week and a half in the hands of some of the world's outstanding space authorities. We also realize that our visit to Brooks came at a time when we were eager to hear more about men and less about machines.

Your briefing that Wednesday morning was one of the most stimulating communications sessions of the week, and we knew as we listened how fortunate the country is to have the facilities as well as the staff of dedicated people who work at Brooks. The overriding impression of our group was

one of continuing high caliber and devotion of all of the individuals concerned with the space effort.

During the tour I had an opportunity to talk briefly with Mr. Webb. Later, apparently uninhibited by the sacred aspects of military channels and believing it was still possible for two people with mutual interests to communicate on a friendly basis with each other, he wrote me a very nice letter:

...You made us all feel proud of the Air Force and of the Government service.

Prior to my visit to Brooks I had heard a great deal about you, not only from President Johnson, but from many of your admirers. I must say that both you and your work are impressive and I gained many good ideas from the visit. If you plan to be in Washington, I hope you will let me know a little in advance as I would like to arrange for you to get a somewhat broader view of some of the things we at NASA are doing in the space science field. One of the greatest values of man in space is the fact that we are moving from the laboratory type of experimentation, where we isolate smaller and smaller forces and particles and measure them, to the synthesis of this kind of information into broader structures. Our space exploration efforts are to use the great laboratory of the universe and new computer technology so that we can take many synoptic measurements of many factors and then put them together almost in real time so that we have an understanding of a very complex environment without having to isolate each factor—something that is practically impossible in this situation.

The role of man will become very much more important both on the ground and in space.

General Chuck Roadman was stationed in Colorado as the Command Surgeon of the Air Defense Command after his reassignment from the post as Director of Life Sciences at NASA headquarters. I had visited with him again at the time of President Kennedy's dedication of the Aerospace Medical Center, and on other occasions when he had visited the School. We remained good friends and he invited me to come to Colorado Springs to address the professional staff there. I flew to Colorado Springs in April, in a small, jet-powered T-39 military aircraft.

Chuck met me at the base airport (flight operations in military jargon) and we went to his home. That evening, we had a splendid dinner and a fine turnout. A good time was had by all. Mindful of the past, his introduction referred to me as being a very tough fighter: an obvious reference to the days of the difficulties related to the Slayton affair. General Niess, who had also retired to the Colorado Springs area, was seated at the speakers table—he also laughed. The magic of time had done its wondrous work. Those of us who had been involved in the situation could now look back and laugh without experiencing pain. There appeared to be nothing but friendship and harmony among the principals there that evening.

Chuck and I sat up until very early in the morning hours, long after his wife had left for bed, and thoroughly enjoyed talking about how we thought things should be done. Such occasions during my years with the Air Force occurred all too infrequently, and when they did, they always stood out in my memory as singularly enjoyable events.

21

GENERAL RELIEVED OF COMMAND

THE WHITE HOUSE

WASHINGTON

June 18, 1965

Dear Dr. Lamb:

I appreciate very much your thoughtfulness in writing to me
about your decision. While I could never encourage one who
serves the country with such value and distinction to leave
public service, I certainly can realize -- and fully appreciate --
your desire to turn to a teaching career.

In my own scale of values, there is no service higher than
that of teaching our young people. With your background of
unique experience, I am sure your contribution in this capacity
would be unusually great -- and if your services would not be
entirely lost to the Government's needs, as I am sure they
would not, I think you should go forward with your plans.

Your interest and helpfulness personally have meant much to
me. I wish for you every success and a full measure in
happiness, whatever you do.

Sincerely,

Lawrence E. Lamb, M. D.
Chief, Aerospace Medical Sciences Division
Brooks Air Force Base, Texas 78235

21 July 1965

Dr. Lawrence E. Lamb
School of Aviation Medicine
Randolph Air Force Base, Texas

Dear Larry:

I wish to take this opportunity to thank you for taking the time from your busy schedule to come to the Space Science Board's Summer Study in Space Research and make a report on your studies on weightlessness, and to otherwise participate in two days of the deliberations. I felt that your review of deconditioning as arrived at from your studies made a substantial contribution to our study.

It was a pleasure to see you again and, as Chairman of the Session in Medicine and Physiology, I again thank you for your contribution.

With my best wishes, I remain

Sincerely,

Loren D. Carlson

Astronaut Ed White, the first American to walk in space, visits the School of Aerospace Medicine.

From the left; His son, Dr. Lamb, Astronaut Ed White and General Ted Bedwell, Commander of the Aerospace Medical Center.

21

⤷ May of 1965 was a particularly pleasant time. No major crises loomed upon the horizon for the moment. During this rare interlude, I journeyed to Los Angeles to present the annual banquet address for the Los Angeles County Heart Association. California had long been one of my favorite states. I had been invited there to participate in scientific programs and had always enjoyed those exceptionally pleasant occasions. The people were gracious, hospitable, and enthusiastic.

The meeting proved to be everything that I had hoped it would be. I got to see many of my friends in the area, including Dr. Toby Freedman, then of North American Aviation. He had lost 20 pounds before he came to the banquet because he knew he would be seeing me. He was always a delight. The huge Biltmore Bowl was packed with people and a festive air prevailed. I reviewed some of the observations concerning exercise and activity compared to inactivity and weightlessness as the exact opposite ends of the spectrum. These occasions of contact with the "other world" as opposed to my relatively daily experiences of living from crisis to crisis gradually reminded me there really was another way to live. That was when I seriously considered returning to the academic environment. Since most of the programs that interested me were launched, and my major goals achieved, it appeared that I had done most of what I could do. The rest was a maintenance operation. The medical evaluations to select the Apollo astronauts for the Moon project were done.

After the years that I had spent at the school and the numerous times I had seen President Johnson—and considering our friendship—it would not have been right, or possible, to have left the School without telling him of my plans. Having firmly decided to return to the university environment, I wrote him of my decision and to express my appreciation for the many kindnesses and favors he and his family had extended to me. It wasn't long until he replied. In a letter dated June the 18th, 1965, the President wrote to me,

I appreciate very much your thoughtfulness in writing to me about your decision. While I could never encourage one who serves the country with such value and distinction to leave public service, I certainly can realize—and fully appreciate—your desire to turn to a teaching career.

In my own scale of values, there is no service higher than that of teaching our young people. With your background of unique experience, I am sure your contributions in this capacity would be unusually great—and if your services would not be entirely lost to the government's needs, as I am sure they would not, I think you should go forward with your plans.

Your interest and helpfulness personally have meant much to me. I wish for you every success and a full measure in happiness, whatever you do.

Sincerely,
Lyndon B. Johnson

It was so like President Johnson to encourage me to return to the field of education. He had been a teacher himself, and had known the joy of seeing the gleam of understanding light up young faces.

My last year at the School was truly a year of harvest. The National Academy of Sciences had a planning effort for a Mars mission that summer. This called for a review of our studies related to man-in-space obtained to that date. For me, this was an occasion for Woods Hole revisited. I was asked to return to discuss the area of weightlessness, specifically to review our ground-based studies and to project their implications for future long-term space flights. I landed at the Hyannis airport and motored on to the little community that was the frequent summer gathering of many scientific brains of the nation. The summer season was just beginning. The air was still crisp, but already boats dipped their sails and moved out across the water.

Things had not changed greatly since my trip in 1958—before any astronauts had gone into space. Then, I had come at Dr. Lovelace's invitation to talk about the selection of space crews and the problems of weightlessness. The seven years that had elapsed had proved that most of the things which had concerned us then were of importance for prolonged space flight. The problems of fainting in the post-flight period and the loss of calcium from bones had indeed proved to be areas which needed attention. Data from the Mercury project and the early experiences with the Gemini project compared well with the ground-based studies we had been doing with our bed rest experiments. The changes noted during bed rest were often referred to as "deconditioning."

The major difference was that during the intervening seven years our team had obtained a large volume of data, using a variety of experimental studies and confirming them with a suitable number of observations. There had been ample opportunity to confirm that these studies had definite counterparts in manned space flight, and represented a meaningful contribution to our knowledge.

Revisiting Woods Hole was a brief but pleasant occasion—an opportunity to see old friends again, including Dr. Stu Bonderant, Dr. Charles A. Berry and many others. Just before the meeting, our group had completed the medical examinations for the first scientist-astronaut selection for NASA. These were the first astronauts who were not pilots, but scientists with backgrounds that would help accumulate new facts about the moon. That concluded evaluating all the future astronauts who would go to the moon for the Apollo project.

Afterward, Dr. Loren Carlson, Chairman of the Sessions in Medicine and Physiology for the National Academy of Sciences and the National Research Council's Space Science Board's Summer Study, wrote me a thank you letter and to say he felt my "review of deconditioning, as arrived at from your studies, made a substantial contribution to our study."

Dr. Herbert Shepler also wrote, in part,

I want to take this opportunity of telling you how much we appreciated your very fine presentation to the Summer Study Group. It was certainly appropriate, timely, and concise, and brought forth very favorable comments from all who heard it. We feel that you made a very fine contribution to our efforts at Woods Hole this summer.

I would also like to thank you for the compilation of current material on bed rest studies, etc., which you sent us. As you may have noted, I had an additional copy made and then placed both copies in our reference library at Woods Hole. Our librarian informed me that it was used quite extensively for reference during the Study.

I commented to some of my friends at the meeting that I was seriously considering leaving the School. They were apparently shocked at my comment. My decade of being associated with the medical efforts supporting the man-in-space program had so identified me with the project it was assumed I would stay at the School indefinitely. While a number of different personalities in the Air Force had come and gone from the scene during those 10 years, I had supplied a thread of continuity and a personal identification for many of the programs carried out by the School of Aerospace Medicine. I prepared a written summary of the ground-based studies applied to the problem of weightlessness for man-in-space flight which was published in the proceedings of the Scientific Sessions of the National Academy of Sciences.

One of the great thrills of the summer that cheered the nation was astronaut Ed White's spectacular space walk. Once again, the Soviets had beaten us with an earlier walk in space. Floating through space, on the end of a tether at orbital velocity, was called EVA (extravehicular activity) and, whatever it was called, Ed White did it well. A whole world watched and listened while he performed this spectacular feat. The unbelievable color movies gave the entire world an opportunity to see a man speeding past Earth in outer space—unshackled from the forces of gravity—achieving one of man's oldest dreams of soaring far above the Earth like a bird, floating through the vistas of space. In that short span of time, Ed White became the nation's hero.

Ed White claimed San Antonio as his home town. He was born in an Army Hospital at old Fort Sam Houston. It was there, on June the 17th, 1965, that the Alamo City turned out to give him a hero's welcome. He spoke to the populace in the downtown area and motored on to the Aerospace Medical Center. The events for "Ed White Day" at the School were reminiscent of an earlier day when a youthful President, also with red-brown hair, came to speak of men and space. Now, one of these men had come to this same spot, returning from the nation's most advanced man-in-space adventure to that date. The slender, young astronaut stood behind the same podium that President Kennedy had used to deliver his last official address. He returned to thank the people at the school for the many things they had done to make his space flight possible. At the conclusion of his address, he was given a handsomely framed picture of President Kennedy standing behind that same podium.

After the ceremonies were over, a small reception was held in the patio of the large building used for classes and lectures. As soon as Ed arrived, his quick eye caught sight of me and he came over and seized my hand. It was great to see him again. We had much to say, but very little time in which to say it. We talked about his weight loss in space, and how much of it must have been due to water loss. He told me he had lost 9 pounds in space but regained almost all of it the first day after he returned to Earth. We talked again about exercise and physical fitness. Ed told me that he was in the best physical condition he had ever been in before he made his space flight. In Ed's case, that would have represented a fitness level equivalent to an Olympic athlete.

I considered Ed's visit as our team's personal reward for one of the areas of our research. The biodynamics group at the School that did centrifuge studies, and the team doing bed rest studies teamed up to determine tolerance to g forces after prolonged periods of bed rest. The goal was to establish how high horizontal g loads like those encountered in reentry from space flights would affect man. A series of studies done before and after four weeks of strict bed rest had given us the necessary information to be reasonably certain that the reentry profile planned for a manned orbital space flight would not cause serious difficulties after exposure to prolonged weightlessness.

Later, I learned from Dr. Berry at the Woods Hole meeting that the NASA team used this information in planning the reentry phase for Ed White's and Jim McDivitt's space flight. The on-board computer used to land the spacecraft exactly in the pre-planned area at sea during reentry developed a malfunction. There were two alternatives available to the ground crew covering the space flight: they could either use a higher level of exposure to gravity loads than previously planned during reentry, or they could give up the idea of a specific landing area at sea, which might produce some problems in recovery.

On the basis of the information from our experiments, it was decided to go ahead and use higher g loads for reentry, since the levels they needed were well within the range our studies had shown were safe. This enabled them to bring the Gemini spacecraft down in the pre-planned area and immediately recover the astronauts from the sea. These were the kind of results I liked to see from our team's work—the acquisition of knowledge that had a direct application in protecting our astronauts' and space pilots' safety, even during the unexpected.

Almost like a replay of President Kennedy's visit, Ed White went to the same altitude chamber that President Kennedy had visited a year-and-a-half earlier. We walked together to the chamber area with Ed White's son at his side. At that particular time, our group was continuing our studies on hypoxia (low oxygen) during bed rest. I explained the experiment to Ed and he took the headphones, as had President Kennedy, and spoke briefly with the young airmen inside the chamber. Ed White told them how important the contributions they were making were to him and his fellow astronauts in being able to carry out their space missions. This was a real morale boost for the airmen participating in that kind of a boring contribution to the nation's space effort.

We walked on from the space chamber and passed out to the street. The time had come for Ed to go. We paused, shook hands with each other, and bid our good-byes. That was the last time I would ever see Ed White. Once again, I had seen someone who was important to me—vibrant and healthy—for the last time, as he visited the School. Ironically, the similar pattern of the ceremonies for Ed White's visit to that earlier visit by President Kennedy carried with it a prophecy of the future, too grim for the imagination, and totally out of keeping with the festive air that occasioned his visit.

That fall, one of my most cherished goals was reached. W.B. Saunders, one of the largest and most prestigious publishers of medical textbooks, published my large textbook on electrocardiography and vectorcardiography. It contained much of what I had learned about that subject during my 10 years of research. The preparation and publication of the book had not been a simple task. I had to draw upon all of my training and experience throughout my earliest years in cardiology. I was determined that the things I had learned from my unique experience to study this large population of Air Force aircrews would not be lost to medical knowledge. The half-million electrocardiograms that had been studied, and the studies of people under a variety of conditions, all provided important facts that could readily be used by the medical community. With its publication, I had a sense of having met an obligation—a reporting to my colleagues of these studies. This was to become one of W. B. Saunders' most popular textbooks and helped many doctors to understand electrocardiography. Even 20 years later, an internist from Los Angeles who was attending a medical meeting in San Antonio told me that he learned how to interpret electrocardiograms from my textbook.

The mellowing days in October brought still another harvest, and this was in recognition of the achievements of the Aeromedical Consultation Service. I had organized the first formal consultation service at the School. For many years it had provided support to the medics responsible for the care of the flying population through out the Air Force. Our studies resulted in many changes in rules concerning medical safety for flying. The consultation service had also provided the medical evaluation program for test pilots, astronauts, and space pilots.

The public information personnel at the Aerospace Medical Division did some paper and pencil work and found out that the evaluations of air crews at the School saved the Air Force over 50 million dollars a year. Prior to the development of the service, a large number of skilled pilots had to be removed from flying duties because there was no good way to resolve their problems and to be certain that they didn't compromise flying safety.

The consultation service resulted in salvaging almost half of these people and returning them to the cockpit and their careers. The study found 1,273 rated personnel out of 2,608 evaluated were returned to flying duties. Each one of the individuals represented a major financial investment in his training and experience. Some of the experienced command pilots responsible for some of our major aircraft represented investments of over 1.2 million dollars each.

In recognition of the importance of the service, I was invited to the Department of Defense Noon News Conference in the Pentagon to present a briefing. Many of the newsmen promptly dubbed the School as the "Medical Court of Last Resort." The briefing was well received by top-level officials from the Department of Defense. It also gave me an opportunity to talk to them a bit about exercise and physical fitness as a preventive program in the control of heart disease. Such efforts had been very successful in improving the health of a lot of our flying personnel. A certain number of these individuals, after adequate improvement, had been able to continue their flying careers. This would have been impossible otherwise. The pleasant fall day and convivial atmosphere was a welcome contrast to some of the earlier experiences I had survived in the Pentagon, related to the wrangling between the Department of Defense and NASA over primacy in the nation's man-in-space mission.

Fall ushered in another significant event. For some time there had been a desire to see if difficulties related to the Aerospace Medical Division could be corrected by a change in personnel. Reassignment was one of the solutions commonly used when there were problems in the Air Force. Surgeon General Bohannon told me that he had offered General Bedwell the post as Surgeon for the Pacific Air Command and he had refused it. I was well aware that General Bedwell had not been an active supporter of my team's efforts or me. Some of his immediate staff confided to me that he spent a lot of time trying to check my activities to the point that it was "harassment."

Evidently, the Air Force Systems Command under General

Schriever had lost confidence in General Bedwell and had requested some changes in the Aerospace Medical Division Headquarters. I do not know what all the facts or reasons for this were, but I am sure there were many more than I ever knew.

In any case, General Don Wenger, formerly of the Surgeon General's Office, had been reassigned as the Command Surgeon to the Air Force Systems Command Headquarters, which immediately supervised General Bedwell's division headquarters. He flew to San Antonio to meet with General Bedwell and other members of the division headquarters staff to announce imminent and major personnel changes.

There had been a lot of backstage shuffling going on for several months. General James Humphreys, formerly commander of the Wilford Hall Hospital at Lackland AFB, was serving in Vietnam. General Tom Crouch, the new hospital commander, had made some quiet trips to General Wenger's office at Andrews AFB. Apparently, General Bedwell had become quite concerned over these various gambits. His immediate staff was given new guidelines about telephone calls to and from Air Force Systems Command Headquarters. Under this tense atmosphere, some of the staff and other players in the game suspected their telephone calls were being monitored—probably not true. It was difficult to know who was doing what to whom, and what undercover agreements had been made. It was the "time of the long knives," and no one was safe.

One late afternoon, a plane bearing General Wenger and other members of General Schriever's staff swept across the runway at Kelly AFB at the edge of San Antonio. General Bedwell was standing stiffly on the ground, waiting for General Wenger. An effort had been made earlier to set up a meeting at Wilford Hall Hospital at Lackland AFB. General Bedwell, as division commander, demanded that the meeting take place at the division headquarters. The scene was set for the bloodletting. They all squeezed into their Air Force vehicles, General Wenger stoically puffing on his aromatic cigar. In tense silence, the vehicles moved down the highway, on to Brooks AFB and the Division Headquarters.

Soon, most of the players were assembled in General Bedwell's large conference room. Nobody laughed and nobody smiled. General

Wenger laid his well-chewed, soggy cigar in a nearby ashtray and began the announcement. He had come at General Schriever's request to announce that General Bedwell would be relieved of command. It was anticipated that General Humphreys would return from Vietnam the following summer to be the new Division Commander. In an unprecedented move, an interim commander would be appointed. General Crouch would be both commander of the Wilford Hall Hospital and the division headquarters for the Center. Apparently, that was why General Wenger had requested the meeting be held at the Hospital. Something of considerable importance—what, I don't know—must have occurred to replace General Bedwell so swiftly with a temporary appointment.

When General Bedwell asked what his new assignment would be, he was told that it was not a matter for either General Schriever or his staff, but the responsibility of the Surgeon General. The Director of Research at Division Headquarters was also relieved of duty, effective immediately, and other personnel changes at high levels were announced. The air was charged with electricity and hostility oozed from the assembled players. The event reminded me of when President Truman flew to meet and to fire General McArthur during the Korean War.

Fate had been kind to me and I was out of town on announcement day—a fact I did not regret. A dinner party scheduled for the evening and attended by General Wenger, General Bedwell and a number of the other personnel involved in the reshuffle, soon became known as "The Last Supper."

During the following months, the power struggle between factions within the Air Force Medical Service continued unabated. For once, I was able to watch a crisis with a certain degree of detachment. My decision to leave had already been made, and it was only a question of deciding where and exactly what day. My activities during this eleventh year were directed almost solely toward finishing as many of the tasks I had begun in the preceding decade as possible. Shortly after Christmas, General Bedwell departed and was assigned to the Surgeon General's Office. General Crouch became the interim commander for the Division Headquarters until General Humphreys returned.

General Bedwell had many good qualities. In my opinion, he

was unfortunate in having been assigned as the Aerospace Medical Division Commander. He didn't appreciate the need for a free flow of communications and ideas so essential to such an environment. He had followed the concepts of a highly structured, rigid management method characteristic of his past military experiences.

Also, the School was dependent upon a large number of civilian scientists. He didn't seem to appreciate that civilians had any role within a military organization. I must have been a particularly painful thorn in his side because I was a civilian scientist established under Public Law 313. In the civil service ranking system, that was equivalent to his rank in the military. He had achieved his rank by years of service and I was a young whippersnapper. Worse, I occupied an administrative post within the chain of command, which usually would have been occupied by someone in uniform. He couldn't have me transferred to some place like Thule, Greenland. I'm sure I didn't help matters since I recognized rather early what his attitude was by the actions that came from the division headquarters as soon as he became the commander.

As the events of the year unfolded, Colonel Ellingson, the School Commander, had kept his ear to the ground, his nose to the wind and looked carefully at his future. He was 50 years old, had a distinguished military career and every reason to expect to be promoted to general officer's rank. But he had suffered greatly under the constant attacks and intrusions on his prerogatives by the division headquarters during the Bedwell days. The uncertain possibility of his advancement in view of these recent years compelled him to choose another career path. We discussed it on many occasions as we were good friends. With his excellent background in education, as well as his professional credentials, he was quite naturally offered a post as a professor and chairman of a department at Ohio State University. That spring, he announced his imminent retirement.

The Vietnam War delayed General Humphreys return, and General Chuck Roadman would become the new commander of the division, an appointment that I was pleased to hear. However, I had already made my decision to leave.

22

A GLORIOUS REENTRY

From the left: Dr. and Mrs. Hubertus Strughold, Dr. Lamb and Marie Fehmer, secretary to President Johnson.

Colonel James Nutall, Commander of the School of Aerospace Medicine, on the right, presents Dr. Lamb with a framed picture of President Kennedy giving the dedication speech the day before he was assassinated. The board for the backing of the picture was from the platform President Kennedy was standing on.

22

⌒ One reason I decided to return to a university environment was to apply what I had learned in studying a healthy population—astronauts and aircrews—to patients with diseases. I wanted to use our exercise testing procedures to study coronary artery disease and to evaluate the effects of such procedures as heart surgery. Also, I was interested in using the monitoring techniques that we had used in healthy people for sick patients, during and after surgery or in other circumstances. The idea of teaching medical students, interns, and residents again appealed to me.

I had been actively teaching during my 11 years at the School. Each year I taught a week's course in electrocardiography and a short course in cardiology, as applied to the needs of managing heart problems in Air Force flying personnel, to the residents in aviation medicine. They were flight surgeons making a career of the Air Force. I gave shorter courses to over 300 young doctors entering the Air Force each year who would be aviation medical examiners. That way, I came to know many graduates from medical schools from all over the United States and some from other countries.

My future role at the School would have to be a maintenance activity. We had done the medical evaluations for Gemini, Apollo, and the first scientist astronauts. The consultation service was well established and would continue to do essentially the same things. The problems with NASA-MSC no longer existed, and I was looking for a new challenge.

Why didn't I just leave much earlier, in view of the constant turmoil—especially as related to the Slayton problem? Actually, those events were all the more reason I had to stay the course. I couldn't just walk away without doing everything I could to support the nation's man-in-space objectives. It was too important to do the basic ground studies that we did, which proved to be so essential in future man-in-space activity. Once I had done all I could do, I felt it was "Mission accomplished."

During that year, I visited three university medical centers: the University of California in Los Angeles (UCLA); Duke University in Durham, North Carolina; and Baylor College of Medicine in Houston. I believed all were outstanding medical centers, and I was offered an appointment as a professor of medicine at each of the three universities. One of the things that attracted me to Duke, in addition to its excellent reputation, was Dr. Eugene Stead, chairman of the department of medicine. We were friends and I admired his professional reputation. However, when I visited Duke at his invitation, I learned that he planned to retire the following year and they were looking for a new chairman for the department. That left a degree of uncertainty in my mind regarding who would be in charge.

At Baylor, Ray Pruitt was the chairman of the department of medicine and also the Vice President for Medical Affairs. He was a friend and I knew him to be an honest and fair individual, and thought this would be a good place to locate.

My first duty was to my immediate staff—to try to provide ample opportunity for them to complete their own areas of research. My second obligation was to complete as many of the things that I had started as I could. Finally, I owed it to myself to depart on a good note. The change in command at the division headquarters was a big step in that direction. I wanted to eliminate, as much as possible, any element of doubt or rumor concerning my impending resignation.

I decided to make a simultaneous announcement in written form to incoming School Commander, Colonel James Nutall, who was just arriving to replace Colonel Ellingson, and to General Roadman, the new commander for the division headquarters. This would avoid any thought that I was unhappy with either, since we would not have had an opportunity to work together yet. The timing was perfect to cause the least amount of trauma and speculation.

I met with Colonel Nutall shortly after he received my memorandum. He was an old friend and a well-chosen successor to Colonel Ellingson. The opportunity to have worked with him would have been a pleasant one. And I would have enjoyed working with General Roadman. Colonel Nutall and I discussed my future plans and the changes that would be necessary. Other than the German scientists who had arrived at the end of World War II, I had been at the School longer than any physician on the staff, either civilian or military.

A significant number of my staff arranged to transfer to other locations. The small group of civilian physicians within the Clinical Sciences Division also left. The team that had worked so effectively together was breaking up.

I was pleasantly surprised by the large volume of thoughtful letters from many colleagues I had met during the preceding 11 years—from within the Air Force, from other services, from NASA, and from university colleagues. Some notes came from pilots. One, which amused me, came from Smitty, the test pilot Dr. Travell had seen with me some years before. We had developed appropriate nicknames for each other. He often addressed me as "Boy Cardiologist." And, because of his newly acquired knowledge on the management of musculoskeletal problems from his personal experiences, I always referred to him as the "Quack." He wrote,

> *Boy Cardiologist,*
> *Heard just a few minutes ago of your imminent departure from the Air Force. I feel the Air Force is suffering a great loss, but don't let this impress you too much as I have never been noted for perception. Seriously, Larry, sorry to see you leave us.*
> *Best wishes to your new future. Come visit us whenever you pass through Washington, D.C.*
> *"The Quack"*

Although I received some personal letters from General Bohannon, who had been promoted by then to the rank of lieutenant general (the first surgeon general of the United States Air Force to hold a three-star rank), he took time to write a more official letter:

Dear Larry:

Your impending departure from the Air Force family represents a great loss for our Medical Service and is a source of deeply felt regret on my part.

During your association with the Air Force you developed methods which greatly improved the reliability of selection and protection of many previously unexplored environments. Your contributions have enabled man to proceed with confidence into every advanced flight and space operations.

Your extensive original research, including well designed scientific methods for analysis of human capability, have provided definitive and dependable means in evaluating and predicting human responses. Your efforts have thus provided the basis whereby the United States has successfully met the challenge to space exploration.

Air Force flight operations have depended heavily upon and profited greatly from your monumental contributions in the field of Aerospace Medicine. Concurrently you have provided the medical community, worldwide, with long sought answers to many problems in clinical medicine.

Your contributions as a physician, teacher, and author and your untiring search for a scientific truth have placed you among the great men of medicine.

I wish you every success in your continued endeavors. I congratulate you upon your new appointment and upon your choice of Baylor University as a place for continuing your work.

I have the reassuring realization that men of your stature, although nominally associated with a particular institution, actually belong to the medical world at large. In this light I feel confident that we will continue to benefit by your wise counsel.

Sincerely yours,

R. (Dick) Bohannon

As my official correspondence with the Office of the Surgeon General ended, the last letter I received was somewhat different from an earlier one from General Niess, which had included an extensive distribution list.

I also received a welcome letter from Colonel Ellingson from his new post, in part, as follows:

Dear Larry,
Your fine letter and the copy of your letter of resignation were waiting for me when I checked in at the office. Your kind remarks were indeed appreciated. You may be extremely proud of your contributions to medicine and to the Air Force during your service at the School of Aerospace Medicine, and I am pleased you feel that I helped a bit. I must say that it was an interesting experience for both of us. I am certainly grateful for the support of you and others at the School.
Wish I might have been around to hear the reactions to your letter.
Sincerely
s/Hal

Since I was officially a consultant to NASA and had had a continuing obligation to NASA, I also sent a copy of my letter of resignation to James Webb at NASA Headquarters. He wrote a very nice letter in response:

Dear Dr. Lamb:
This is much delayed, but I still want to write to say that your letter of May 13 with the enclosed memorandum of resignation generates a strong reciprocal feeling of admiration for your own work, and I must admit some concern as to the great loss to the Air Force which your leaving entails. I know of no one connected with aviation or space whom I admire more or is more universally admired than you. I have understood the strong desire you have had to utilize the existence of the records on Air Force personnel for your research program and for the projection of knowledge and operational improvements. Also, I believe I can understand your desire to extend and expand this base of knowledge at Baylor. I really wish it were possible within the structure of the United States government to offer you the expanded and continuing opportunity which you seek.

Do you plan to be in Washington anytime soon? I would certainly like to sit down for a long conversation as to the things you have in mind and how I, personally, and NASA, as an organization, can continue to work with you and provide through this for increased strength for both our efforts. Also, I am most anxious to do all possible to strengthen Air Force operations and help create the kind of opportunities in-house in Air Force installations that would offer the kind of challenges men like you seek. I have had some talks with senior Air Force personnel about this and would welcome an opportunity to work with you on it.

Sometimes help toward the solution of a problem can be accomplished by friends of good will working from the outside and assisting those still on the inside. If you think of anything that I can do, or you and I together can do, I will certainly extend every capacity I have in this direction.

Also, I should like very much to find a way to continue the close association and interest which you have had in the field of aerospace medicine through some relationship with NASA that is not inconsistent with your obligations at Baylor. Not only can you be of the greatest help to Bob Gilruth and his associates at the Manned Spacecraft Center, but I am sure you can contribute a very great deal to the concepts and problems, as well as opportunities for leadership, which come to Bob Seamans and myself here at the national level.

The nation needs to utilize men like you to the fullest of their ability and I would welcome the opportunity to help contribute to this result in your case.

Most sincerely,
s/ Jim Webb
Administrator

Oddly, I realized much later, I did not answer Mr. Webb's gracious letter. Why? I am not certain. By the time I had received the letter I was already at Baylor and had turned my thoughts toward new goals. The 11 years of struggle had resulted in a bad case of "burn out." But I should have responded.

I was invited to the LBJ ranch for a farewell dinner with the Johnson family. Once more, I drove down the curving drive below the dam, passed by the security guards, and to the lovely old ranch house that was the Johnson home.

Mrs. Johnson was her usual warm and gracious self. The President had gained weight and seemed preoccupied. The heavy burden of the Vietnam War was ever on his mind. At moments like this, when there were no immediate observers around, you could learn what he really thought. There was no press or others that he was speaking to. He was simply speaking his mind. In the middle of dinner he started commenting on the Vietnam War and I was struck by one of his remarks, "I can just see some Indiana boy dropping a bomb on one of those Russian oil tankers at Haiphong and there would be hell to pay."

I interpreted the President's remarks to mean he wanted to keep the Vietnam War from escalating into World War III as a result of a confrontation with the Soviets. Lyndon Johnson had inherited the burdens of the war from the previous administration. I knew from his numerous remarks that the war had kept him from doing so many things he wanted to do for the country. The simple truth was, he never wanted the war. He hated it.

The war had another cruel effect on the President that those who knew him understood. Lyndon Johnson wanted to be loved. He was a care giver, a man who liked to do things for other people and wanted the whole nation to love him. Unfortunately, that usually doesn't happen to any President in his lifetime. The divisiveness and hate that grew out of the Vietnam War gnawed at his soul. How he must have cringed ever time he heard, "Hey, hey, LBJ. How many kids have you killed today?"

I discussed President Johnson's medical support—for the time he would be in the San Antonio area, after I was gone—with Admiral George Burkley, then the White House physician. I recommended it should be provided by the medicine department at Brooke Army Medical Center at Fort Sam Houston in San Antonio. That was arranged. They had an excellent staff and I had been a consultant to their cardiology service during the years I was in San Antonio.

There were the usual farewell parties marking my departure. The enlisted personnel in the Clinical Sciences Division had their own party for me in San Antonio. I considered this to be a special honor as such recognition for the "brass" was unusual. They took pictures and prepared an album of them for me. They were all my friends and were used to having me check their work, seeing what they were doing, or listening to whatever was important to them. I would miss them all. They had given me a nickname—because of my insistence on things being top quality, I was known as, "Old Iron Ass."

The Division Headquarters and the School of Aerospace Medicine had their farewell party for me at the Officer's Club. General Roadman was there. Colonel Nutall was there. Marie Fehmer, President Johnson's secretary, was with me. Dr. Chuck Berry and his wife, Dell, came over from MSC for the occasion. I was pleasantly surprised that Astronaut Joe Engle also came over to say good-bye. Joe was a friend and one of the nation's top test pilots. Before being selected for the astronaut program, he was a pilot for the X-15 rocket plane. He was also one of the best examples of preventive cardiology. He had significantly lowered his cholesterol level with a good diet and exercise program.

On this occasion, I was presented with my own framed picture of President Kennedy delivering his dedication address for the Aerospace Medical Center—with the backing made from a piece of the platform where he had stood that historic day.

I had made some enemies during my 11 years with the Air Force—mostly ones you could be proud to have as enemies—but I had made many more friends. I had worked with some difficult people and many more really terrific ones. I would always treasure them in the years to come. As I looked back, it was quite remarkable that the Air Force medical service gave a 28-year-old whippersnapper the responsibility and opportunity afforded to me when I first arrived in the Surgeon General's Office 11 years earlier. I had come a long way from a four-room shack in Kansas as a child, mired in poverty, to work with national leaders and to play a meaningful role in the greatest adventure of this century. Now, it was time for a new beginning.

23

THE EAGLE HAS LANDED

23

Just six months after I had left the School, the nation received a terrible shock. I was devastated. It happened at the Cape, the evening of January 27, 1967. The groundwork by NASA and the thousands who had contributed to the goal of landing a man on the moon had been accomplished, but the goal itself had not yet been achieved. The huge new Apollo vehicle was finally ready. It was to be the United States' first three-man spacecraft. Many at NASA, including the astronauts, had complained about some of the workmanship while it was being built. Nevertheless, it was readied for its maiden voyage into space. It had undergone numerous tests; finally it was time for a last, full dress-rehearsal. All the personnel who would be involved in the flight were in place. The astronauts were inside, in their suits, exactly as they would be at the time of launch. The hatch was sealed and Apollo was filled with 100 percent oxygen at Earth's atmospheric pressure.

The checkout continued for hours as numerous glitches were found. During the final stage of the checkout, one of the sloppy wire connections produced a spark. That turned into a glow in the oxygen enriched atmosphere. Soon, the flame devoured all the flammable material within the spacecraft and Apollo became a ball of fire. The hatch could not be removed. In minutes, it was all over. The three astronauts—Ed White, Virgil Grissom and Roger Chaffee—were dead.

I have never been one to tolerate death easily. The combination of the loss of these vibrant young men and what the catastrophe meant to the United States' moon mission was a heavy blow. Apollo had burst into flames on the ground. The brave astronauts did not die in space, but on Earth. This was a direct result of the 100 percent oxygen environment combined with shoddy workmanship on the vehicle itself. From the beginning, the American space vehicles utilized 100 percent oxygen. That did not pose a threat during space flight when the cabin pressure was reduced to about one-third the atmospheric pressure at sea level—but at Earth environment it can be dangerous.

The space program and the nation had lost three gallant men. I knew all three of them, but I knew Ed White best of all and considered him a personal friend. I brooded over the event and wondered if it could have been prevented. I remembered the last day I had seen Ed, at the School, when he was accorded a hero's welcome. I thought about him rushing over to see me and excitedly telling me about how much weight he had lost during space flight and how quickly he regained it after he returned to Earth. I remembered how he had his young son with him as we walked between the buildings at the Center. I would miss him. The catastrophe would delay the man-in-space program, but it would not stop it. Ed White would have wanted it to go forward.

The United States had lost valuable time in the race with the Soviets to reach the moon, but soon the Soviets would have their own tragedy. They launched *Soyuz 1* on April 23, 1967, piloted by Vladimir Komarov. Technical difficulties in flight made it appear impossible for him to return to Earth. His wife was brought to the monitoring facility to bid him good-bye, and he was promised a hero's funeral. But he almost made it. He reached the final stage of descent and had deployed the spacecraft's chute for landing. Unfortunately, the chute twisted on itself and did not open. *Soyuz 1* crashed to the ground, killing the brave cosmonaut. The tragedy would slow the Soviet space program as well.

In the aftermath of the Apollo fire, NASA had the vehicle reengineered. The fire demonstrated why nothing less than perfection could be tolerated. The success of the moon mission required zero tolerance for sloppy workmanship. It took 21 months for a new Apollo to be readied. Everyone was happy with the new spacecraft. It was first tested in unmanned space flight in November, 1967. A huge Saturn 5 rocket launched it into orbit. This was followed by two more unmanned space flights.

Finally, Apollo 7 was launched with a three-man crew on October 11, 1968. Other than bickering between Wally Shirra and Mission Control, the flight was picture-perfect. Although Shirra had a reputation of being a fun guy, he could be testy and he liked to be in control. He was in command of Apollo 7 and took exceptions to changes being made in the flight plan on the spur of the moment by Mission Control. He was a very capable astronaut and had learned the value of eliminating all but those aspects of a flight that were essential to the success of the mission. That way he could concentrate on turning in an A-one performance. He had proved this originally during the Mercury project. There were glitches in all the first Mercury flights, but when the nation needed a shot in the arm with a perfect flight, Wally Shirra delivered with Mercury's *Sigma 7*. He delivered again with the first manned checkout of Apollo.

NASA was preparing for a manned lunar landing in incremental steps. Finally, a decision was made to leave Earth orbit and go directly to the moon. The idea was to orbit the moon and take pictures for the future landing. Frank Borman, Jim Lovell, and Bill Anders boarded Apollo 8 and blasted off into space on December 21, 1968. For the first time, a manned spacecraft would not just orbit Earth, but would accelerate fast enough to escape the pull of gravity and move into deep space. They sailed through the emptiness of space and orbited the moon. It was a spectacularly successful flight. Apollo 8 sailed past the back side of the moon in utter darkness and, as they came around the moon into the light, they looked out over the lunar horizon and saw the brilliant colors of Earth in the distance. The vivid blue Earth was shrouded in an irregular white cloak of the atmosphere. One of the world's famous pictures from space was of the curved lunar horizon topped with the blackness of empty space, and just above this was the spectacular view of planet Earth.

The lunar orbit of Apollo 8 could not have occurred at a better time. It provided an upbeat end to a year of turmoil. The Vietnam

War was going badly, resulting in widespread discontent and rioting. Riots occurred in cities throughout the country in the wake of Martin Luther King's assassination. Many universities became battlegrounds. Senator Robert Kennedy was assassinated in June, and there were bloody riots at the Democratic National Convention in Chicago. Then, millions of Americans listened to a message of hope from the moon as the astronauts read from the Bible. The fantastic achievement was a Christmas gift to the world.

Of course, I formed opinions of the astronaut candidates as they came, once or several times, to the School for evaluation. I reviewed the complete reports by the various specialists, including the psychological testing and psychiatric evaluations. All had intelligence tests done as part of the examinations.

I was quite impressed with Frank Borman. He was one of the brightest and most capable of the test pilots that we evaluated. He was also about the closest to perfect health of any of the candidates. Jim Lovell was equally capable and had a wonderful personality. I followed his space career closely, and would know Jim again when he was the Chairman of the President's Council for Physical Fitness and Sports. I was a medical consultant for the Council from the Kennedy through the first Bush Administrations. I often gave the keynote address for meetings for teachers sponsored by the Council and for national and international meetings. Jim's heroic efforts became well-known in his epic adventure in Apollo 13, the one lunar flight that sustained an explosion in space, nearly ending in a disaster.

NASA's next step was to simulate anticipated lunar operations in Earth orbit with Apollo 9. The lunar excursion module (LEM) that would be used to land and take off from the moon was tested in space above the lunar surface with an Apollo 10 flight. The final steps had been completed. Landing on the moon was next.

Apollo 11, *Columbia*, would carry the first men in the history of the world to land on the moon. *Columbia* was launched July 16, 1969. A mass of humanity began to converge upon the Cape as many as two weeks before the launch. They came in vehicles of all descriptions. Nearly one million people clogged the roads and beach areas to watch the event of the century. There were thousands on boats of all descriptions on the Indian and Banana rivers. As the morning sun warmed the area, many men stripped to the waist and stood in shorts, squinting into the sun. It was reported that 1,782 journalists were there to cover the event. Over 800 of these were from countries from all over the world, speaking everything from English to Asiatic tongues.

All manner of dignitaries were there: senators, governors, ambassadors, and those from the entertainment world, including Johnny Carson and Jack Benny. Charles Lindbergh was there, too. One of the distinguished guests who most deserved to be there was Lyndon B. Johnson, the man who had spearheaded the nation's space program from its inception in the early 1950s. He was representing President Nixon. He stood there in his dark blue suit, light blue tie and white shirt, with a white handkerchief in his coat pocket, also squinting into the sun. Lady Bird was by his side in her sleeveless polka-dot dress, wearing sunglasses and an unpretentious straw hat.

In the darkness of the early morning, the giant Saturn 5 rocket stood on its launch pad, a towering 363-foot structure with the comparatively small Apollo 11 spacecraft nestled at its peak. Saturn 5 was bathed in floodlights that gave it the appearance of an enormous monument—which it was: a monument to man's first journey to land on the moon.

Even though *Columbia* appeared tiny aloft the giant rocket, it was not small. It was 12 feet high, 13 feet in diameter and conical in shape. The three astronauts were inside. Immediately below *Columbia* was the service module, 12.8 feet in diameter and 22 feet long. It contained the engines to power the spacecraft. Below the service module was the LEM adapter. It contained the LEM (*Eagle*) that would transport the two astronauts on the surface of the moon. The LEM itself was 21 feet long and 11 feet in diameter. All of this was sitting on top of the largest rocket ever built: Saturn 5.

Neil Armstrong, Edwin Aldrin, and Michael Collins were lying on their astronaut couches, waiting for the eventual blast-off into space. The crowd standing in the morning sun buzzed with small talk as the clock ticked away. Then, a voice boomed out "T-minus-two minutes;" just two minutes until launch. A hush fell over the crowd and the morning was still. The countdown began and, suddenly, the huge engines of Saturn 5 ignited. The roar of the engines was awesome—even the ground shook. Slowly, ever so slowly, the giant rocket lifted from its pad and rose above the plume of its exhaust flames. As it rose off the pad it shook off over 1,000 pounds of ice that had frozen to its sides from the cooling effects of the rocket fuel.

Columbia orbited Earth until Houston cleared it for "translunar insertion," meaning the spacecraft could speed up sufficiently to escape the pull of earth's gravity and begin its epic journey through deep space to the moon.

The Soviets were not out of the picture. Just three days before the launch of Apollo 11, they had launched *Luna 15*, a moon probe. There was a major difference. There were no cosmonauts aboard. They would not make a lunar landing. No one knew just what the Soviet intentions were. Some speculated that they would attempt a lunar landing to scoop up some moon soil and beat the United States in returning samples of the moon to planet Earth. The Soviet efforts were shrouded in secrecy, characteristic of their space program. The outside world never knew what the Soviet agenda was. This contrasted to the United States' open effort, with the whole world watching—whether the efforts were a success or a failure.

The Soviets had frequently been invited to witness the American space activities. Ambassador Anatoly Dobrynin was invited to the Apollo 11 launch, and he had accepted. At the last minute, it was announced that Dobrynin could not attend the launch, since he would be out of the country. It was suspected that one reason for his sudden absence was that diplomatic niceties would require the Soviets to make a similar gesture to the United States in the future. Evidently, the Soviets intended to keep their agenda and their successes or failures hidden from the rest of the world.

Apollo continued into deep space. When the spacecraft was 200,000 miles from Earth and only 43,495 miles from the moon, the pull from the gravity of the moon equaled the pull from Earth's gravity field. Since the moon is only one-sixth as heavy as Earth, its field of gravity is much weaker. After passing the point of the overlapping gravity fields, the moon's pull was the stronger and Apollo was pulled into a lunar orbit. As the astronauts sailed past the moon, Apollo was traveling at a speed of 5,645 mph. It slowed as it passed behind the moon to a speed of only 3,736 mph. In its first orbital path behind the moon, all radio contact with Earth was blocked for 34 minutes. These were anxious moments at the Lyndon B. Johnson Space Center in Houston, Texas, as NASA waited for Apollo to emerge around the moon. Apollo orbited on a path as near as 70 miles and as far away as 196 miles from the lunar surface.

It was July 20, 1969. Apollo carried the vehicle that Armstrong and Aldrin would use to land on the moon, the LEM, named *Eagle*. Collins would stay in *Columbia,* the command module, and orbit the moon while the other two astronauts explored the lunar surface. The LEM undocked from Apollo while it was orbiting behind the moon. This was another critical phase, as the LEM would now be on its own. The undocking occurred during one of the long periods of radio silence, and mission control sweated every second, wondering if everything had gone according to plan. As contact was reestablished, Armstrong reassured them, "The *Eagle* has wings."

The tricky part was still ahead. *What would the lunar surface be like? Was it suitable for landing the somewhat clumsy LEM?* The descent engine was fired and *Eagle* skimmed the moon's surface. It was strewn with large rocks and boulders. If they crash-landed, there was no escape. The fuel for the descent engine was near exhaustion. They had less than two minutes before they had to land or abort the landing, fire the ascent engine and return to the mother ship.

The automatic landing system for the LEM was propelling it directly into a crater filled with large boulders—and time was running out. Armstrong took over manual control and searched for a better landing area. The LEM was down to 40 feet above the surface of the moon. Some moon dust swirled up around the LEM. Armstrong had found a suitable area that had previously been mapped as Tranquility Base. Relief flooded the men on board the LEM and also those at Mission Control. Armstrong called in, "Houston, Tranquility Base here. The *Eagle* has landed." This was at 4:17:41 EDT. Pandemonium broke out at Mission Control Center. The 16-ton LEM had landed without mishap and in good condition.

It was imperative to be certain that every aspect of the LEM was in perfect working condition. Armstrong's and Aldrin's lives depended on it. They spent over three hours reviewing the checklist to make sure *Eagle* would be able to take off. The two astronauts put on their boots and all their equipment to enable them to move about in this new environment. When they were ready, they opened the hatch. Neil Armstrong started down the ladder. He hesitated a moment as he placed one foot on the surface of the moon. His boot sank into the soft, powdery surface as he spoke to Earth, *"That's one small step for man, one giant leap for mankind."*

As Armstrong descended, he activated the camera to photograph their arrival. Buzz Aldrin followed down the ladder and the two literally romped across the lunar surface. For two hours the astronauts explored, took pictures, and gathered samples of soil and rocks. They left plaques and mementos and planted a large American flag. Not long after the flag was in place, mission control called and asked them to move within the field of the camera: President Nixon wanted to speak to them. The two astronauts stood near the flag as the President told them, *"This certainly has to be the most historic phone call ever made. All the people on this Earth are truly one in their pride of what you have done, and one in their prayers that you will return safely."*

Exactly two hours and 31 minutes after Armstrong had stepped on the moon, the two astronauts were back in the *Eagle.* Within the safety of the LEM, Armstrong and Aldrin relaxed, ate, and finally slept. Just 21 hours after the lunar landing, they were preparing to blast-off, returning to *Columbia* and to Earth—but the suspense was not over yet.

Lift-off was the new challenge. If the LEM didn't have enough thrust, it would fall back to the moon and crash. There was also that moment when you waited for the ascent engine to ignite. If it didn't, the astronauts would be stranded. If the lift-off was too high, it would not be in sync with Apollo, causing the rendezvous and docking procedure to fail. The engine started and *Eagle* rose from the lunar surface in perfect trajectory to the proper position for a flawless docking. And what of the Soviet *Luna 15*? It made its own orbit around the moon, but there was no lunar landing. The United States had triumphed, demonstrating in an open manner the nation's technical competence and mastery of space. The chief architect of the Soviet project, Vasily Mishin, was disappointed, but also impressed. He said, "It pained me, but it was wonderful." The era of manned space exploration of the planets had begun.

I was in New York City on a book tour when Armstrong stepped on the moon. My book, *Your Heart and How to Live With It*, had just been published by Viking. This was my effort to raise public awareness about the cause of heart attacks and how to prevent them. Everywhere I went, throughout the United States, to interviews with newspapers and for TV programs, everyone wanted to ask me about the three brave heroes. Of course, I was thrilled with their success. I was proud of having had a role in developing the means to evaluate men for such a mission and of the support our group at the School had provided for the program. Our methods to test men under dynamic conditions had paid off. We had used these methods to evaluate the first men ever to land on the moon—in fact, everyone who went to the moon as part of the Apollo project. I was even more proud of the three highly trained, intelligent men of courage who were the first to visit the moon.

I thought of the morning Neil Armstrong came to the School for his evaluation. I met him in the conference room next to my office. I already knew a lot about him. He had been a Navy test pilot and later became a civilian flying the X-15 rocket plane. I recalled his rounded face with such smooth skin you might have thought it was plastic. He was a pale, blue-eyed blond. I was struck with his quiet demeanor. He did not emote and I thought his personality was somewhat flat. His aura was one of cool, calm confidence. I thought that his expressionless face would make him an outstanding poker player. I was certain he could deal with any emergency, and his past history supported that feeling.

Buzz Aldrin was at the other end of the spectrum. He was also blond and gave the appearance of being very alive and active. He was the best educated of the pilot astronauts at the time of his selection. He had a Ph.D. and was a Phi Beta Kappa. Buzz was also an Air Force test pilot. I thought he had a complex personality. He had a terrific imagination and an inventive mind. Ed White's space walk looked easy, but when the astronauts tried to work in space, it was almost impossible. There was no traction. It was Buzz Aldrin who solved the problem. He tested methods in a swimming pool and eventually learned that you didn't walk in space, you swam in space.

Then there was Michael Collins, designated to remain in *Columbia*, the Command Module, while Armstrong and Aldrin explored the moon. Michael was halfway between the two extremes in personality. He gave the appearance of a very mature individual who could well serve as a diplomat. He was raised in a military family, was an Air Force test pilot, and very patriotic. I always thought of him in regard to an observation I made about one group of astronaut candidates. Almost all—28 out of 32—were the first born son in the family. Michael was one of the exceptions. But, he was born years after his siblings, long enough to be essentially an only child. The observation intrigued me. Michael was at the Edwards AFB Test Pilot School when I visited there, and I thought of him calling after me to have me meet his attractive wife.

Columbia orbited the moon then headed home. It splashed down in the Pacific on July 24, 1969. But the astronauts' journey was not quite over. No one knew what might be on the moon. NASA did not want to take a chance on contaminating the Earth with some new organism. The astronauts were quarantined. Every precaution and decontamination procedure was carried out. It was not until the middle of August that the three astronauts could emerge and receive the hero's welcome they so richly deserved.

The moon project achieved what President Kennedy hoped it would. It stimulated vast new technological advances that led inevitably to the many marvels of the modern world. It was not just going to the moon, but the ability to do so and the achievements needed to reach the goal: advancements that would benefit all mankind.

The men who entered the space program and flew in Mercury, Gemini, and Apollo were not "Spam in the can," as some feared when the project was first conceived. The astronauts often made the difference in the success or failure of the mission. It was John Glenn who manually steered Mercury's *Friendship 7* to a successful conclusion. Gordon Cooper made the difference in whether his

Mercury flight was successful or not. The astronauts proved that man could survive the space environment and would be able to survive and work on other planets. Al Shepard even proved you could play golf on the moon! Most importantly, developing the capability to operate in space—the huge rockets and the spacecraft—provided the United States much needed protection from any hostile presence in space. The nation's space program conquered the vastness of space and prepared the way for the exploration of the universe. The astronauts expanded the possibilities for all mankind beyond the limitations of Earth into the vast reaches of the unexplored universe.

EPILOGUE

President's Council on Physical Fitness and Sports photo

Left: Carson Conrad, Executive Director of the President's Council on Physical Fitness and Sports, Secretary of Health, Education and Welfare, Casper Weinberger (center) and Dr. Lamb (right) the speaker representing the United States at the International Fitness Conference.

Left: Astronaut Jim Lovell (Apollo 13) Chairman of the President's Council on Physical Fitness and Sports, Leen Akkers (center) the speaker representing the Netherlands and Dr. Lamb, speaker representing the United States, at the International Fitness Conference.

Dr. Lamb, keynote speaker for the First National Conference on Fitness for All, greeting President Carter (center). This was the occasion when President Carter announced that the United States would not participate in the Olympics being held in Moscow that year because of the Soviet invasion of Afghanistan.

EPILOGUE

⤳ The Deke Slayton case surfaced again in the summer of 1975. I was not involved with either the Air Force or NASA and could sit this one out. Slayton was no longer an Air Force pilot either. He was going to be on the crew—but not the commander—of an upcoming joint mission between the Soviets and the United States Apollo-Soyuz mission. The two space ships would meet in space and dock with each other. This was far different from being a solo astronaut in the marginal Mercury or even the two-man Gemini flights. By then we knew how the weightless environment of space flight affected the heart and body from the Mercury, Gemini, and previous Apollo flights. As a crew member, Slayton was not essential to obtaining vital information about weightlessness. If he did develop atrial fibrillation, it wouldn't jeopardize the mission. An Apollo flight was not so demanding. It was not comparable to either the Mercury or Gemini flights. The difference between the Mercury and Apollo spacecraft was something equivalent to the Wright Brothers' first primitive airplane compared to a modern jet aircraft. The concern about the space environment had begun to be replaced with knowledge.

On the eve of Slayton's maiden voyage into space with the joint U.S.-U.S.S.R. mission, I received a call from a reporter. He had been talking to the people at the Lyndon B. Johnson Space Center (formerly called the Manned Spacecraft Center) in Houston. He had talked with Slayton about his medical problems and with Bill Douglas—then back on duty with the Air Force. He said that in these conversations, it was apparent that Slayton and his group still "hate your guts." This wasn't exactly news to me. After all, I had lived with that for years.

The reporter again raised the question of who informed Lyndon Johnson about Deke Slayton's medical problems. Did I know who wrote the letter to Johnson? There was no letter to Lyndon Johnson. He was briefed by Dr. Dryden. After all those years and the success of the Mercury project, the same basic propaganda was still being pumped out. The line was still that it was a personal vendetta between myself and Slayton. The basic goals of the Mercury project continued to have escaped the grasp of some of those involved.

Of course, it was not a vendetta on my part. I hardly knew Slayton. Actually, I was happy for him. He had made many contributions to the man-in-space effort, although the nation's space projects were not a rewards program. Considering his role in the man-in-space program after being grounded, he may have made a bigger contribution on the ground than he would have in space. There was no reason for me to recommend that he not engage in a Mercury flight other than my professional opinion about his heart disorder and the purpose of the Mercury mission. My opinion—and the opinion of the other cardiologists who saw Slayton—was not what he wanted to hear and that's what made Slayton and his supporters angry. If I had recommended he be allowed to make a Mercury flight, it would have endangered the nations' man-in-space program. That, I would never have done.

History proved it wasn't necessary to risk the nation's immediate goals of the highest priority. The Mercury project was a success, so was the Gemini project. They provided the basic information needed for man-in-space flight and the stated national goal of sending a man to the moon. There were six other Mercury astronauts. Slayton was not the nation's one and only indispensable astronaut for the mission—no matter how capable he might have been. He was not allowed to jeopardize the nation's man-in-space program, but he was given a major role in the manned space flights, rather than being dropped from the program. NASA and the Air Force were very good to Slayton and gave him every opportunity to use his talents. They did everything for him except allow him to pilot a Mercury flight: for very good reasons.

It was of the greatest importance that the first manned space flights be successful. The United States started late, remained second, and had a national goal of sending a man to the moon. The stakes for the entire free world were high. To have allowed an unnecessary risk to cause a failure could have seriously delayed, or even prevented, landing men on the moon. If we failed, the Soviets could have remained first in space and a threat to our national survival. It could have resulted in the Congress refusing to adequately fund the man-in-space project.

There are times in life when a person may be called upon to stand up and be counted, no matter what happens or how distasteful the situation may be. My decision, whether to recommend Slayton for a Mercury flight or not, was such an occasion for me. I paid a high price for standing behind my belief, but I would do it again under the same circumstances. The continued efforts to retaliate and to cover up the medical opinions—opinions made by many of the world's leading authorities—only served to cause dissension and problems in NASA, in the Department of Defense, and even in the White House. Such an obvious situation should never have had to go all the way to the President to protect the nation's best interests.

Looking back on the things I accomplished in my life, I would say one of the most important ones may well have been stopping the steamroller effort to cover-up Slayton's real medical problem and to risk the nation's man-in-space project in the process no matter what.

There was an interesting follow-up to the questions raised about Slayton's heart. New ways to study the heart were developed. It became possible to directly examine the coronary arteries. It was reported that Slayton really did not have coronary artery disease. But that was never the question. The cardiologists did not say he had heart disease. They said he had idiopathic (unexplained) paroxysms of atrial fibrillation—which were well documented. The mission of the Mercury project was to find out how space flight affected man. You couldn't find that out if he had experienced atrial fibrillation during his space flight. You wouldn't know what was caused by atrial fibrillation and what was caused by the space flight environment.

While you cannot say that every person who has such a form of atrial fibrillation will have a serious complication, a significant number of them do. Dr. White pointed this out in his consultation. If he had an attack that lasted for 18 hours, or 60 hours, that was long enough for a blood clot to form in the heart, become dislodged, and cause a stroke or other serious consequences. No one can predict who will and who will not have such a complication. Since then, the frequent occurrence of strokes from such clots in patients with atrial fibrillation has led to the practice of prescribing anticoagulants (blood thinners) to patients with this disorder.

It was reported that Slayton's attacks of atrial fibrillation eventually disappeared. Actually, there is no way anyone could have been sure that was true, unless continuous recordings of his electrocardiogram were obtained. And, if true, that would not guarantee they would not recur. Nevertheless, that probably had some bearing on why he was allowed to be on the joint U.S.-U.S.S.R. flight.

Deke thought his atrial fibrillation stopped—if it did—because he had begun taking a lot of vitamins. There is no evidence that taking any vitamins by a person who does not have a significant vitamin deficiency will do anything for atrial fibrillation. He fell into one of the oldest of logic traps. Just because two things occur simultaneously does not mean one caused the other. In logic, simultaneous events do not prove a cause and effect relationship. Such simultaneous events, if they occur, may simply be a coincidence. This is like a person with a cold taking sugar pills when he was almost over his cold, and thinking the sugar pills cured him. He would have gotten well anyway.

That is why research on the effectiveness of medications is done with a double blind study. One group of subjects gets the medicine and another group gets a placebo (something that resembles the medicine but is not). Neither the subjects nor the investigator knows who is getting what until after the study is over. Then the results are compared to determine if the medicine really is more effective than the placebo. If it is not, any improvement in both groups is more likely just the normal recovery from the illness without taking medication. Deke's unsound conclusion was just a testimonial. If his attacks of atrial fibrillation stopped, at least temporarily, they would probably have stopped spontaneously regardless of what he was taking. In any case, it was great that he got to go on an Apollo space flight without any problems and realize that part of his ambitions.

Later, Slayton left NASA to start his own private space company,

Space Services, Inc., of Houston. Although Deke did not realize all of his ambitions, he did achieve many of them, and I was sorry to learn that he had died from a brain tumor. I doubt that his brain tumor had anything to do with the atrial fibrillation that was noted much earlier.

Perhaps the strangest thing about the Slayton affair was why so many seemed to have totally forgotten what the Mercury mission was all about. It was the United States' first effort to find out how weightlessness and space flight affected people. It was to gather facts to learn if people could even survive the space environment. You couldn't do that if you sent astronauts on space flights who had significant medical problems. *What if Slayton had a stroke during a Mercury flight?* Without any facts yet about weightlessness and the effects of the space environment, would anyone know if it was caused by the space environment or a blood clot from his fibrillation? Such a comparable situation had already happened once, with astrochimp Enos. His space flight was suspected by Air Force flight surgeons assigned to NASA of causing runs of ventricular tachycardia, a serious heart irregularity. Actually, the ventricular tachycaradia was caused by a catheter in his heart and had nothing to do with space flight. In regard to Slayton, evidently, the people involved simply got so focused on atrial fibrillation and heart disease they couldn't focus on the real purpose of the Mercury mission: finding out how space flight affected the heart and circulation in healthy astronauts. Then, unfortunately, there were some involved who had their own agendas, leading to the problem of turf wars.

After Apollo, the manned missions to the moon began a long sleep. But that was not the end, only the beginning of man's exploration of the universe. There will be new sources of power developed. It will be possible to send space ships at enormous speeds from planet to planet. It requires little power to move a spaceship through space after it has escaped the major pull of a planet's gravity field. In the absence of gravity, a spaceship has no weight. The enormous power required to launch a rocket to send a space vehicle from Earth to the moon is because of Earth's gravity.

***

It may be possible to gradually accelerate a space ship to ever increasing speeds until it reaches the right point, then progressively decelerate it for a soft landing on a target planet. That means we could travel to the moon in hours and to other distant planets in days or weeks—not months or years. The shorter the travel time to distant planets, the fewer supplies will be required to make the journey. That also would permit a smaller space vehicle for supplies. There would be a big difference between a six-week and a six-month journey to another planet. Mars is not the only target for exploration. Far out is Jupiter, which has some moons that can be used as space ports and some may have environments to support life, even as we mammalians know it. Europa, in particular, is of interest.

There are other possibilities as well. The force of gravity is still not well understood, any more than electricity was understood before learning how to use it? Then there is the role of "antigravity," the force that is pulling the planets apart to expand the universe. Mankind does not know everything yet.

Neil Armstrong's lunar landing really marked the beginning of man's exploration of the universe. The moon is actually planet Earth's spaceport. It is a giant, permanent space station. Since its gravity field is only one-sixth that of Earth's, it will require only one-sixth as much power to lift space vehicles off its surface to journey to distant planets. Indeed, that is why a fragile lunar excursion module (LEM) was able to liftoff from the moon to rendezvous with its mother ship, *Columbia*, to return the astronauts to Earth.

The effects of gravity on lifting huge space ships could be limited by building them, or assembling them, on small planets that have low gravity fields—such as the moon. It would require far less power to launch a spaceship from the moon than from Earth to journey to distant planets. The planets that have a spaceport—like Earth's moon are likely target planets for exploration. Man has begun his first efforts to explore and perhaps inhabit other planets.

The moon can be colonized with permanent structures just as bases have been built at Antarctica. It can have its own permanent launching facility as the jumping-off point to other planets. Once that is accomplished, inhabiting the moon will be easier than working on the space station. It provides a solid surface and, unlike the space station, it has a gravity field that will keep objects and astronauts from floating off into space. Astronauts will have traction, making work much easier. The low gravity field will also make it easier to work with objects that are heavy on Earth.

NASA plans to build a permanent lunar base that will permit crews to live and work on the moon's surface. Space crews may inhabit the base for as long as a year. It will probably be located at the south pole of the moon. The base camp can be used to determine how to build and operate a base on Mars. The point is, the moon will literally become the base of operations to explore the planets in our solar system. The ultimate goal is not just to land and live on the moon, but to extend man's capability to survive and function on other planets.

Materials can be ferried from Earth to the moon to build the base. Crews and supplies can be transported with the new Crew Exploration Vehicle (CEV), a moon ship, planned for missions to take over where Apollo left off. Component parts of the CEV system can be launched separately from earth and actually assembled in space. This will require less energy than if the CEV system were assembled on Earth and launched as a single unit. There are basic things on the moon that will help to establish the lunar base. The surface is covered with a fine powder called regoliths, created by the constant bombardment of its surface with small meteorites breaking up moon rocks. Regoliths contain lots of oxygen; work is under way to find ways to extract this oxygen. The abundant sun rays are a source of solar energy that can be used to produce electricity. There may be significant amounts of frozen water beneath the lunar surface, at its poles.

A lunar base can be used to monitor events in space, including any hostile activity. If a giant killer meteoroid threatens to impact Earth, a rocket from the moon may be used to change its orbit and protect planet Earth.

Will the decay in national preparedness that can occur when there is no apparent challenge, similar to what I found in the military when I first arrived at the School of Aviation Medicine in 1955, happen again and lead to deterioration of the nation's capabilities in the space arena? The United States quickly disarmed after World War I, and let its

411

guard down again immediately after World War II. The invasion of South Korea by North Korea was a wake-up call for the free world. After the Korean War, there was another period when the nation became complacent, enjoying a feeling of superiority—one that ended suddenly with the bark of a dog from space. The security of the free world depends on free nations remaining first in space. To be strong, we must remain strong. If we fail to progress, others will take up the challenge, just as the Soviets did and threatened the world by their unquestioned superiority before, and in, the early days of the space race.

Mankind's evolution is usually thought of in terms of his physical and mental changes through time, as exemplified by the Darwinian concept. But man's understanding and use of those things in his physical universe is also a form of evolution. This is exemplified by the first use of stone in the Stone Age to today's age of technology in the conquest of space and exploration of the universe. Only fifty short years ago, there were no satellites. Now, they are an integral part of our lives and possibly our survival. Within the 20th century, Goddard's first rockets—which could travel faster than sound—have lead to landing on the moon and our network of global satellites. The prescient vision of Kepler and Galileo in 1610 has become a reality. New discoveries may significantly prolong man's healthy life span beyond anything envisioned today, which would provide more time to travel to distant planets. As President Kennedy expressed several times, it wasn't just going to the moon, but achieving all the things necessary to make that possible, which would improve life on Earth. One need only look at the role of satellites in our modern life now compared to the days before the first satellite was successfully launched into orbit to see how true that is. *Who can foresee the future?*

Landing men on the moon was one of mankind's greatest achievements. It required the efforts of many great and talented individuals from all disciplines—and it stimulated a period of enormous scientific advancement. There were lots of hurdles on the way to the moon. The many scientists and heroic astronauts who overcame them made the lunar landing possible. I shall always remember and cherish every detail of the role I was privileged to play in that great adventure in the history of mankind—"...One small step for [a] man, one giant leap for mankind"—in the exploration of the celestial bodies.

END

APPENDIX A

Significant excerpts of Dr. Lamb's consultation provided to Lt. Colonel Bill Douglas, flight surgeon for NASA-MSC in September, 1959, regarding Major Donald "Deke" Slayton's atrial fibrillation:

In reference to recurrent atrial fibrillation, it is not unknown to occur in the absence of heart disease in apparently healthy individuals.... The chief problem associated with this arrhythmia is its unpredictability. It may be precipitated by fatigue, stress, excessive tobacco, excessive ingestion of alcohol or excessive ingestion of caffeine. On other occasions, it may occur without any apparent precipitating cause. There are no particular examinations which can be carried out which will enable one to predict in advance whether a person is gong to have fibrillation the next day or even the next hour. The complications attendant to it are hemodynamic (ability to pump blood) and occur when the rate is too rapid. Atrial fibrillation may occur at a very rapid rate, resulting in inadequate filling of the heart during a short diastolic period and resulting even in circulatory collapse. The question might be raised if the one episode of syncope (fainting) in 1946 following the ingestion of alcohol might not have been associated with a transient episode of atrial fibrillation.... The other complication of fibrillation which is most infrequent is the possibility of formation of an embolus (clot) in the fibrillating atria with subsequent dislodgment of the embolus to either peripheral or pulmonary areas, producing infarction (tissue death) at the site of the embolus.*

His future management should be to avoid excessive exertion and known precipitating factors, otherwise, he should lead a normal life....

Concerning the relationship of this arrhythmia to flying performance, it must be stated unequivocally that the recurrence of such episodes of atrial fibrillation are unpredictable and there are no tests which will enable us to predict when such episodes will occur or how long they will last. During such episodes, it is quite clear that such an individual is not at his peak performance level. There have been numerous hemodynamic studies done in recent years on the influence of the arrhythmia associated with atrial fibrillation and it is definite that there is a diminution in cardiac output (how much blood the heart pumps) in the presence of fibrillation. Under normal circumstances, in such healthy individuals as this person, the variation in cardiac output is not of clinical significance; however, if one is to consider using such an individual to carry out strenuous physical tasks of the most exacting nature, such a compromise in circulatory dynamics (function) would definitely be a limiting factor to his overall performance and to the maximum capability of his cardiovascular dynamics. The study of circulatory function in the presence of atrial fibrillation as...published in *Modern Concepts of Cardiovascular Disease* has adequately demonstrated the point that there is a compromise in normal cardiovascular hemodynamics in the presence of atrial fibrillation. Thus the problem in this case is not so much one of disease, but it is a question of hemodynamic action due to a disturbance in normal rhythmic mechanisms....

---

*In more recent times it has been established that atrial fibrillation greatly increases the risk of a stroke, from a clot that forms in the heart from the fibrillation alone, that can dislodge and go to the brain. It is now usually recommended that patients with atrial fibrillation take medicines that prevent the formation of blood clots.

APPENDIX B

Dr. Lamb's letter to General Charles Roadman, Director of Life Sciences, NASA Headquarters, March 5, 1962, in part, was as follows:

This letter is prepared in response to your telephone conversation of 3 March, 1962, requesting my opinion and recommendations concerning the medical qualification of Donald Slayton to engage in Mercury orbital flights. The medical selection of the seven Mercury astronauts and the specific medical problem which involves Donald Slayton occurred prior to the time that you became affiliated with NASA and prior to the time that you were responsible for the Life Sciences Division of NASA. For this reason, I will review the pertinent medical aspects of this case as I remember them. (The medical findings and history have been previously included in Dr. Lamb's consultation of August, 1959, detailed in Appendix A)

...If the ventricular rate should become rapid in the presence of atrial fibrillation, a major compromise to cardiac output occurs predisposing to circulatory collapse, loss of consciousness, or relative coronary insufficiency. For these reasons the United States Air Force has wisely followed the policy throughout World War II and up to the present time, to exclude individuals who present with atrial fibrillation from the flying population unless it was a single isolated episode associated with an adequate, acceptable cause such as occurs during an acute illness of the magnitude of pneumonia or severe gastroenteritis.

Unless such an adequate precipitating cause is known, and can be demonstrated, and unless the episode was isolated in nature, these individuals are not returned to flying. The only exceptions to this which have occurred are those rare instances in which a waiver has been granted to a senior general officer whose duties do not require primary control of high performance aircraft. This policy was established many years ago on the recommendation of nationally-known cardiologists and I concur in the wisdom of this policy.

...In view of the above facts I would have no hesitancy to recommend that Donald K. Slayton continue an active normal healthy life and would be qualified for general military duty. As a matter of record, however, were he to present himself to me as a candidate for retention in the unrestricted flying category for the United States Air Force, I could not in good conscience recommend a waiver of the usual medical standards for this category in his case.

While I agreed verbally at the time of his previous evaluation with the concept that he might be retained in the Mercury project to utilize his engineering skills, and refrained at General Flickinger's telephone request from making any further recommendations, I did not, and do not now, feel that it is good medical judgment that he should at anytime participate as a subject in orbital flight.... The dangers imposed by his (Major Slayton's) medical condition include: (1) danger to his own personal health and welfare due to the possibility of underlying heart disease, or in its absence, the possibility of recurrence of previously documented atrial fibrillation compromising the cardiovascular response on a straight mechanical or dynamic basis. (2) Aside from the personal considerations for his own welfare there remain those factors which are in the nation's interest. The possibility that the presence of atrial fibrillation could compromise his ability to perform during such an event and compromise the success of the mission remains. (3) It must also be recalled that the presence of atrial fibrillation, at any time during his flight can and will be detected by various receivers throughout the world and it would be known in countries not friendly to the United States as well as within our own country that an individual with recurrent atrial fibrillation had been used as a subject for Mercury flights. While it is quite conceivable that an individual with the apparent general good health that Donald

Slayton has could complete such a mission, and it is conceivable that atrial fibrillation might not occur during such a mission, it remains that a considerable risk is involved in hoping that such an event will not occur and this approach is a straightforward gamble which does not appear to be justified since he is not the nation's only Mercury astronaut.

I fully recognize the desire of those who are directly affiliated with Donald K. Slayton to see him fulfill his ambitions and there is no question but what he is an extremely capable, well-motivated individual. I also recognize the motive and desire of those members of the Air Force to see an Air Force candidate participate in such flights, however, I cannot allow either of these motives to influence my professional recommendation that it is not in the best interest of Donald K. Slayton or the national program of man-in-space flights to utilize him as the pilot for Mercury orbital flights and I am compelled to recommend that his retention in the program should be restricted to a point short of primary control of high performance aircraft.

APPENDIX C

Excerpts from Dr. Paul Dudley White's consultation regarding Major Donald K. Slayton, in June, 1962:

Certainly there are no abnormalities, with the exception of the paroxysms of fibrillation, in the case of Major Slayton that would deter one from considering him fit for almost any activity on earth. These frequent paroxysms of atrial fibrillation are, however, distinctly abnormal and a bar to his inclusion under any heading of perfect health. It is this arrhythmia which, it seems to me, cannot be regarded as of minor significance, even though the heart rate is usually not elevated during the arrhythmia and even though he were not to be subjected to the strains of outer space. To be sure, paroxysmal fibrillation occurring even as frequently as in Slayton's case can go on for many years without harm. But on the other hand, it can lead to more prolonged arrhythmia quite possibly with faster rates and with some hazard of the eventual development of intracardiac thrombosis and embolism there from. Also it is possible, although not immediately threatening, that in such cases the heart can eventually dilate and fail without any other cause. Such cases are not common but they are seen by almost all cardiologists of long experience. Furthermore, other arrhythmias can complicate such arrhythmic hearts. One such case, with paroxysmal tachycardia and fibrillation, to whom we had given a favorable prognosis, expired unexpectedly and suddenly at middle age with extreme ventricular tachycardia and fibrillation.

Another feature of atrial fibrillation is that it detracts from a perfect circulation. Although the blood is probably still propelled to a variable degree from the atrium into the ventricles, and naturally flows itself there into, there is nevertheless a defect in the circulatory mechanism. Moreover, there is to be taken into consideration the individual's awareness of the presence of fibrillation. This is true at least some of the time in Slayton's case, and so has a distracting influence. Thus there is a psychological handicap presented by such paroxysms.

...I believe that the hazards from the arrhythmia under these particularly stressful present circumstances are too great both for the individual himself and his family, as well as for the program which is still in its infancy and under study, to recommend that he face the same conditions faced by Glenn and Carpenter (the previous two Mercury flights).

I am quite sure, as has been the thought of some of the others who have seen Major Slayton, that we must demand as perfect a circulation as possible for anyone exposed to this program as it is set up at present. Not only must the heart itself be considered but the efficiency of the brain is at least equally important and must not be handicapped by such an arrhythmia as atrial fibrillation.

...Risks are needed in such pioneering but surely it is not necessary to add materially to the risks that we are already acquainted with (Mercury space flights) by introducing this unknown hazard of important cardiac arrhythmia. It might be regarded as an interesting experiment to find out, but are we justified in recommending such an experiment?

...I regret to express this opinion in view of the disappointment that it is bound to cause, but in all honesty and objectively from my own experience and the careful study of Major Slayton himself, and of the records of Glenn and Carpenter, I cannot do otherwise.

APPENDIX D

Excerpts from Warren Burkett, reporter for *The Houston Chronicle*, to Dr. Lamb, December 16, 1962:

Thank you for your most complimentary letter. I am glad that Vice President Johnson enjoyed reading the series, since he had such an instrumental part in our coverage of the meaning of the aeromedical evaluation results to the general physician and patient.

...I know that you must have found much more data there than was obtainable from the SAM (School of Aerospace Medicine) staff alone. There was so much information at hand before and after my visit to San Antonio that the sheer bulk presented a problem in handling the subject.

I understand that a few *naive* persons delude themselves into believing that some corporate or military information man decides what a reporter writes or an editor prints. We know this certainly is not the case, and the information specialists know only too well that it never has been.

Our decision on illustrations went through several stages. Since these people were living, breathing entities, we decided upon photographs. We first wanted to use a head or portrait shot of every man; from our files and through correspondence we collected photographs of every man who had taken the physical examination and been named to astronaut training. The photographs of the NASA crew came from our morgue, given us originally by NASA and its

Public Affairs Office for various purposes. Every newspaper in the country must have dozens of these; we maintain a good file and had 150 to choose from. We also had on file most of the Air Force astronaut trainees and test pilot school personnel. If we did not have them, or where the photographs lacked quality, we wrote Air Force: Washington, Edwards Air Force Base, and other places for suitable poses. We had more than 50 such formal head and shoulder pictures to use if we wanted.

Naturally we assumed that such an occasion as the selection of the new team of astronauts would not go unphotographed. We contacted Public Affairs Offices, Astronaut Affairs Offices, and others at Manned Spacecraft Center and I learned that this was true. Through our normal contacts with Colonel Powers, Mr. Chop, and the local astronauts we learned that the photographs were not of the type that could be considered offensive. Prints of these   photographs were made for our examination, and in consultation with the Houston MSC Public Affairs Office, we selected the pictures that would best illustrate the procedures involved. Some were new and had never been published before. The NASA-MSC newspaper published a suitable Schirra photograph only a week before the series opened. Others showed the specific tests so well we did not mind prior publication.

The Houston Public Affairs Office saw each of the photographs and assisted in identification. So much has been published about the NASA astronauts and about the Air Force crews that we did not need to look any further than our files and NASA's for such things as age, height, weight, families, etc. Naturally we are grateful to NASA-Houston for supplying us with this background of biography and photographs; this is the function of any competent Information Service.

Thusly did our selection of formal, family, physical-exam photographs evolve to illustrate the specific stories. It was unnecessary to get any of this material from you and your people at SAM, and I did not trouble you with such a chore since I knew there would be more than adequate information of this kind available elsewhere.

Although exciting and interesting to me, some people find the clinical details of such a procedure rather dull. Therefore we (I) read appropriate books, press conference texts, magazine articles, etc.

and talked with the subjects and their friends. From these published and otherwise available sources I selected appropriate anecdotes and situations to add something concrete, specific, and illuminating at what I considered proper points in the stories. The physicians at MSC (air force flight surgeons assigned to the Manned Spacecraft Center) were in many ways the source of some of the better ones. It really became a matter of throwing away appropriate material because I could not possibly use all that was available.

As your speech in Washington made clear, the interest lay in the implications that your examinations had for the average man. I wanted to satisfy myself that a statistically significant number of people had gone through the examination first.

I hate to waste the time of someone like yourself, or mine for that matter, going into an interview about some medico-technical subject, unless I'm somewhat prepared. As you know, I opened our interview with about six pages of questions compiled from reading a special Senate space committee report on manned space flight and astronaut selection. In all our discussions on medical evaluation purposes and procedures, it was essential that I sift out which of the Apollo procedures had been used and which ones were suggestions. I have found it practical to double check much of the material printed about the space program for just this distinction. I also had read both the Senate and House appropriations hearings' transcripts and a book called *America On The Moon* by one Jay Holmes, who is a NASA information consultant in the capital. This material also covered the Lovelace work.

I also made myself familiar with certain astronautical facts given in documents written by the astronauts, Dr. Charles Berry, Dr. Robert Voas, Dr. William Douglas, Robert Gilruth, D. Brainerd Holmes, James E. Webb, Walter Williams, and others. I do try to keep up with certain key speeches made by NASA personnel, articles in technical and scientific-medical journals, and some of the more reliable popular writers. (As I go to some trouble to keep up with information relating to the specialties of others, I am often astonished to find they know so little about mine or don't take the effort to learn before passing out third-hand opinions based on often mythical and undocumented generalities. But one can't keep up with everything. So I was very pleased to deal with your staff, which is very knowledgeable or accepts the advice of competent PIO counsel.) I suspect your people thought it a little odd that I did not appear either desperate or disappointed that you did not give me any personal stories or recollections about either the Air Force or NASA trainees. I recall I asked one time 'for the record' and again just to see if the reply by this particular doctor would drag up something about medical ethics or if there might be some other reason given for your staff being unable to remember anything about a specific member of the astronaut trainees sent there. Later, in Los Angeles, Dr. Berry told me about some agreement whereby NASA would release any photographs or intimate personal details.

Your people kept your end of the agreement very well, and so did NASA in releasing the pictures and other data.

…The series then becomes a synthesis of interviews, public documents, NASA's official biographies and photographs, published speeches, and other material cleared by the agencies involved. I must have discarded at least three times as much as we published.

Enough! I shan't impose on your time any more. If this entertains or enlightens anyone, well and good. It was a pleasure to work with you and all the others at SAM (School of Aerospace Medicine) If I can ever be of assistance, please call on me.